Being the Body of Christ

Gender, Theology and Spirituality

Series Editor: Lisa Isherwood, University of Winchester

Gender, Theology and Spirituality explores the notion that theology and spirituality are gendered activities. It offers the opportunity for analysis of that situation as well as provides space for alternative readings. In addition it questions the notion of gender itself and in so doing pushes the theological boundaries to more materialist and radical readings. The series opens the theological and spiritual floodgates through an honest engagement with embodied knowing and critical praxis.

Published

Resurrecting Erotic Transgression: Subjecting Ambiguity in Theology
Anita Monro

Patriarchs, Prophets and Other Villains
Edited by Lisa Isherwood

Women and Reiki: Energetic/Holistic Healing in Practice
Judith Macpherson

Unconventional Wisdom
June Boyce-Tillman

Numen, Old Men: Contemporary Masculine Spiritualities and the Problem of Patriarchy
Joseph Gelfer

Ritual Making Women: Shaping Rites for Changing Lives
Jan Berry

Sex and Uncertainty in the Body of Christ: Intersex Conditions and Christian Theology
Susannah Cornwall

Forthcoming

For What Sin was She Slain? A Muslim Feminist Theology
Zayn R. Kassam

Our Cultic Foremothers: Sacred Sexuality and Sexual Hospitality in the Biblical and Related Exegetic Texts
Thalia Gur Klein

Through Eros to Agape: The Radical Embodiment of Faith
Timothy R. Koch

Baby, You are my Religion: Theory, Praxis and Possible Theology of Mid-20th Century Urban Butch Femme Community
Marie Cartier

Radical Otherness: A Socio/theological Investigation
Dave Harris and Lisa Isherwood

Catholics, Conflicts and Choices
Angela Coco

Telling the Stories of Han: A Korean, Feminist Theology of Subjectivity
Jeong-Sook Kim

Reinterpreting the Eucharist: Explorations in Feminist Theology and Ethics
Edited by Anne Elvey, Kim Power, Claire Renkin and Carol Hogan

Elsie Chamberlain: The Independent Life of a Woman Minister
Alan Argent

Not Behind our Backs: Feminist Questions and Public Theology
Edited by Stephen Burns and Anita Monro

Being the Body of Christ

Towards a Twenty-first Century
Homosexual Theology for the Anglican Church

Chris Mounsey

Published by Equinox Publishing Ltd
UK: Unit S3, Kelham House, 3 Lancaster Street, Sheffield, S3 8AF
USA: ISD, 70 Enterprise Drive, Bristol, CT 06010

www.equinoxpub.com

First published 2012

ISBN   978-1-84553-951-1 (hardback)

British Library Cataloguing-in-Publication Data

A catalogue record for this book is available from the British Library.

Library of Congress Cataloging-in-Publication Data

Mounsey, Chris, 1959–
   Being the body of Christ: towards a twenty-first century homosexual
   theology for the Anglican Church/Chris Mounsey.
      p. cm. — (Gender, theology, and spirituality)
   Includes bibliographical references and index.
      ISBN 978-1-84553-951-1 (hbk.) English fiction — 20th century — History and
criticism. 2. Homosexuality in literature. 3. Christianity and literature — Great
Britain — History — 20th century. 4. Homosexuality — Religious aspects — Anglican
Communion. I. Title.
PR888.H67M68 2011
823'.91093538--dc22
                              2010031028

Typeset by SJI Services, New Delhi
Printed and bound in the UK by MPG Books Group

CONTENTS

INTRODUCTION: HOMOSEXUALITY AND ANGLICANISM

I started work on this book after a conversation I had with Elizabeth Stuart about our disappointment at Rowan Williams's failure to bring the Anglican church into the present tense and accept its homosexual clergy. We felt it was a pity that so many ministers would have to continue to hide their sexuality rather than present a model of spirituality to their congregations that was derived from their particular gift. We agreed that all gifts were from God, and sexuality was one of those gifts, as blindness is my new gift.

I have always been homosexual, but am newly blind. What my new gift taught me was that God's gifts may be meant to challenge us, and this book will argue that the challenging experience of homosexuality has led many British writers of the twentieth century to find new ways of expressing their spirituality outside mainstream Anglicanism. This seems to me to be a great loss to the Church, and though I have now rejoined, my attendance is something more like an armed truce than an untroubled communion. A catholic church ought to welcome all people with all their gifts in all roles. If we are the body of Christ then should I not be able to be his feet, his hands or his mouth according to my gift? But my experience as a homosexual has been one of rejection and incomprehension. It is as though the Anglican Church regards the gift of heterosexuality as the image of God, but I can find no place in the Bible where He took a wife, and I remember Jesus saying that we should all be brothers and sisters in heaven. Who needs sex in heaven anyway? Souls are hardly going to have children: they are immortal after all.

After 20 centuries of heterosexual western history, maybe it is time to learn from homosexuality. Homosexuals have been part of the human family for as long as we have been human, and if we learn anything from our fellow people, then maybe we ought to learn from all our fellows rather than from those who it is convenient to class as normal. In fact, if it is true that homosexuals have always made up about 10 percent of the human population, it would make us a normal minority. Refusing to listen to homosexuals and to learn from their experience is like refusing to listen to black people and learning from theirs. And I am sure there are some homophobic racists out there but what I learn from them is how to forgive them for they know not what they do. But when I received recently a letter sent by my bishop laying down the law to me about the fact that the Anglican Church was happy to accept homosexuals in its congregations, but did not believe the lifestyle was compatible with the ministry, unless same-sex relationships were celibate, I did not feel so forgiving.

Even as a child I never believed that my sexuality was a lifestyle. I grew up in a household where homosexuality had never been mentioned other than in a term of abuse 'queer', but nevertheless, I knew I was attracted to men from reading my first illustrated *Tales from Troy* by Roger Lancelyn Greene. The pictures of Achilles and the heroes with their long, lithe limbs and shiny, plumed helmets attracted me to read on and on, turning the pages to find another illustration of a nearly naked man, and hurrying past the stories of Iphigenia in Aulis and Tauris because the scantily clad woman just did not do the same for me. I heard the word 'homosexual' on TV, and looked it up in the family *Encyclopaedia Britannica* where I discovered that it was a form of self-abuse practiced by humans and some higher apes. Well at least if apes did it, it would seem to be natural behaviour and not a conscious choice.

My intellectual development, based on early reading of the classics for all the wrong reasons was another cuckoo in my family's nest. I have dyscalculia and have to count on my fingers (I have to touch each finger to believe I've counted it) or write down numbers in words in order to understand them. Neither my mother nor my father could understand me because they could add up figures at the same speed they could run a pencil down a column. And they could do old money too, pounds, shillings and pence: 12 pence one shilling, 20 shillings one pound. I was glad when decimalization came in because I only had ten fingers. My parents also had an unflinching belief in genetic inheritance, so I was pushed into doing science A-levels because they believed I was a late developer and would soon understand how mathematics worked. When they saw my results they were convinced I must either be lazy or stupid. Only after my parents heard me discussing literature with my aunt could they believe that I was different from them.

More importantly, just as my sexuality and intellectual curiosity burgeoned without nurturing, so did my spirituality. I grew up in a Godless household, with two siblings for whom science was their only way of expressing themselves emotionally: both are now successful medical doctors, helping the sick. My mother had only ever been taken to church as a child when the aunt, who brought her up, was angry with her father. My father expressed some interest in being a minister after leaving the army, but my mother put her foot down. She was not going to be a vicar's wife. I think I went to church once between the ages of 6 months (when I was baptized), and 11 when I joined my school choir and sang services every day seven days a week during term-time. Before this I always said I wanted to go to church, but somehow Sundays were kept as sleep-in days followed by a brisk walk then dinner in the evening. When I had to be taken to school chapel for the service, the family Sunday underwent a sea change around the parental taxi journeys. Neither sibling ever came to hear me sing, and often I was simply taken to chapel by one or other parent and picked up after the service.

I was confirmed as a matter of course, the first of my siblings though I was the youngest, and when it came to going to university, because of my failure in my science A-levels I decided to read theology with an eye to ordination. While the robes and incense never caught my imagination, the incantation of words 'that have become valid' held me in their spell. I joined the choir the first day I was in 'Big School', and eagerly learned how to chant Psalms, first as a treble, then as an alto, then tenor and bass. As my balls dropped and my education continued, I lost what little faith in science I had picked up from my family, preferring the more evanescent truths offered by literature and the more certain truths of faith. I argued continually with my sister who couldn't understand why James Joyce's *Ulysses* was not readily comprehensible to her. She was at Oxford University so was clever, and that meant she could lay the law down about *Ulysses*. It could not be great literature because she did not understand the story. When I told her it was grown up Homer we simply came to blows.

I remember the embarrassed conversations with my mother about wanting to be ordained. She was pleased in one sense because, I think, she thought it would be good to tell her friends about her son the minister. However, I always felt during the conversations that she would have been happier if I had wanted to become a doctor. Helping people surely ought to make them well again from some disease? I persisted in my spiritual life in the same way I persisted in my sexual and intellectual lives: against the tide of expectations. I arranged a talk with the Dean of my local cathedral about vocation, and booked myself into a retreat after which the decision would be made. I was truly excited by the prospect of working in the Anglican Church and prayed fervently to be accepted into the life that I felt sure was calling me.

The priest in charge of ordinands put a stop to my dream. I have never met a more unlikeable man. There was something patronizing and insinuating in his tone both at the same time. He read me as a homosexual as I walked in to speak to him in the way that I learned later that only homosexuals can do with one another: Gaydar, or the homosexual gaze. I could not keep my eyes off the gold wedding band on his finger, and he knew I had read him too. I think that it was I who left the room before his bidding. I have seldom wanted to be out of someone's company so quickly. At the time I had not 'come out' to my friends and was hardly out to myself, so I had never encountered homophobia, but it was as though I was physically being hit by every word that he said to me. After I walked out of the audience with this man I did not go into a church for ten years.

The rejection was so bruising that I spent five years living by myself in London trying to work out what I would do with my life. I made an attempt at a science degree but flunked the first year. There really was nowhere for me but the Anglican Church and the Anglican Church did not want me. I lived a precarious existence working in and around the theatre: the proper place for homosexual men. I came out to my friends and met with the usual, casual homophobia. I found new friends and eventually my long-term partner.

Robert did not tell me he was a Unitarian minister until we were so thoroughly involved with each other that it did not matter. In fact I was pleased, though I never did feel at home in his services so seldom went. Nevertheless, watching a vocation in practice brought me one step back to being able to walk into an Anglican Church. Furthermore, with the stable background of a loving relationship, I was able to find my niche teaching English Literature in a university where I became a specialist in the eighteenth-century. What interested me in the century was the acceptance that everyone was a Christian. It was also the century that saw the founding of Religious Dissent, so I had something to talk about with Robert and we would chatter on for hours about religion.

It was these talks that laid the foundation for the end of our partnership as it became increasingly obvious that I could not accept or adopt Robert's faith in the rational basis of his religion, and I was not happy with its rejection of the personhood of God in Christ. However, by this time I was interested in Christianity again, if only in its history: I realized that like my sexuality it wouldn't go away. I wrote a book about Christopher Smart the mid-eighteenth century religious poet and cross-dresser, and found his *Jubilate Agno* fascinating.

> Rejoice in God O ye tongues. Give the glory to the Lord and the Lamb. Nations and Languages and every Creature in which is the breath of life. Let Man and Beast appear before Him and Magnify His Name together.

Writing about a man who took his religion as seriously as he did his politics, drinking and theatre was refreshing. I'd never wanted worship to be po-faced and I admired Smart's puckish humour that existed side by side with his poems on the attributes of God.

What struck me about the eighteenth century was the amount of writing published on the subject of Christianity. It was as though people could not get enough sermons and religious tracts, and a quick computer search of published material in the century produces 14,000 items with the word 'sermon' in the title. The same search carried out on the twentieth century garners only 220 items. The energy that went into religious writing must have been immense. But then why did it dissipate in the twentieth century? To argue that the fall in interest in religion might be due to the rise of science and rationality in the age of Enlightenment is to miss the point that science had been rising for a hundred years before the eighteenth century began and it didn't affect the output of religious material in that century. To the contrary, the failure of science to cure every ill is argued to have led to the rise of the gothic horror novel in the mid-eighteenth century, a marker of people returning to faith in irrational explanations.

This is not to say that the Enlightenment was an illusion, but rather that where its philosophies of rationalism and empiricism pulled people away from faith, their old beliefs did not vanish in the brilliant light of scientific discoveries. The prefatory poem of Isaac Newton's *Principia Mathematica* uses the metaphor of the great man's work appearing like sunshine through the clouds of uncertainty. But the English translation was followed quickly by John Hutchinson's *Moses*

Principia, which reread all of Newton's theories through the lens of the Pentateuch. Until the twentieth century nearly all Anglican Ministers were, either knowingly or not, Hutchinsonians. There was no need to give up Christianity in order to be a scientist, and few did.

There must have been many reasons why the twentieth century saw such a reduction in the level of interest in religious affairs, but I am interested in the way people behaved when faced with the same problem I had with the Anglican Church. This book will therefore explore parallel histories of twentieth-century homosexual writers.

We shall begin with Oscar Wilde, who tried to move from the Anglican Church to the Roman Catholic, in the hope that personal confession might shrive him of the guilt he felt about his homosexual activities. I shall argue that the general confession would have suited him better, because no sin need be named, and in effect, one might choose which acts one has done that week that one would like to think of as sinful while one repeats the words. There are questions of conscience and true repentance, but as St Paul said in his letter to the Galatians 'It is for freedom that Christ has set us free.' The statement leads to further questions about slavery to sin, but in the event the Anglican Church could not satisfy Wilde because he would not ask to be forgiven for following what he believed to be a natural desire. The chapter therefore reads closely Wilde's story 'The Fisherman and His Soul' where the hero cuts himself free of his soul so he can marry a mermaid. When conscience strikes and he reluctantly reunites with his soul, losing the love of his life, he begins to do evil things and drowns himself in disgust. Fisherman and mermaid are buried in unhallowed ground, which subsequently flourishes with flowers, but when the priest comes to bless the graves, the flowers are no more. The fisherman's willing separation of himself from his soul so he can marry the mermaid is a powerful evocation of the feeling of rejection by the church for sexual irregularity. The flowers that spontaneously grow on the graves signify the naturalness of irregular sexual desire. The intransigence of the priest in not letting the fisherman marry the mermaid is what the story seems to suggest is at fault. The smell of the flowers alters his sermon from one on the God of Wrath to one on the God of Love: but it is too late for he will only accept the irregularity of the fisherman's love when both he and the mermaid are dead. As if the story were a prophecy, the Catholic Church finally embraced Wilde in an article in *L'Osservatore Romano*, the Vatican newspaper, in July 2009.

However, the immediate aftermath of Wilde's trial for 'gross indecency' was unsettling for early twentieth-century homosexuals. The fierceness of the attack on Wilde in his third trial was probably led by Lord Rosebery, the Prime Minister, who, like Wilde, had been sexually linked with one of the Marquess of Queensberry's son's (Francis, Rosebery's private Secretary, who subsequently committed suicide). To be a homosexual was not safe and many men hid their sexuality in one way or another. Thus we move to E.F. Benson who did not, like Wilde, leave the Anglican Church because of his sexuality. Rather he left his sexuality because of the Anglican Church.

E.F. Benson was the son of Edward White Benson, Archbishop of Canterbury, and like his other three siblings Arthur, Maggie and Hugh, was homosexually inclined. I have devoted four chapters to *David Blaize*, a hitherto unexplored trilogy by E.F. Benson because it is so fascinating in the detailed twists and turns that describe a man coming to terms with the Anglican Church's demand for continency of homosexuals. Whether or not it is autobiographical is irrelevant: all novels are to a certain extent autobiographical but novels also allow writers to tell the truth through stories that are made up. In the trilogy we follow David through his first same-sex love affair, learning about masturbation and how it can be used to take the pressure off his desire for sexual encounters, discovering that he cannot find women sexually attractive, learning how to use his sexual allure to get what he wants, and finally to his asexual marriage to Frank, his first boyfriend. More importantly the book is read as E.F. Benson's lesson for all homosexuals that even though their sexuality will not go away only continency will do for the Anglican Church. And in this sense I read it as a tragedy. I have called the section 'A Sexuality fit for My Lord' because E.F. Benson published the portrait of his father as the frontispiece to the first part of his autobiography *As We Were*, with the subscript 'My Lord'. The impression one gets from the trilogy is that he was terrified out of his sexuality, all of it, though it put up a good fight.

Generally then, the first part of the book presents the Anglican Church as an authoritarian institution that did not allow sufficient interpretation of conscience for homosexuals such as Wilde, and which effectively crushed Benson, like Salome in Wilde's play, beneath the shields of the Roman soldiers. And it has not moved very far from that position in the last century. I was crushed by it and still wonder sometimes why I went back. But the reason may lie in the parallel history of homosexual theology that follows in the second part.

I noted above that there is not much published in the twentieth century that looks like practical theology compared with the eighteenth century. But the search was to make a point, rather than to capture all that has been written about Anglican Theology, and we can look for religious writing in other forms. Daniel Defoe's novel *Robinson Crusoe* has a third volume appended to it of serious religious reflections on the story of his shipwreck. Since Defoe was a Dissenter, other writers, for example Penelope Aubin, satirized his theology in their novels from an Anglican point of view. Defoe's may be claimed erroneously to be the first in the English language, but my perspective on the novel is that from its earliest manifestation it was an outlet for religious as well as imaginative writing. So when considering the writing of homosexuals in the twentieth century who shared my disappointing experience with the Anglican Church, we might find that they are writing on theological issues in other ways than might be expected, and using language that we might find strange.

The parallel history will begin with a look at the poetry and tracts of Edward Carpenter. Unlike Wilde, Carpenter was not tried for 'gross indecency' though he lived openly as a homosexual, beginning a life long partnership with George Merrill three years after the Wilde trials. Unlike Benson, he left the Anglican Church, after serving as curate to the Christian Socialist F.D. Maurice, believing that homosexuals could bring about social change if people would learn from them. Although one might style Carpenter an atheist, I will argue that in his term 'Democracy' he captures much of Christ's final message that we love one another as He loved us. In this word he also argues for a society that is less hierarchical than the one he left in the Church of England. Another challenge to Anglican tradition is Carpenter's adamant assertion that people should not forget their bodies in their spiritual struggle to find meaning, and his work suggests that revelations are possible from bodily experiences. His reading of the homosexual gaze is important here as it takes the first steps towards what I shall call the theology of the body, which is the theme that holds this part of the book together. When two men look at each other and recognize what they both are, what I had seen in the look of the priest in charge of ordinands, the revelation of a possible 'us' occurs like a third person that is made up of neither one objectifying the other nor vice versa. The 'us' is irreducible to either and is a moment of respect in respect of each other.

From Carpenter we move to Alan Hollinghurst, whose religion I do not know, and whose book never mentions Anglicanism. Hollinghurst's education at Canford School and Magdalen College, Oxford would suggest that his formative years were associated with Anglicanism, and the characters of *The Swimming-Pool Library* share a similar public school and Oxbridge background. But despite the lack of overt engagement with theology, the novel squarely takes on the subject of morality in terms of vengeance or forgiveness towards those who have deliberately sought to harm you. Furthermore, the framework of the story is Herman Melville's *Billy Budd* in the setting as an opera by Benjamin Britten, which transforms Melville's ambiguous treatment of the question into a clear call for spiritual absolution for those who have knowingly committed an injustice. More specifically, Hollinghurst argues that we should not allow ourselves to be conditioned either by the heterosexual or the homosexual worlds if we want to find out who we are as individuals. What is fascinating about his book is that though it contains much truly erotic writing it does not devolve into pornography. Hollinghurst shows us a world where the homosexual body in all its sexual actions is just like Carpenter's taken one stage further: but where the sex acts are real rather than implied within the look, the questions of self-delusion, manipulation of others and free will (and Will is the name of the protagonist of the book) become more important. In effect I shall argue that Hollinghurst's novel takes on authoritarian institutions and tells us that only by forgiving the worldly forces that try to mould us according to their image can we be free of them and free to be what we want to be.

The final author to whom the book turns is Jeanette Winterson and *The PowerBook*. That her writing is theological is not difficult to argue, though her split with her Elim Pentecostalist childhood might suggest otherwise. Winterson also writes erotic prose, but in what I shall argue is a theology of here and now that leads us to the body. What we shall see is that she is engaged in theology because she writes in a way that promotes the idea that her words will lead directly to the things she describes. In order to reach her theological point, she explores the problems in postmodern, scientific and religious theories of language, and finds each fails to some extent. Instead, Winterson turns to fiction, specifically love stories, and love stories that involve sexual encounters, where we see that the ecstatic caress of a lover on the body of their beloved can be caught in language *about* the caress. I argue further that in this theory of language, Winterson is much indebted to Luce Irigaray's metaphors of the body as a way of understanding meaning, but taken further and applied to lesbian love. In this way, Winterson shows us writing that has become a human parable, where a secondary meaning appears unexpectedly in the story in moments of desire that break the boundaries that usually separate two people. More importantly, this is the gift of the homosexual writer to the heterosexual world, she tells us to invent ourselves in love. Because this revelation comes to us spontaneously, it is not deferred to another place or time, but is here with us now.

The last brief chapter draws conclusions from the other chapters based on autobiographical writing about my own vitiated body. In this chapter I use my changed perception to illustrate the problems and difficulties of bringing the theology of the body into our lives and loves as we are so used to embodiment that we do not understand how it works. What I argue is that if we are the body of Christ then we need to be challenged by our bodies in order to learn how fully to comprehend our perceptions: and then we can be like Christ in the way Oscar Wilde so wanted us to be.

Chapter 1

OSCAR WILDE, 'THE FISHERMAN AND HIS SOUL' – THE FAILURE OF ORGANIZED RELIGION

Typically, critical writing on Oscar Wilde's religion centres upon his several unsuccessful attempts to convert to Roman Catholicism, his personal association (Jesuitical?) with Christ found in works dating from during and after his imprisonment, and a discussion about whether his deathbed conversion to Roman Catholicism was conscious or whether he was in a terminal delirium. What seems wanting about the response to Wilde's religious conviction is that it never moves far from the question of a lifetime dabbling with Roman Catholicism that tends to be read in opposition to atheism. Whereas, and a fact that is conveniently forgotten, Wilde was a nominal Anglican all his life. In terms of religious belief the adjective 'nominal' may seem strange, however, the designation all but defines the religious life of the majority of British Protestants, and before the 1920s, Irish Protestants as well. Church going at the local parish church was expected, unquestioned and largely unengaged.

I shall argue in this chapter that throughout his life Wilde was always inspired by spiritual concerns and worried about the fate of his soul, and in this sense, unengaged nominal Anglicanism did not suit him. However, nor was there a place for him in the Catholic church because of his sexual preference for men, something which it thought of as a sin, and moreover, a sin which the Catholic church could not bring itself to forgive. Had either the Anglican or Catholic churches been able to welcome him as a homosexual, they would have had a devoted servant. However, since each form of Christianity with which he associated himself attempted to turn him against his immutable sexuality, he rejected both for their obduracy.

The chapter will look first at certain critical studies of Wilde's religion and argue that they tend to misread his spiritual and devotional life. Then it will briefly explore Wilde's biography and letters to demonstrate that however hard he tried, he was unable to find a place for himself within either Anglicanism or Roman

Catholicism. Finally, I will read Wilde's story 'The Fisherman and His Soul', a children's tale written in 1891 at the height of his literary output, which will show that Wilde did not want to be assimilated into mainstream Christianity because it rejected his homosexuality. Furthermore, we shall see that the story suggests that he did not believe that mainstream Christianity could ever assimilate homosexuality, and that he did not want it to try.

Critical Address to Wilde's Religion

As though having the privilege of the last word on the subject of his father's religious tendency, Vyvyan Holland tells us that:

> All his life, my father had an intense leaning towards religious mysticism and was strongly attracted to the Catholic Church, into which he was received on his death bed in 1900.[1]

Famously, Richard Ellman's monumental biography of Wilde argues against the validity of the deathbed conversion.[2] But it is hard to argue from Ellman's position that Wilde was never really interested in Christianity given the evidence of the little boy bearing stigmata in *The Selfish Giant*, or the subject matter of *Salome*.[3] What is difficult to discern, however, is what Wilde himself might have thought about religion and the use of its imagery. Did he use the language of Christianity as a disguise for something else? Or was he interested in spiritual salvation through the action of a personal saviour?

On the one hand, Jack Zipes, in *Fairy Tales and the Art of Subversion*, argues that Wilde used Christian imagery for the purpose of social critique:

> Wilde's [critique of society] was stamped by a unique commitment to Christian Socialism which celebrated individualism and art.[4]

---

1. Merlin Holland, Vyvyan Holland, Owen Dudley Edwards, Terence Brown and Declan Kiberd (eds), *Collins Complete Works of Oscar Wilde* (Glasgow: Harper Collins, 1999), p. 12. [Cited as Complete Works]

2. Richard Ellman, *Oscar Wilde* (London: Hamilton, 1987).

3. It must be remembered that *Salome* was banned, not for lasciviousness, but because no play with a religious subject could be performed on the British stage until after 1967.

4. Jack Zipes, *Fairy Tales and the Art of Subversion* (London: Heinemann, 1983), p. 111.

Thus, Zipes reads Wilde's fairy stories through the lens of *The Soul of Man Under Socialism*, arguing that:

> Christ made no attempt to reconstruct society, and consequently the Individualism that he preached to man could be realised only through pain or solitude. The ideals we owe to Christ are the ideals of a man who resists society absolutely. But man is naturally social ... Christ is upheld as the model of anti-authoritarianism and humanism, but ... he must be transcended through a common struggle of joy towards socialism ... [Thus] Wilde used the figure of Christ to show the need to subvert the traditional Christian message.[5]

Zipes' argument is tantalizing. He captures the paradoxical way in which Christian images appear in Wilde's writing. So many important characters die, or are dead before the beginning of Wilde's fairy tales, that it appears the world is populated by Christ-like models. But if this is so, then why has society not learned its lesson and become better? Only the purveyors of the traditional Christian message can be to blame. Thus, for Zipes, Wilde tells us that in the dyad 'Christian Socialist', Christianity is less important than the resultant Socialism.

On the other hand, Patrick O'Malley, writing on Wilde's religion[6] argues that although

> Wilde's religious yearnings ... challenge religious orthodoxy ...
> they serve as a stumbling-block to those who would read Wilde
> as the prophet of a gleefully aesthetic queerness.[7]

While Zipes' Christian Socialist Wilde may not simply be equated with a gleeful aesthetic queer Wilde, O'Malley's insistence that Wilde's religious yearnings were significant of a genuine religious conviction, albeit unorthodox, challenges the idea that Wilde's religion was simply a sign of, or a way towards, something else. For O'Malley, Wilde's religion was both sexual and devout: in fact to use the term technically, it was 'queer'.

But what is significant about these two readings is that Zipes' religion as socialism is typical of the academic climate in which he was writing (1983), and O'Malley's queer religion, typical of the time

5. Zipes, *Fairy Tales*, pp. 115–16.
6. In Frederick Roden (ed.), *Palgrave Advances in Oscar Wilde Studies* (Basingstoke: Palgrave, 2004). [Cited as O'Malley].
7. O'Malley, p. 167.

at which his essay appeared (2004). But was not religious conviction typical of, if unengaged, in the time in which Wilde was writing? Likewise, was not guiltily hiding homosexuality *de rigeur* for the late Victorian man? Reading Wilde in his own context, ought we not understand Wilde's religious yearning as religious yearning? Ought we not read this yearning alongside and distinct from his hidden sexual yearning, and therefore as two forces in his life that might come into conflict?

Owen Dudley Edwards points out that Christianity was never far from Wilde's childhood experience:

> Perhaps the most neglected biographical item in Oscar Wilde's life is that he was the nephew of three clergymen.[8]

What is not neglected in Wilde's life and writing, however, is his self-identification with Christ, which has infected much of the critical writing about Wilde. Even Merlin Holland, his grandson, makes an easy comparison between Wilde and Christ on the first page of the Collins Complete Works:

> The same public which crucified him for his lack of conformity and respect for Victorian values in 1895, today holds him up as a martyr for individuality. "I was a man," he says in *De Profundis*, "who stood in symbolic relations to the art and culture of my age. I treated Art as the supreme reality, and life as a mere mode of fiction: I awoke the imagination of my century so that it created myth and legend around me: I summed up all systems in a phrase, and all existence in an epigram." The unabashed arrogance of that must have been difficult to swallow, but today we are forced to see the truth of it. Wilde's life and his work survive side by side, in symbolic relationship with each other, and despite all attempts by his critics to prise them apart and subject each to scrutiny, they remain more closely entwined than ever.

But for Holland, as in Zipes, Wilde's religion is equated with something else, this time art, and is not left to be what it is: religion. What Holland loses in this reading of the crucifixion of his grandfather is the fact that Wilde was fired by the idea of being an intercessor between people and that which is greater than they, in this case between people and their art and culture. Wilde explains God's world to people as Jesus did before him. His area of intercession is paltry to

---

8. Complete Works, p. 15.

be sure (the meaning of art is hardly as important as the meaning of life) but his model is Jesus, and we must not miss this fact.

O'Malley notes that the problem is common among writers on Wilde. Just as Holland loses Wilde's religion while maintaining his use of religious language, so have many others used religious words in the titles of their works on Wilde while few have actually written about the subject itself. But then, O'Malley is writing from the perspective of a Roman Catholic with the purpose of challenging Ellman's view that Wilde's deathbed conversion was not sincere, and thus his project is to demonstrate to us Wilde the Roman Catholic. The task is not easy, given his own admission that Wilde's religion was never orthodox, and so he uses the terminology of queer into which the unorthodox fits. But while this aspect of O'Malley's essay may be limited by the literary theory current at the time he was writing, what remains of longer lasting use is that he reads Catholicism to explore Wilde's sexuality and vice versa, even given the fact that

> It is hard for us to believe that Wilde may well have had attractions simultaneously to Catholicism and to other men, both sincere and both subject to irony.[9]

If there is a difficulty here it lies in the word 'attractions' which elides sexual and spiritual desire. In order to shed some light on how the two can be understood to coexist more or less happily, O'Malley notes two trends in writing about Wilde, homosexuality and Catholicism. First, that the Catholic Church was attractive to Wilde since it provided a place of aesthetic excess (bells and smells) which made it easy for the homosexual in him to give vent to his emotions: the Catholic Church as a place of aesthetic identification. Second, that the Catholic church was essentially at odds with same sex desire, and presented 'a type of orthodoxy' ...which ... 'trumps' perversity:[10] the Catholic Church as a cure for homosexuality.

Ellis Hanson offers a discussion of these ideas in *Decadence and Catholicism*,[11] where he argues that the Roman Church offered Wilde the enactment of his 'dandyism and his aestheticism, there was beautiful ritual and passionate faith.'[12] This is, however, once again

9. O'Malley, p. 177.

10. O'Malley, p. 172.

11. Ellis Hanson, *Decadence and Catholicism* (Cambridge MA: Harvard University Press, 1997).

12. Hanson, *Decadence and Catholicism*, p. 271.

to read aestheticism as the subtext to Wilde's religion, and as such reads religion as something other than it is. Both the excessive ritual and the substance behind the enactment of a service are reduced to dressing up and art.

To be fair, Hanson notices the problem, and argues for a productive dialectic between Wilde and Catholicism. But his argument remains one which rests on the idea that Wilde's sexuality was external to his faith:

> If Wilde were simply a pagan, why did he consider conversion so often? Why did he attend Catholic services so often? Why did he return over and over again to Christian themes in his work?[13]

Here Hanson's dialectic disguises a mutually exclusive opposition: If Wilde is a homosexual engaging in casual homosexual sex then he cannot be Catholic, so he must be a pagan. When Wilde went to Catholic services he was attempting to slough off his homosexuality and become pure. That is, you cannot be a practising homosexual and a practising Catholic. But is this so?

Hanson's unresolvable paradox leads us to another in the question about the sincerity of Wilde's conversion. Could it be called sincere if he waited to convert on his deathbed when he could not have any more sexual relations? And the answer would seem to be 'Yes' because he felt Catholicism could only shrive him of his sins if he were sincere, and would not accommodate them without instilling him with intolerable guilt about his immutable sexuality. Thus, Hanson has to argue that Wilde was a pagan, in order that he did not have to submit himself to guilt and self-doubt.

But guilt of this type is only possible if the sin becomes known to a third party, which is the priest in the private confession of Roman Catholicism. On the other hand, the general confession of the Anglican Church would have allowed Wilde to continue to be forgiven for a sin that was otherwise unnamed and invisible. Therefore, we could argue that being a nominal Anglican allowed Wilde unhypocritically to continue to use the religious language, which was so important to him, and to attend religious service. When Wilde speaks of religion in the same language as he does beautiful things or beautiful men, it is not in opposition to his sexuality, because weekly (or daily when he was at Trinity or Magdalen) his sins were forgiven. Thus, guilt

---

13. Hanson, *Decadence and Catholicism*, pp. 231–32.

need only be seen to be the product of his sexuality in the Catholic ritual, which demanded that he alter his sexual behaviour when he confessed it to a priest.

However, this is to offer too simplistic an answer, for if Wilde was a nominal Anglican he was an unhappy one, and he *was* as Vyvyan Holland tells us, always attracted to the Roman Church. But even if this was so, he was wary of it too. Perhaps then we should turn to Declan Kiberd as the best account of Wilde's ambivalent position on the Roman Catholic Church. Writing about the poem 'Easter Day', he argues that the poem:

> shows a man at once fascinated and repelled by Popish opulence, though the final note is a Miltonic disapproval of a false and garish priesthood which betrays the true simplicity of Christ ...[14]

But as the argument continues, Kiberd becomes taken up with the opposition between Roman Catholicism and paganism, and commenting about 'On the sale by Auction of Keats's Love Letters' falls back into this opposition, disregarding the influence of the Protestant Milton:

> [Wilde] develops his image by likening the poet's fate to that of the crucified Jesus, for whose garments the squalid Roman soldiers cast lots. Such a complex of ideas conflate ... artistry and sacrifice, combine [...] pagan energy with Christlike suffering ...[15]

Interestingly, but perhaps rather suspect and even perhaps homophobic, is Kiberd's gloss of Wilde's paganism with a reference to Greece which acts as a synecdoche for homosexuality:

> Again and again in the poems, Wilde's breath is taken away by the baroque magnificence of Rome, against which he usually sets the more chastely proportioned symmetries of ancient Greece. If Greece tends to win out in the contrast, that is because so often Wilde's Greece is no more than a version of his own ideal England.[16]

But in failing to discuss religion together with sexuality, Kiberd misses the central issue in Wilde's writing: that sex and religion are both vitally but mutually exclusively important, and remain always in dynamic tension. We see the tension at work in *Salome*, where

14. Complete Works, p. 741.
15. Complete Works, p. 741.
16. Complete Works, pp. 741–42.

the eponymous heroine represents a sexual being who passionately wants religion, since it seduces her and makes her feel good, and is potentially better than sex. The tragedy in the play lies in the fact that in order to have religion, she must kill it (she must have John the Baptist's head) because if she takes religion on 'alive', it will kill her, since it will stop her from being sexual. It is therefore interesting that the addition that Wilde makes to his biblical source (the soldiers turning on Salome to kill her) represents that very death of the sexual, for, as we know, John the Baptist was not the Saviour, but only the first to recognize Jesus as such. Thus, in the ending of his play, Wilde demonstrates the potential danger of religion which comes back to take its revenge when you are least expecting it.[17] And thus also, Salome's tragedy may be seen as embodying the homosexual Oscar Wilde's dilemma with religion: why should he accept a religion which condemned his private behaviour as unacceptable, but whose saving grace he wanted and needed.

Therefore, in terms of his sexual life, as Neil McKenna puts it in *The Secret Life of Oscar Wilde*[18] '[Wilde] was torn between the desire to proclaim the existence of his secret life and the need to conceal it.' Although we can now develop this idea to suggest that he was trying to conceal it from other people, from the ministers of organized religion, but not from God. It is as though Wilde is saying, with Salome, God made me as I am, therefore my desires must be good, and I will follow them albeit that you will kill me. And here we must remember that before Wilde went to gaol he attended a private performance of *Salome* given by friends.

However, and as Kiberd argues, this acceptance by Wilde about his homosexuality was not consistent throughout his life. After imprisonment, Kiberd writes:

> In [*The Ballad of Reading Gaol*] Wilde finally rejects Greek ideas of self-creation through joy and instead resigns himself to a Christian notion of purgation through pain.[19]

Although we still have to read 'homosexual' in place of the word 'Greek,' Kiberd's point is valid for both in terms in this late work.

17. And it must also be remembered that the soldiers turning onto Salome is the only addition to the plot which Wilde made in his version of the story.

18. Neil McKenna, *The Secret Life of Oscar Wilde* (London: Century, 2003), p. xiii.

19. Complete Works, p. 742.

The message is one of paying for sexual sin and becoming 'clean' through personal suffering. This is the second element of Wilde's association with Catholicism which O'Malley noted, a point which Kiberd backs up:

> ... for all its Greek colourings, the Wildean personality was finally placed in service to a theory of beauty which "at its very base is the truth inherent in the soul of Catholicism: that man cannot reach the divine except through the sense of separation and loss called sin."[20]

But then, if one part of Wilde wanted purgation through pain, to be rid of his homosexuality, the other part wanted to express his sexuality physically, and we will see his dilemma writ large in the story discussed below. Two such influential drives cannot have controlled him equally at all times in his life but must have alternately surfaced and receded, with sexual fulfilment being followed by a feeling of guilt and sin. In the late nineteenth century, the homosexual drive was conceptualized in terms of inversion and perversion, and it is hard to believe that Wilde did not wonder on which side of that opposition he fell. Likewise the question of feeling sinful and desiring a cure had an irresolvable opposition at its heart. Is sin original, and part of the fallen nature of humans, or is it the result of trying and failing to follow an impossible moral code?

We find a useful source for Wilde's views on both of these debates that he mentions in a letter written while he was at Oxford. Wilde says that he is going to bed to read a chapter of *The Imitation of Christ* by Thomas a Kempis, of which he notes ironically: I think half-an-hour's warping of the inner man is greatly conducive to holiness. As we shall see, 'the warping of the inner man' cannot simply mean the moral code that a Kempis suggests all men must follow in order to be like Christ, but might equally well refer to the homoerotic terms in which he addresses his love for Christ.

I shall discuss the context of Wilde's comment later, but for the present will offer a few paragraphs of a Kempis without comment, paragraphs which relate to sexual purity, clean living and purgation of sin, and are written in the language of desire of one man for another: the writer for Jesus. I have refrained from detailed exposition of the quotes, however, I suggest that when you read them, you think of

20. Complete Works, p. 743.

them ironically as well as devotionally. Thus, for example, when a Kempis writes that 'we should love all men, but not make close companions of all' the secondary sexual meaning of the word 'love' should not be discounted, and nor should the idea that the second part of the sentence condemns all homosexual encounters.

> *He that followeth me shall not walk in darkness,* saith the Lord. These are the words of Christ, and they teach us how far we must imitate His life and character, if we seek true illumination, and deliverance from all blindness of heart. Let it be our most earnest study, therefore, to dwell upon the life of Jesus Christ.[21]

> He, therefore, that will fully and with true wisdom understand the words of Christ, let him strive to conform his whole life to that mind of Christ.

> It is vanity to follow our desires of the flesh and be led by them, for this shall bring misery at the last.

> [Of Aestheticism]

> Be oftentimes mindful of the saying, The eye is not satisfied with seeing, nor the ear with hearing. Strive, therefore, to turn away thy heart from the love of the things that are seen, and to set it upon the things that are not seen. For they who follow after their own fleshly lusts, defile the conscience, and destroy the grace of God.

> [On being a student]

> ... because many seek knowledge rather than good living, therefore they go astray and bear little or no fruit ... Of a surety at the Day of Judgment it will be demanded of us, not what we have read, but what we have done ...

> [Of inordinate affections]

> ... if ... he yield to his inclination, immediately he is weighed down by the condemnation of his conscience: for he hath followed his own desire, and yet in no way attained the peace which he hoped for. For true peace of heart is to be found in resisting passion, not in yielding to it. And therefore there is no peace in the heart of a man who is carnal nor in him who is given up to the things that

21. The translation I have used is nearly contemporary with Wilde's reading of the text, though is not the one he would have read. It is by W. Benham B.D. (Leipzig: Tauchnitz, 1877). I chose it because Tauchniz' publications attempted to popularize texts, and because it is available on Google Books.

are without him, but only in him who is fervent towards God and living the life of the Spirit.

Be not familiar with any woman, but commend all good women alike to God. Choose for thy companions God and His Angels, and flee from the notice of men.

We must love all men, but not make close companions of all.

Our great and grievous stumbling-block is that, not being freed from our affections and desires, we strive not to enter into the perfect way of the Saints.

If we look upon our progress in religion as a progress only in outward observances and forms, our devoutness will soon come to an end. But let us lay an axe to the very root of our life, that being cleansed from our affections, we may possess our souls in peace.

It is a hard thing to break through habit, and a yet harder thing to go contrary to our own will. Yet if thou overcome not slight and easy obstacles, how shalt thou overcome greater ones? Withstand thy will at the beginning, and unlearn an evil habit, lest it lead thee little by little into worse difficulties.

[Of the uses of adversity]

It is good for us that we sometimes have sorrows and adversities, for they often make a man lay to heart that he is only a stranger and sojourner, and may not put his trust in any worldly thing. It is good that we sometimes endure contradictions, and are hardly and unfairly judged, when we do and mean what is good. For these things help us to be humble, and shield us from vainglory. ...

Therefore ought a man to rest wholly upon God, so that he needeth not seek much comfort at the hand of men.

All saints have passed through much tribulation and temptation, and have profited thereby.

Many who seek to fly from temptations, fall yet more deeply into them. By flight alone we cannot overcome, but by endurance and true humility we are made stronger than all our enemies.

Thou art called to endure and to labour, not to a life of ease and trifling talk.

How great is the frailty of man, which is ever prone to evil! Today thou confessest thy sins, and to-morrow thou committest again the sins thou didst confess.

Biography, Letters and Poetry

If a Kempis represents, for Wilde, the impulse to be free from sexual
desires in order to be pure, set in tension with the equal and opposite
urge to express his sexuality in relationships with men, then it is
now time to look at both of these in play at important moments in
his life and letters. We shall consider six moments, three of which
demonstrate that there was no place for Oscar Wilde in Anglicanism,
with its general confession, and three of which demonstrate that
there was no place for Oscar Wilde in Roman Catholicism with its
personal confession.

Certainly the most famous incident which suggests that there
was a place for Wilde otherwise than in the Anglican Church was
his mother having him re-christened into the Catholic Church as a
child. However, since he had no volition in this, there is no conclusion
which can be drawn from it. Nevertheless, due to the fact that this
was brought about under his mother's auspices, we might well
conclude that she predisposed him towards the Catholic Church in
the divided religious community of Ireland in which he was brought
up. How far his mother's Irish Nationalism influenced his intellectual
development is an argument outside the realms of this chapter, so
we shall not consider this aspect of Wilde, in terms of his sexuality
and religion.

The first time we can be certain that Wilde showed a conscious
interest in the Catholic Church was while he was at Oxford University.
He was known to have many Catholic images in his bedroom, and
wrote in a letter to his friend William Ward, on 3 March 1877:

> I now breakfast with Father [Thomas] Parkinson [SJ], go to St.
> Aloysius, talk sentimental religion to [Archibald] Dunlop and am
> altogether caught in the fowler's snare, in the wiles of the scarlet
> woman – I may go over in the vac.[22]

Two things are interesting here, that Wilde thinks he might go over
in the vacation, as though it were something for which there was no
time during term, or which had to be hidden from the university;
and that he uses a very ambiguous terms 'the fowler's snare' and
'the wiles of the scarlet woman' to describe the effect of Roman
Catholicism upon him.

22. Rupert Hart-Davis (ed.), *The Letters of Oscar Wilde* (London: Rupert
Hart-Davis, 1962), pp. 30–31. [Cited as *Letters*].

Of the first of these, going over to Roman Catholicism during the vacation may have had something to do with the current religious climate at Oxford University. To have become a Catholic while a student could have caused him a great deal of trouble, since it was only four years earlier, in 1873, that Roman Catholics (along with Dissenters) had been allowed to study at the university.[23] Although it was now legal for him to be a Catholic and a student, for so prominent a personality to be known to be a Catholic might have prejudiced his degree result in an academy unused to anything but High Church Anglicans. That Wilde chose instead to become a Freemason while at Oxford, suggests his outward conforming to a group which was more acceptable to the Protestant majority, while his letter tells of his yearning for something else: Catholicism.[24]

But exactly how Wilde viewed that 'something else' is difficult to ascertain from the evidence of this letter. Much has been said of Wilde's use of the descriptor 'the scarlet woman' – the whore of Babylon – to describe the Catholic Church. But that the defeat of her overt sexuality is one of the heralds of Apocalypse or Revelation, suggests the tension which will become apparent in his interest in the Roman Church, with all its vermillion finery, as a portent for future spiritual cleanness. The other descriptor 'the Fowler's snare' is equally ambivalent. The term in itself suggests that Wilde was unable to escape the Roman Church, and felt helplessly trapped. When we look at the two references in the Bible (one in Psalm 91 and the other in Hosea) the way he viewed Catholicism does not become any clearer.

The Psalm reference suggests that 'the secret place of the most High' will protect him from 'the snare of the fowler,' but since Wilde writes that the fowler's snare *is* the Catholic Church, the question remains as to what he believed was 'the secret place of the most High' – was it the Anglican Church? If so, then maybe this is why he could 'go over in the vac', since he would not be attending so many Anglican services while on holiday in Ireland.[25] This seems a

23. It may even be that Wilde thought of Catholicism as a fashion accessory as it was so new, but this view does not tally with his serious approach to spiritual matters which we shall see in his writing.

24. In the same letter, Wilde says that he would be sad to give up freemasonry if he went over to Catholicism since he 'believe[s] in it awfully'.

25. While in Magdalen as an undergraduate, he would be expected to attend chapel every day during term.

hopelessly cynical position to take. The Hosea reference gives less help. The verse reads: *The watchman of Ephraim was with my God: but the prophet is a snare of the fowler in all his ways, and hatred in the house of the Lord.* And the question remains as to whether Wilde sees the Protestant Church as hateful to the Lord, or the Catholic Church. Hosea describes the House of Israel in turmoil while in captivity, and perhaps it is to this turmoil that Wilde refers, reading his dilemma as equivalent to that of Israel. Whatever, the letter suggests that the only way out of turmoil is to 'go over' to Catholicism, as had his friend Dunlop. That Wilde did not, in the event, 'go over', does not erase the fact that he thought he might: and for unknown reasons which had to lie in the failure of his own religion.

But the early steps toward Rome were made at a cost: literally.[26] In a letter to Reginald Harding, of 16 June 1877, Wilde wrote of a financial loss incurred by his early Romish leanings.

> A cousin of ours to whom we were all very much drawn has just died – quite suddenly from some chill caught riding ... My brother and I were always supposed to be his heirs but his will was an unpleasant surprise, like most wills. He leaves my father's hospital about £8,000, my brother £1,000, and me £100 on condition of my being a Protestant.
>
> He was, poor fellow, bigotedly intolerant of Catholics and seeing me "on the brink" struck me out of his will. It is a terrible disappointment to me; you see I suffer a good deal from my Romish leanings, in pocket and mind.[27]

Read in terms of Wilde's desire to move away from Anglicanism, we can easily see how the cousin's response was typical of the ferment between the two religions which was expressed daily in Irish life then and now. But that Wilde himself felt it so important to 'come out' to his family as being 'on the brink' of Catholicism shows just how strongly he felt about his choice of religion: that he let it be known how he felt.

What is further interesting for the subject of this chapter is that we also see a developing ambiguousness in Wilde's desires for the

26. It is tempting to suggest that the loss of the inheritance was the reason Wilde did not 'go over in the vac', but the timing of the letters is wrong since the Easter vacation came in between these two letters, and would surely have provided time for Wilde to convert had he so wished to.

27. *Letters*, pp. 42–43.

Catholic religion and homosexual love in two early poems: *San Miniato* and *Ave Maria Gratia Plena*. The first poem describes the ecstasy derived from a visit to a Church on the outskirts of Florence. San Miniato, which is the architectural pattern for several other famous churches in Florence itself, is notable for its mosaic of Jesus between the Virgin and San Minio. Wilde addresses the poem to Mary 'The Virginal white Queen of Grace' who, as the mother and wife of Christ, can act as intercessor for him by praying at the time of death. In the Protestant tradition Mary is reduced in importance and no prayers are addressed to Jesus through her. Just as in the general confession, Protestantism leaves the sinner very much to their own devices with their sins and their conscience. On the contrary in the Catholic tradition, where the priest hears the details of the sin and sets penance, the sinner is led to salvation and knows just where they are and what must be done. Mary, who takes the role of the priest in contacting Jesus, is the model of intercession, and being a mother figure, offers an identifiable structure of offering comfort to the afflicted child/sinner. It is probably this relationship with Mary that Wilde calls 'sentimental religion.'

Thus, Wilde is 'coming out' about his association with the Catholic Church in the lines:

> Mary! Could I but see thy face
> Death could not come at all too soon.[28]

The evocation of Mary in this way demonstrates Wilde's impatience with the arid Protestant tradition, and his desire for 'sentimental religion.' He clearly wants a personal relationship with his intercessor, which is not on offer in the Protestant tradition in which he was brought up.

Ave Maria Gratia Plena, which was placed directly after *San Miniato* in the 1882 collection of poems, makes clear the link between religion and sexuality. Once again, the poem concerns an ecstatic vision, opening 'Was this His coming!' But this time, the effect of the ecstasy is ambiguously religious and sexual. At once, after the initial 'I' to whom the vision shows itself, the sex of the person visited by (a) God is altered, in the two references to Danae and Semele. However, the actuality and physicality of the sex act remains along with its orgasmic and forbidden quality. In both Greek models, prohibited sex is fruitfully, if disastrously enacted.

28. Complete Works, p. 749.

Danae was imprisoned in a tower so she would not have a child who might fulfil a prophecy and kill her father, but Zeus visited her in the form of a shower of golden rain. Perseus was born, and though Danae and he were set adrift in a box, they were rescued, Perseus returned to his homeland and killed his grandfather accidentally with a discus.

In revenge for Zeus impregnating Semele, Hera suggested to her rival that she ask Zeus to come to her in the glory that he did when he approached her, his wife, for sex. Semele demands this of Zeus, who comes to her in a thundercloud, killing her, although he managed to rescue her unborn son, Dionysus.

If we are to read the 'I' narrator as Wilde, the use of these two images suggests the illicitness, fruitfulness and disastrousness of a passionate relationship with 'Him', which is homosexual if 'he' is just a man or which is religious if He is Jesus of the Roman Catholic Church. Wilde's concluding lines give a clear resolution:

> With such glad dreams I sought this holy place,
> And now with wondering eyes and heart I stand
> Before this supreme mystery of Love:
> A kneeling girl with passionless face,
> An Angel with a lily in his hand,
> And over both the white wings of a Dove.

The last three lines of the poem describe the typical iconography of Annunciation paintings which suggests the sexless birth of Christ through Mary. The linking lines, which bring us back to the 'I' narrator, draw our attention to his quest to understand 'Love.' Thus, the poem moves, as though from the mistakes of the Old Testament[29] to the fulfilment of the New, where Wilde seems to be calling to Mary to cleanse him of his forbidden sexual desire by making his love sexless. Clearly, Wilde believed that if he remained an Anglican he would succumb to the power of his homosexual drive, and only through the person of an intercessor – in this case 'Hail Mary Full of Grace' – could he escape from himself and the disastrous consequences of his love.

In terms of sexuality and religion, we might therefore read Wilde's longing to become a Roman Catholic as equivalent to his longing to have sex with men. Both were forbidden and might be dangerous if

---

29. Here instead, of course, Greek Mythology, and its concomitant permissible homosexual love.

he gave in to them. Both were nevertheless attractive to him and all but out of his control. As far as Anglicanism was concerned, it was the religion away from which his desire, either sexual or religious, was leading him so it cannot have been fulfilling him.

Reading his attitude to Catholicism together with Wilde's sexuality, we can understand Wilde's response to desire for the forbidden as one which began with self-justification, led to 'coming out' to others about the desire, and then was full of surprise and hurt at the negative response to his being truthful. And being truthful to himself and others was probably the strongest driving force in Wilde's life: it could tear him away from established social and religious norms. For a man who had been brought up as a Protestant in a country which contained such bigoted people as his cousin, he knew from early on that his being truthful about his behaviour could lead to trouble. The same attitude would lead to more trouble in England where the people were even more bigoted against his homosexuality. Nevertheless, from the beginning, Wilde attempted to be truthful to himself and to other people: most probably so that he could be truthful to God.

But if he were trying to be truthful to God, it was not acceptable for him to be truthful to the ministers of the Roman Catholic Church. There was no place for Oscar Wilde in Catholicism with its personal confessions and intercessors: it was too limiting and claustrophobic for him. And it would not take him as he was.

Beginning with another incident which demonstrates the ambiguity of Wilde's religious and sexual yearnings, and which connects his reading of St. Thomas a Kempis with sexual gratification, we can see that it is difficult to argue that Wilde looked at Roman Catholicism in any other way than he looked at young men bathing: with distant unfulfillable desire. To complete the quotation from the letter of Wednesday, 26 July 1876 that Wilde wrote to William Ward:

> ... although always feeling slightly immortal when in the sea, feel sometimes slightly heretical when good Roman Catholic boys enter the water with little amulets and crosses round their necks and arms that the good S. Christopher may hold them up.
>
> I am now off to bed after reading a chapter of S. Thomas a Kempis. I think half-an-hour's warping of the inner man daily is greatly conducive to holiness.[30]

30. *Letters*, p. 21.

David Alderson reads the incident in the sea as an indication of Wilde's nascent Englishness, set against the Irishness of the boys,[31] but this seems to miss the point of the juxtaposition of the second paragraph about reading Kempis. Wilde is captivated by the swimmers[32] and describes them without abashment, in the manner of Walt Whitman. They are beautiful and wear gold crosses, which would not be seen if they were not naked. He calls them Catholics since he has been brought up in Ireland, where one's religion is always the question, and he concludes they are Catholic because of the crosses. In the same gaze he desires the bodies and notices the religion. Thus in one second of recognition, he realizes that their religion does not, as he hoped, curtail his desire, but nor does it permit it. The dilemma leaves Wilde in the same position he was in with the Anglican Church: an outcast homosexual.

The apparently insouciant attitude to the problem, which we associate with Wilde's later writing, is demonstrated by his masturbating over Thomas a Kempis later in the evening of the same day. A Kempis represents the holy life that Wilde wants in Catholicism, but the saint's ban on sexual gratification runs counter to the feelings incurred in Wilde by the beautiful Catholic men he has seen that afternoon. Wilde *has* to give way to his God given sexuality which has arisen in seeing the object of his desires, but if he does, he is damned by the messengers of God whom he wants to bring him to salvation. Thus, to masturbate while reading a Kempis ironizes the conventional religious curtailment of non-procreative sexual gratification: either in bed alone, or in the actual sight of naked men on the beach. The only question that remains for Wilde is: with two such contradictory desires, where is *my* place in Catholicism?

Wilde formally asked the question of his desired religion in April 1878 when he entered into a series of confirmation talks with the Revd Sebastian Bowden at the Brompton Oratory. He also took part

---

31. 'Momentary Pleasures: Wilde and English Verse', in Eibhear Walshe (ed.), *Sex, Nation and Dissent in Irish Writing* (New York: St. Martins Press, 1997), p. 43. [For]Wilde – from a Protestant, Anglo-Irish background, and a student from Oxford who suppresses the signs of his Irishness – finds the alterior appeal of the boys in their apparent freedom and naïve faith …In this way the sexual desirability of these boys is clearly bound up with their cultural otherness; indeed, this very fact seems to enable the desire.

32. And are they 'boys' or potential sexual partners? The term 'boy' is used in Anglo-Irish slang by homosexual men to describe another homosexual.

in an informal confession of his sins, receiving a curt rejoinder in a letter from Bowden.

> You have like everybody else an evil nature and this in your case has become more corrupted by bad influences mental and moral, and by positive sin.[33]

Neil McKenna explains succinctly what he believed happened:

> Reading between the lines, it seems clear that Oscar had confessed some or all of his sexual experiences ... to Father Bowden. And this was the "positive sin" Bowden was referring to. ... Bowden fervently urged Oscar to take the plunge and convert to Catholicism. "As a Catholic," he told him:
>
> > you would find yourself a new man in the order of nature as of grace. I mean that you would put from you all that is affected and unreal and a thing unworthy of your better self.
>
> ... by becoming a Catholic, Oscar would not only enter a state of grace, but that he would also throw off the burden of his unnatural sexual desires – that "thing unworthy of himself" – and take his assigned place in the natural order as a normal man, a man who loved women.

But, instead of converting, Wilde left a bunch of lilies on the steps of Brompton Oratory to signify his withdrawal from Catholicism: lilies being the sign of the sexless Annunciation of her pregnancy to Mary. It was as though Wilde was saying 'Sexless sex is not what I am capable of. Celibacy and chasteness are not the gifts I have been given by God.'

For one wracked by the paradox that the only religion that will give him the strength to defeat temptation by giving him human witnesses to help him, also leads him into temptation both religiously and sexually, Wilde responded with a sidestep. In the same letter that he called the Catholic Church 'scarlet woman' and 'snare of the fowler', Wilde showed that since there is no place for him inside, he must construct a place for himself outside it.

> If I *could hope* that the Church would wake in me some earnestness and purity I would go over *as a luxury*, if for no better reasons. But I can hardly hope it would, and to go over to Rome would

---

33. McKenna, *The Secret Life* (London: Century, 2003), p. 15.

be to sacrifice and give up my two great gods "Money and Ambition".[34]

Although these words were written a year before leaving the lilies at Brompton, they give the direction that Wilde would take: they mark the first steps on the road to his becoming the man who stood in symbolic relations to the art and culture of his age. That is, the man who took the Roman Catholic Jesus and Mary for his model to become intercessor between people and their art and culture.

But this was no sham religion of Art. Wilde did not put his 'faith' in art. Art is plastic and, although criticism is based upon judgments that do not coincide with the empirical, at least there is an object to see and from which to make a judgment, and upon whose elements one can justify the judgment. 'Faith' in God has no referent, and as we shall see, God remains in Wilde's writing as its central theme: and as a resolution to the paradox in which he found himself.

The Fisherman and His Soul

On the surface, 'The Fisherman and His Soul' reads like an extended version of one of Wilde's counter-aphorisms ('all bad art springs from genuine feeling') written in mockery of Victorian English sincerity. Certainly Wilde inverts Hans Andersen's[35] *The Little Mermaid*, in which it is the mermaid who wants to marry the prince, and in order to do so she has to *find* a soul. But if we take the spiritual aspects of the story seriously we can read it as a representation of the religious and sexual paradox in which Wilde found himself. 'The Fisherman and His Soul' was written in November 1891, a month before Wilde wrote *Salome*, and it can be read as another version of that play.

The first thing we have to understand is what the love between the fisherman and the mermaid represents, and in the terminology of this chapter, I would suggest that it is the illicitness, fruitfulness and disastrousness of a passionate relationship that falls outside the accepted religious norms of sexual behaviour. We see this in the priest's denunciation of the Fisherman when he asks to be rid of his soul so he can be like 'the Fauns that live in the Forest' and

---

34. *Letters*, p. 31.

35. The striking similarity between Wilde's and Andersen's sexual identities could call for comment here, but there is no space in this chapter for the discussion.

'the Mermen with their harps of red gold.'[36] It would be very easy to make the mistake of reading this as the Fisherman wanting to be like an animal, that is, without a soul. However, his choice of models is not from the animal kingdom, after all, Psalm 150: 6 declares 'Let everything that hath breath Praise the Lord.'[37] What distinguishes the fauns and merpeople is their being outcast, and partaking in perilous joys which can tempt people from the normal way, as the Priest says:

> the pagan things God suffers to wander through his World. Accursed be the Fauns of the woodland, and accursed be the singers of the sea. I have heard them in the night time, and they have sought to lure me from my beads. They tap on the window and laugh. They whisper into my ears the tale of their perilous joys. They tempt me with temptations, and when I would pray they make mouths at me. They are lost, I tell thee, they are lost. For them is no heaven nor hell, and in neither shall they praise God's name.[38]

It would therefore be reductive to read the fisherman's love for the mermaid as representative of a homosexual liaison. Rather, it represents the topos for Wilde's paradoxical dealings with the church and his sexuality. In the same way, the priest is neither specifically Anglican nor Catholic, but represents the voice of denunciation of that which lies outside his experience.

Thus, to find help, the fisherman has to go to another outcast, a witch, who, after sexual dancing at a black mass, gives him a knife with which to separate himself from his soul. In so doing, the fisherman cuts himself off from the sexual and social norms of his group, but is unquestionably happy to live with and love the mermaid. This is demonstrated by the first of his two yearly meetings with his soul, at which we learn that his love for the mermaid is worth more than all the wisdom and riches in the world.

When his soul comes to tempt the fisherman for the third time, the conventions of the Fairy Tale demand that this time it will be successful. It is therefore not unexpected that what tempts him out of

36. *Complete Works*, p. 238.

37. I have written on the question of whether animals have souls in *Christopher Smart: Clown of God* (Lewisburg: Bucknell, 2001) but it is not at issue here since the *Jubilate* suggests that animals can praise God whether or not they have souls.

38. *Complete Works*, p. 238.

his outcast position are the social and sexual norms of the life which the fisherman has given up. The soul tells him of a dancer whose

> face was veiled with a veil of gauze, but her feet were naked. Naked were her feet, and they moved over the carpet like little white pigeons. Never have I seen anything so marvellous …
>
> Now when the fisherman heard the words of his soul, he remembered that the little Mermaid had no feet and could not dance. And a great desire came over him …[39]

The desire to be normal, when the fisherman is happy being outcast, marks the beginning of his journey from joy to pain. Immediately he leaves what is natural to him – loving the mermaid and living in the water – the fisherman is led astray.

What runs counter to intuition, however, is that it is his soul, which the priest has called 'the noblest part of man'[40] which tempts the fisherman to perform evil acts, stealing and murder. In one sense, the inversion of our expectations is forced upon Wilde because of *his* inversion of the Hans Andersen story. But in another sense, this paradox becomes the point of the story. The Soul is bad, and blames its badness on the fisherman for not leaving him with a heart. Of course the fisherman needed his heart to love the mermaid, so here the story demonstrates Wilde's problem of wanting to give vent to his homosexuality (to give his heart to the mermaid) in a society whose religion will not allow it (the requirement that the fisherman gets rid of his soul to marry the mermaid). That Wilde thinks the situation is iniquitous is demonstrated by the soul's tempting the fisherman into evil when they are rejoined.

The fact that the fisherman cannot detach himself from his soul again demonstrates the power of society to impose itself upon the individual: and here we might think of Wilde writing the story, trapped in a marriage of convenience and with two children and a wife whom he loved. All he can do is shut his desires up inside of himself and pine for the lost opportunity to be who he really is. When the soul tempts him again with a sexually available woman, all the fisherman can do is think of his real love for the outcast mermaid.

> Her eyes are coloured with stibium, and her nostrils are shaped like the wings of a swallow. From a hook in one of her nostrils hangs a flower that is carved out of pearl. She laughs when she

39. Complete Works, p. 252.
40. Complete Works, p. 238.

dances, and silver rings that are about her ankles tinkle like bells of silver. And so trouble yourself no more, but come with me to this city.

But the young fisherman answered not his soul, but closed his lips with the seal of silence and with a tight cord bound his hands, and journeyed back to the place from which he had come, even to the little bay where his love had been wont to sing. And ever did his Soul tempt him by the way, but he made it no answer, nor would he do any of the wickedness that it sought to make him do, so great was the power of the love that was within him.[41]

The impasse is made complete when the fisherman finally gives in to his soul, and says that it can return to his heart. The soul cannot find a way in, and the fisherman must tell his soul that he wants it to return to his heart, at which, there is a cry of mourning from the Sea as the Mermaid dies. When the fisherman has finally lied to himself in giving in to the demands of religion, he has shown that he must no longer love the object of his sexual desire.

The image of the fisherman drowning himself beside the corpse of the mermaid is interesting. When he was outcast, and knew himself outcast, he could live in the sea – an alien medium for a normal human. When he has let the soul back into his heart, and lied to himself declaring that he wants to be a normal human, he dies in the medium where he had been happiest – the outcast medium of the sea. But his death comes when he has let the soul into his heart: dramatizing the problem of the desire for religion pulling against the desire for unauthorized sexual congress.

We can see that Wilde saw no solution to the problem in the ending of the story. The flowers which have grown on the fisherman's and mermaid's grave cause the priest to preach about love rather than wrath. This is a new definition of love, it is an active sexual love, and not the sexless love of Mary's Annunciation, and we see it in the fact that the priest

> blessed the Sea and all the wild things that are in it, The Fauns also he blessed, and the little things that dance in the woodland, and the bright-eyed things that peer through the leaves. All the things in God's world he blessed, and the people were filled with joy and wonder.[42]

41. Complete Works, p. 255.
42. Complete Works, p. 258.

While this ought to be a rainbow sign for the future happiness for homosexuals and others outcast by the church, the final lines of the story are bleak:

> Yet never again in the corner of the Fuller's Field grew flowers of any kind, but the field remained barren even as before. Nor came the Sea-folk into the bay as they had been wont to do, for they went to another part of the sea.[43]

The absence of those affected by the tragedy from the places the priest blesses, suggests that Wilde believes that the Priest will only bless what he thinks is good. His opinion of the merpeople has not changed because they will not conform to the priest's view of what they should be.

The paragraph, I would argue, marks Wilde's exit from organized religions. Although he uses the terminology of religion, and was keen to continue to do so throughout his writing (in *Salome* for example) which demonstrated his continuing interest in his spiritual life and salvation (of which *The Selfish Giant* is probably the most poignant) Wilde could not do so within the confines of the Anglican or Roman Catholic Churches.

43. Complete Works, p. 258.

Chapter 2

E.F. BENSON, THE *DAVID BLAIZE* TRILOGY, A SEXUALITY FIT FOR MY LORD – E.F.B., GOD AND THE ARCHBISHOP

Introduction

What little critical heritage Edward Frederick Benson enjoys, seems either to read the author of some 70 novels as the creator of the camp characters in the Mapp and Lucia cycle,[1] to make speculations in brief and unfootnoted introductions to reprint editions about which character is the closest self-portrait,[2] or to try to explain the author through the gossip of others who knew him.[3] And if there is one biographical fact that is reported again and again, it is that E.F.B. was one of the six brilliant children of Edward White Benson, Founding Headmaster of Wellington School, Founding Master of the Lincoln Seminary, and Archbishop of Canterbury.

His more thorough biographers, Brian Masters,[4] and Geoffrey Palmer and Noel Lloyd,[5] note that E.F.B. wrote homoerotic novels,

1. See, for example, Rachel R. Mather, *The Heirs of Jane Austen: Twentieth-Century Writers of the Comedy of Manners* (New York: Peter Lang, 1996), and Robert Kiernan, *Frivolity Unbound: Six Masters of the Camp Novel* (New York: Continuum, 1990).

2. Particularly the Hogarth edition of some of his works published in 1985, with introductions by T.J. Binyon and Peter Burton. For example, Peter Burton writes: It is my contention that while David represents Benson's innocence, Maddox represents Benson's awareness; that, in effect, Benson used the duality of his own nature to create *both* his central characters – giving to either David or Maddox the components from his own personality which most suited them. Thus David's horror at his father's appearance and behaviours at the cricket match coincides with something similar from Benson's schooldays, while Maddox's time at the archaeological school in Athens neatly coincides with Benson's own Athens experiences.

3. See, for example, Cynthia and Tony Reavell, *E.F. Benson: Mr Benson Remembered in Rye, and the World of Tilling* (Rye: Martello Bookshop, 1984). The Tilling Society website is another bastion of E.F.B. gossip.

4. Brian Masters, *The Life of E.F. Benson* (London: Chatto & Windus, 1991) [Cited as Masters].

5. Geoffrey Palmer and Noel Lloyd, *E.F. Benson As He Was* (Luton: Lennard Publishing, 1988) [Cited as Palmer and Lloyd].

but each claim that it is not possible to be certain about the question of his sexuality, concluding that he was very private about it and that we shall never know for certain whether or not he was a homosexual. Speculation about his same-sex desire has been constant.[6] After the success of his first novel *Dodo* (1893) E.F.B. moved in a fast literary set which included Oscar Wilde and Lord Alfred Douglas. But to base any conclusions about homosexuality on information of that sort is an attempt to prove guilt by association.

Geoffrey Palmer and Noel Lloyd demonstrate how unsuccessful it is to try to make this type of clear assignment of homosexuality, and gloss E.F.B.'s friendship with Wilde and his associates very circumspectly:

> It was likely that Fred and Oscar Wilde were introduced to each other by Robert Ross, Wilde's devoted friend who spent a year, or part of a year, at King's College ... Lord Alfred Douglas says in his autobiography that he was on terms of great friendship with Fred Benson. Fred attended the first night of *Lady Windermere's Fan* with Max Beerbohm and Reggie Turner (whom Wilde called the child catcher of Clement's Inn), each wearing a green carnation.[7]

This extract seems to demand the reader to believe that E.F.B. was a homosexual because he wore a green carnation in public. But the wearing of the flower could have been unintentional, or might have merely been to show E.F.B.'s support for Wilde and his play. But the problem with guilt by association is that it quickly establishes itself as a clear accusation when repeated at second and third hand:

> Fred met [Lord Alfred] Douglas again in Luxor. They, with Robert Hichens, author of *The Green Carnation* and Reginald Turner, made a vicious quartet, staying in the same hotel before travelling up the Nile together. ... Rupert Croft-Cooke, in *Bosie* called Fred 'one of the three queer sons of the Archbishop of Canterbury' and hints maliciously that the trip to Luxor was made for reasons the reverse of cultural.[8]

---

6. Peter Burton, *David of King's* (Brighton: Millivres, 1991). There is no evidence that E.F.B. ever fulfilled his emotional leanings: in fact the number of spinsters of both sexes in his books suggests that he was without carnal knowledge, a knowing innocent. Unpaginated.

7. Palmer and Lloyd, p. 32.

8. Palmer and Lloyd, p. 50. In Rodney Bolt, *As Good as God, As Clever as the Devil* (London: Atlantic Books, 2011), we learn that Maggie, EFB's sister, accompanied him on this trip to Luxor.

There is no evidence for Croft-Cooke's accusation, but nor is there evidence for Palmer and Lloyd's repeating the implication. And they go further than implying homosexuality, claiming that it was because of the Wilde trial that: 'Fred retired to the sidelines [of the homosexual world] as an observer rather than a participant, knowing what was going on in the underworld of sexual deviation, commenting on it obliquely, but never openly acknowledging its attractions for him.'[9] This is not strictly true. The homoerotic novels, and the *David Blaize* trilogy in particular, discuss 'sexual deviation' in great detail. In *David Blaize and the Blue Door* (1918), *David Blaize* (1916) and *David of King's* (1924), the love between two boys, which grows into the love between two men, David Blaize and Frank Maddox, is the sole topic.

As far as I can tell, the *David Blaize* trilogy has never been the subject of academic analysis. Stanley T. Williams mentions the first in his 'Parent of Schoolboy Novels'[10] only to list it as another book that was influenced by *Tom Brown's Schooldays*. Eona de Vere lists it in 'Wide Reading in the Novel' in a group 'revealing the development of character'.[11] J. A. Mangan notes that David Blaize is a sports hero of a 'lesser extent' in the novel of that name, but says no more.[12] Hugh Brogan points out that Christopher Isherwood says he 'revelled in *David Blaize*' in *Lions and Shadows*, but does not discuss why.[13] Intriguingly, Robert Protherough quotes from an unnamed novel of the 1930s which declares 'People whose knowledge of public schools is based on *David Blaize* … What a Mistake!'[14] Protherough returns to *David Blaize* once more in an account of 'Shaping the Image of the Great Headmaster' noting that the Headmaster in the book (there are two, but I believe that the descriptions are all of David's Private School Head at the beginning of the novel) is an 'object of terror', 'impressive', 'tall' and treated with 'awed respect'.[15] Paul M. Puccio comments that in *David Blaize* David has no mother and Frank no

9. Palmer and Lloyd, p. 50.

10. *The English Journal* 10. 5 (May 1921): pp. 241–46.

11. *The English Journal* 32. 1 (January 1943): pp. 44–45.

12. 'Play Up and Play the Game', in *British Journal of Educational Studies* 23. 3 (October 1975): pp. 324–35.

13. *Twentieth Century Literature* 22. 3, Christopher Isherwood Issue (October 1976): pp. 303–11.

14. 'True and False in School Fiction,' *British Journal of Educational Studies* 27. 2 (June 1979): pp. 140–53.

15. *British Journal of Educational Studies* 32. 3 (October 1984): pp. 239–50.

father, and quotes the passage when David is mortified when his father, the Archdeacon, shouts out his Christian name at a cricket match.[16] None of these amounts to a serious academic study, and none mentions more than the first published of the three novels.

Both biographies spend a little time on the three novels, and both read them as to some extent autobiographical. Masters mines *David Blaize* 14 times for hints and guesses about E.F.B.'s character. Palmer and Lloyd describe Benson's project in writing *David Blaize* as an exercise in memoir:

> Fred had long wanted to write a chronicle about the time in a boy's life when, both impressionable and sentimental, he is without a gender of his own, feeling neither completely male nor female, but indeterminate. Such creatures, Fred claimed, are not bothered by sex, so their energies can be directed into other channels, and in particular into a devotion that transcends the physical ... He thought he could do it by depicting himself under the name of David Blaize as he really had been, or had wanted to be, all those years ago: yellow haired, sunny-natured and of an unbelievable goodness.[17]

Despite the evidence of this opinion, which is taken from a letter from E.F.B. that claims that David and Frank's devotion 'transcends the physical', sex and the question of David's sexuality *is* raised in *David Blaize*. Both Masters, and Palmer and Lloyd draw attention to the scene in their school-house bathroom when David and Frank's relationship nearly becomes physical. The scene will be quoted at length and discussed in detail below, so at this stage, I will simply state that I think that Masters' conclusion that 'it is unquestionably a love scene, [which] makes more sense of the reconciliation a few pages later when Maddox more or less begs forgiveness and makes plain that he has threatened David's innocence with "the miry road that had been in [his] mind",'[18] misses the point. And so does Palmer and Lloyd's conclusion that 'After ... a gruff little scene of reconciliation, and with sighs of relief the two boys resume the old relationship.'[19] It is not reconciliation that comes at the end of the

16. 'At the Heart of Tom Brown's Schooldays,' in *Modern Language Studies* 25. 4 (Autumn 1995): pp. 57–74.

17. Palmer and Lloyd, p. 99. Masters quotes the source of these ideas in a letter from E.F.B. to an unnamed academic, see, Masters, p. 215.

18. Masters, p. 76.

19. Palmer and Lloyd, p. 101.

bathroom incident, it is the awareness that the ever present sexuality at the heart of their friendship has to be negotiated because it will not go away, whether or not they act upon it. Furthermore, the point of writing a trilogy about the same relationship would seem to be that David and Frank have to negotiate and renegotiate the sexual angle of their friendship over and over again, and that physical sex, which is seen in the bathroom incident as a threat to their early friendship, does not become any the less difficult to circumvent as they grow up and their age and status differences become less important. At almost every moment each may lead the other down 'the miry road' to physical fulfilment.

The very fact that in *David of King's*, E.F.B. returned to David and Frank's friendship a third time, eight years after the first two volumes, seems to confirm this, but once again Palmer and Lloyd's conclusion seems to miss the point.[20] They suggest that in the final volume, 'Frank was certain that one day David would "manifest himself in the ways of a man with a maid", and then the private David would be accessible to him no longer.'[21] But this misreads the last third of the book, in which David has written a letter to Frank (which we do not see) telling him that, for him, their friendship has changed. The tension of the end of the story lies in the fact that we do not know what David has written, and whether the friendship will survive the contents of the letter. The relief of the last page comes when Frank, who has brought David the news that he has taken a First Class Degree, explains that what David wrote was that he has grown up, so their friendship can no longer be based in the hero worship that it had formerly. It is clear at the end of the book that the friendship will continue, and will continue to negotiate itself and re-negotiate itself around the question of its founding sexual basis. The one thing it will never be is physical.

The key to this reading of the *David Blaize* trilogy lies in the second written volume, *David Blaize and the Blue Door*, which tells of David's coming to consciousness about sex and his early-childhood dilemma over sexuality. The volume is not popular with either biographer. Palmer and Lloyd describe it as 'a mishmash of surreal incidents

20. Masters does not make any judgement of this volume, and merely recounts Ethel Smyth's 'rapturous if slightly breathless explosion of praise,' p. 255. He also miss-titles the book *David at King's*.

21. Palmer and Lloyd, p. 139.

22. Palmer and Lloyd, p. 190.

that might individually be funny but cobbled together without any connecting thread are definitely not.'[22] Brian Masters believes that it 'seems contrived'.[23] While there is no doubt that *David Blaize and the Blue Door* is a substandard *Alice in Wonderland* in terms of reading it as a children's book, it becomes more interesting when considered as having adult content. I shall argue that it concerns David Blaize's rejection of hetero and homosexual activity in favour of autoeroticism. The reason why he eventually rejects physical sexuality in all of its forms becomes the material for the third volume, when as a man David must put away childish things.

Masters' biography is useful in making my argument since it was he who pointed out the similarity between the subject of *David Blaize* and E.F.B.'s brother Arthur Christopher Benson's book, *The Memoirs of Arthur Hamilton* (1886),[24] which discusses the irresistible, and potentially destructive power of same-sex love, and the need to overcome it in some way. A.C.B.'s book is the story about the perfect friendship between Arthur Hamilton and Edward Bruce, school-master and pupil, who know their desire for sexual gratification with each other, but who have repented it, transcended it, and live instead in the serenity of avoiding sex rather than acting upon their desires. However, expounding on the similarities between Arthur Hamilton, David Blaize and E.F.B., Masters concludes that E.F.B. 'was, in short, a prude. There is a sadness about Fred's self-denial which he only allowed to show, obliquely, in his fiction.'[25] I shall argue the contrary, that E.F.B. explores asexuality and the reasons for making the choice of self-denial thoroughly in the *David Blaize* trilogy. And for E.F.B., sexual self-denial is presented as the epitome of the love that one man may have for another in the eyes of his Lord.

The subjects of the analyses in the other essays in this book have either left the organized church or failed to be ordained. For E.F.B., ordination seems to have been expected of him, given the vocation

23. Masters, p. 225.

24. Keegan Paul, Trench & Co.: London. [Cited as *Arthur Hamilton*] The novel claims to be an edition of Arthur Hamilton's memoirs by his friend Christopher Carr, and so may be read like an internal conversation in Arthur Christopher Benson. If we privilege such an association between author and protagonist, we would be reducing the novel to being an occasional piece, a personal gripe about a particular set of circumstances, rather than a more generally applicable comment on the interface between same-sex relationships and the church at the beginning of the twentieth century.

25. Masters, p. 247.

and position of his father. Of course, having an archbishop for a father does not necessitate that the son should follow in his father's footsteps, but the fact that Edward White Benson's portrait subtitled 'My Lord,' appears as the frontispiece of E.F.B.'s autobiographical sketch, *As We Were* (1930), suggests the depth of the influence of his father. Reflecting this ecclesiastical father-son relationship in the *David Blaize* trilogy, David's father is an Archdeacon, and supervising David's first flight with the birds in *David Blaize and the Blue Door* is Canon Crow, who got the name because he and his wife used to nest in a cathedral close. Whether or not E.F.B. disappointed the Archbishop by not entering the priesthood, the Archdeacon does approve of David's decision to become a writer in *David of King's*, but, as we shall see, only if David fulfils certain conditions. And the major one will be argued to be to give up autoeroticism and remain celibate.

We can find a source for E.F.B.'s championing sexual self-denial in the marriage service in the *Book of Common Prayer*, where we are told that marriage 'was ordained for the procreation of children' and as 'a remedy against sin, and to avoid fornication, that such persons as have not the gift of continency, might marry, and keep themselves undefiled members of Christ's body'. I shall argue that E.F.B. felt that the gift of continency was the only way to come to terms with same-sex desire, and he wrote about it, not as a transcendental place of peace after physical sin, as his brother depicted it, but as a constant battle akin to the battle to keep faith or the battle against sin. E.F.B.'s brother and sister, Arthur and Maggie, suffered terribly from depression, and each has also been associated with same sex love, but where they retreated respectively into trite prose and archaeology to stave off their black dog, E.F.B. appears to have been able to live more or less happily without physical expression of his love. Or at least that is what he writes about in the *David Blaize* novels.

The Memoirs of Arthur Hamilton

Brian Masters suggests that E.F.B.'s brother, A.C. Benson, would rather the first book in the trilogy, *David Blaize* 'had been more distant and detached' since 'it came close to identifying one of the Benson "problems" – homosexuality.' Masters quotes some textual

26. Masters, p. 212.

variants,[26] which demonstrate that there are signs that E.F.B. altered his manuscript in accordance with some of A.C.B.'s suggestions, so *Arthur Hamilton* would seem a good place to start to understand the genesis of *David Blaize*.

A.C.B. was a teacher at Eton College and later Fellow then Master of Magdalene College, Cambridge. In common with other writers who lived and worked at single sex establishments at the turn of the twentieth century, his novel shows he was aware that contemporary work on inversion and perversion by sexologists such as Havelock Ellis and Kraft-Ebing, had identified a tension between being interested in people of the same sex and being sexually interested in people of the same sex. It is also likely that he knew of 'Comrade Love' which was being popularized in Walt Whitman's poetry and in men's clubs, and how it affected his own life as a tutor to boys and young men in whom as a teacher he was defined by being interested in them, and who might in turn hero-worship him. Moreover, A.C.B. had been a member of the Apostles, a homoerotic group of upper-class intellectuals, while he was at King's College, Cambridge, reading for his Bachelor's degree. He had a mental breakdown while taking his degree, and the *Oxford Dictionary of National Biography* suggests that the breakdown was associated with 'a chastely loved friend from school' who entered into a physical relationship, either with A.C.B. or someone else. Thereafter A.C.B. preached abstinence from sex, and was horrified by the fact of schoolboy masturbation (*The School Master*, 1902).

In *Arthur Hamilton*, A.C.B. begins by presenting a philosophy of determinism, which brings with it what we would now call an essentialist view of sexuality, and of homosexuality. Hamilton is writing as a dying man looking back on his career as a teacher, he muses: 'Now, the more I work at Education, the more I am driven into Determinism; it seems that we can hardly regulate tendency ...'[27] A few pages later he repeats himself.

> If I saw the slightest loophole at which free-will might creep in, I would rush to it, but I do not; if man was created with a free will, he was also created with predispositions which made the acting of that will a matter of mathematical certainty.[28]

27. *Arthur Hamilton*, p. 33.
28. *Arthur Hamilton*, p. 42.

A.C.B.'s logic demonstrates the belief that humans have inborn predispositions towards particular patterns of behaviour, and they can only have the free will to decide between acting upon one or more of these patterns. Therefore, they do not have the free will to do a thing for which they have no pre-determined inclination. In terms of sexuality, the theory implies that if one has only a predisposition to same-sex attraction, one cannot use free will to choose to desire members of the opposite sex, which follows the inversion theory of sexuality. A.C.B. comes to sexuality later in the book, and we shall explore his view in detail below.

After introducing his epistemology, Hamilton then begins to tell his story. In order to get over the failure of his friendship with a young man whom he met at school, he takes a trip around Europe and much of the rest of the world, so as to carry out his decision to withdraw from 'Living life to the uttermost' and instead to live a life of contemplation. While in Teheran [sic], Arthur meets an Englishman with two sons, who entrusts the elder to him, to be his tutee after Hamilton has returned to England. The decision is made because of an instant fellow-feeling which arises between man and boy:

> The boy had formed a great attachment to him, and the idea of
> their future sent a strange and unwonted glow into Arthur's mind,
> so that he parted from him on the next day "with wonder in his
> heart," and something like an ache too.[29]

The meeting between Hamilton and the boy – Edward Bruce[30] – sets up the problem of the teacher, who must have a liking for young people in order to carry out his job, but who, in the contemporary sexological climate, is confronted with the idea that his liking might overspill into sexual activity, and the invert might pervert the boy. Moreover, the 'ache in his heart' is happening for a second time for a second boy, and this starts Hamilton thinking about the origin of 'sin and disorder' in God's world. He left England to get away from

---

29. *Arthur Hamilton*, p. 87.

30. The fact that the initials of the boy are 'E.B.' cannot escape notice, along with the hint of homosexual incest which it sets up between the brothers, E.F.B. and A.C.B. Initials are important in this book, since it is presented as a memoir of Arthur Hamilton, written to Christopher Carr, A.C.B.'s first two names. Furthermore, E.F.B. and A.C.B. lived many years together in Rye. However, this is a speculative reading, and as such no more convincing than the idea that E.F.B. was a practising homosexual because he associated with Lord Alfred Douglas.

a relationship in which the object of his attraction has fallen into sensuality, and thus it seems as though the meeting with Edward Bruce, for whom he feels a similar attraction, was somehow divinely inspired to test his resistance, since 'He certainly regarded [sin and disorder] as emanating practically, in some way that he did not comprehend, from God.'[31] Hamilton speaks to himself demanding he:

> Accept my present condition; brace yourself to bear it. I know how much can be borne. Give your sufferings to God nobly. Your patience is none the less noble because you have brought this on yourself; nay, it makes it even nobler.[32]

The remainder of his trip gives Hamilton time to reconsider his actions and failings in various other situations in his life to date, and to ruminate upon on former mistakes concomitant upon his following, or failing to follow his predispositions. He lists how as a shy single man he learned to avoid social situations, how his ability to form close relations with boys fit him to be a teacher, how he came to terms with the fact that he had no literary talent though he wanted to be a writer, how the depression resulting from his failures might be overcome, how to die well and since he discovers he is terminally ill, how to find serenity rather than commit suicide facing his inevitable destiny. All these lessons have been stored up, he believes, so that he can learn how to summon enough strength to counter the sexual aspect of the attraction he feels for Edward Bruce.

When the boy arrives in England, Hamilton's feelings for Bruce try him to the uttermost, so much so that we find among his musings about education, an extraordinary passage about the power of sexual attraction, which regards all forms of sexual gratification as a sin that must be resisted at all costs.

> I must confess that I do not realize the strength of this particular temptation, but I am willing to allow for its being almost infinitely strong. I don't know what has preserved me. It is the one thing about which I never venture to judge a man in the least, because, from all I hear and see, it must hurry people away from the manner of which those who have not experienced it cannot form any conception.

31. *Arthur Hamilton*, p. 112.
32. *Arthur Hamilton*, p. 113.

You ask me what I think the probable effect that yielding to such temptation has on a man's character. Of course, some drift into hopeless sensualists. About those I have my own gospel, though I do not preach it; it has scarcely formulated hope. But of those that recover, or are recovered, all depends upon the kind of repentance. The morbid repentance that sometimes ensues is very disabling. All dwelling on such falls is very fatal: all thoughts of what might have been, all reflections about the profaned temple and the desecrated shrine though they cannot be escaped, yet must not be indulged. I always advise people to try and forget them in *any* possible way – banish them, drown them, beat them down.

But the subject is very repugnant to me. I don't like thinking or talking about it, because it has its other side: the thought of a woman in connection with such things is so unutterably ghastly; it is one of the problems about which I may say most earnestly "God knows".[33]

I have quoted at length since it is only in the final paragraph that one can be certain that Hamilton is writing about homosexual attraction as the 'particular temptation' that is 'almost infinitely strong.' Due to Hamilton's determinist view of pre-dispositions, his not coming to judgement about other people who 'drift into hopeless sensualists' falls something short of magnanimity. But at the same time, the discussion about repentance being 'morbid' or 'manly' suggests empathy and offers hope to those who 'recover, or are recovered,' albeit a barbed hope. For Hamilton, there can be hope only for those who do repent and 'preserve' themselves. It would seem therefore to be almost certain that Hamilton has not preserved himself unscathed with the first of his infatuations, since his discourses in the rest of the book on his own morbid depression that has led to manly repentance, must lead to the conclusion that he has at one time drifted into sensuality, and 'recovered or been recovered'. Hamilton's advice is most interesting, since it is the morbid repentance that 'must not be indulged', not the sin, since the sin is unavoidable if you have a pre-disposition to a temptation that is almost infinitely strong. The alternative of 'manly repentance' which can 'temper and brace the character' is no doubt Hamilton's final position, a position of transcendent abstention after the fact of sin.

33. *Arthur Hamilton*, p. 179.

And this would seem to be the message of the book. Hamilton has fallen into sensuality, has 'recovered or been recovered'. He has indulged in morbid repentance, and moved to the final position of manly repentance, a position of power from which he can face the second onslaught of his feelings for Edward Bruce and yet not succumb. But the end of the book is weak, since both Edward Bruce and Hamilton die, the first in an accident in which he is run over by a dog cart, the second of his illness. Neither has to maintain the life of manly repentance very long, and even the time Bruce is living with Hamilton in Cornwall, when one would think the temptation was at its height, is treated very briefly. All this considered, the book seems to suggest that A.C.B. was more interested in describing than sustaining the state of transcendental abstention. But sustaining abstention over a long period is exactly what E.F.B. attempts to describe in *David Blaize*. For A.C.B. the mathematical certainty of same-sex desire makes the physical act of sex inescapable, and repentance after the fact the only way to defeat it. I shall demonstrate that E.F.B. argues against his brother and sets up, in the *David Blaize* trilogy, a way that could allow for free choice in matters sexual by describing a sex-life that maintains virginity by moving from inviolable innocence, to knowing innocence, to solo masturbation, and ending in asexual marriage. Whether or not this is the working through of a gift of continency, it allows David Blaize to avoid the mathematical certainty of his homosexual nature from leading him into forbidden homosexual encounters.

A clear link is forged between A.C.B.'s novel and *David Blaize* in the manner of Bruce's death. With E.F.B.'s typical insouciant wit, there are two incidents with carts in the *David Blaize* trilogy. The first runs over David at the end of *David Blaize*, and brings Frank back from Cambridge to David's bedside, to hold his friend's hand for an entire night: an act which saves David's life. The cart then reappears in an innocent prank at the beginning of *David of King's,* when David throws a ball over one parked outside King's College, and hits his friend Bags. The effect of the three accidents with carts is identical, leading to mawkish and overly sentimental feelings being shown for a same-sex friend. The horse pulling the cart in the prank in *David of King's* almost causes an accident, and an association is born between apparently innocent fun and its consequences in both *Arthur Hamilton* and the *David Blaize* trilogy.

But the main difference between the two brothers' works is that where Bruce dies while Hamilton is still his guardian, David and

Frank must live on with their mutual desire, moving from an hierarchical relationship as boys in school to one of equal adults who want to continue their association all their lives. For them it is not a case of reaching some earthly transcendence, but of working through the practicalities of celibacy and chasteness: the continual testing of their gift of continency. For them, every day of their lives becomes a trial of strength against their desire. The cross each bears is his love for the other that will never be fulfilled in sexual contact.

The David Blaize Trilogy

My approach to close reading the trilogy has a dissonant logic to it. The books were written out of chronological order according to David's life, but I have resisted the temptation to put them back into their correct order. I will begin with the volume set in school, *David Blaize,* and then move back in narrative time to read the story of David's childhood in *David Blaize and the Blue Door,* because this volume about David's early life expands and explains David's sexuality, rather than sets the foundations for it as we might expect from its position as a chronological first volume. The reason is twofold. First, the very fact that *David Blaize and the Blue Door* was written after, or at least published after *David Blaize,* gives it the look of a sequel, even if it concerns David at nine years old. Second, *David Blaize and the Blue Door* takes the form of the dream of a single night rather than an account of David's day-to-day life, as do the other two volumes. This means that it reads like a sort of flashback in the mind of the grown up David, which suggests in turn, that it glosses the first volume, and so ought to be read with the first volume in mind. In this sense, I would argue that *David Blaize and the Blue Door* is a stylistic innovation, more modernist than any other of E.F.B.'s literary output. E.F.B. concentrates on David's mind, analysing him, his nursery rhymes, toys and games. *David Blaize and the Blue Door* clearly discusses heterosexuality, homosexuality and masturbation, and it might be argued that E.F.B. had the direct intention of psychoanalysing his protagonist. However, I cannot find any references to E.F.B. having studied, or being convinced by Freud's arguments, so the line of reasoning that the book is in any way a technical psychoanalysis is hard to sustain. Furthermore, the lack of father and mother figures in *David Blaize and the Blue Door* and substituting for them, a motley crew of uncles, animals from the ark, tin soldiers, a trout, a pike and Mr Noah, suggests that David is less being imposed with the obligatory superego, than the dream is to be read as a vehicle for saying difficult things in disguise. It would seem that E.F.B. knew little more about Freud than his more famous creation Lucia, who mentions 'that horrid thing that Freud called sex.' If he did know about condensation and displacement in dreams, this would give more weight to my reading of the book as being sexual, but the references to sex through childish toys, ideas and games are so clear cut that it would seem hard to deny them with or without Freudian reading machinery, especially after having read the first volume, *David Blaize*. And, of course, since Freud found no place for homosexuality in his system, and less for asexuality, his work would in any case have been of little help to E.F.B.

My readings of the various actions of the novels will probably also appear a little at odds, as I shall work through each volume in turn expounding upon those incidents that I believe to be important. This is largely because no academic work has been done on these novels, so I have no secondary sources to refer to which might act as short cuts. The method will mean that I shall move back and forth from the point I want to make, but since the overall strategy is to argue that the *David Blaize* trilogy is about asexuality and the intermittent struggle necessary to abstain from sex, then to present the volumes in the order they appeared, and the incidents in the order in which they occur will perhaps give the truest picture of the unpredictable nature of the situations in which sexuality appears.

Chapter 3

E.F. BENSON: THE *DAVID BLAIZE* TRILOGY, A SEXUALITY FIT FOR MY LORD – THE CLOSET OF NIGHTMARES

Sex and the religious disapproval of two of its forms are announced as the royal road to inviolable innocence from the first incident of *David Blaize*. With their class, David and his friend Crabtree (Bags) are writing letters home to their fathers, from their Private [i.e. Preparatory] School, one Sunday afternoon. They are housed in the school museum as their classroom is being decorated. They have done their Catechism and Bible study, and now are watched over by the ineffectual Mr Dutton, who is reading a Maupassant novel hidden in his Bible. While Dutton is 'deep in the misfortunes that happened to Mademoiselle Fifi',[1] Bags throws an inky dart that hits David on the mouth, when all of a sudden the Headmaster enters. However, rather than chide Bags or David for the dart, the Head first turns to the hidden pornographic novel, and tells off its owner:

> By some strange mischance – I repeat – by some strange mischance – I have found this disgusting and licentious book on your desk. How it got there, how it happened to be open at page 56, I do not wish to inquire. It is more than enough for me to have found it there. I am willing to believe, and to tell you so publicly, Mr. Dutton, before the boys whom you are superintending on this Sunday afternoon, I am willing to believe that some obscene bird dropped from its claws this stinking – yes, sir, stinking – carrion.[2]

Albeit that the book is out of place in a junior school classroom, in the public act of humiliating Mr. Dutton, the Head criticizes licentiousness in general as well as the teacher in particular. In so doing, heterosexual desire is denied in the curious concatenation of the boys, the reader and the Headmaster all apparently knowing what happens on page 56 of the Maupassant. The technique is that of comedy, the reader is set up to believe from the moment Mademoiselle Fifi is

---

1. E.F. Benson, *David Blaize* (London: Hodder and Stoughton, 1916), p. 5.
2. Benson, *David Blaize*, p. 10.

mentioned that some disaster will strike. Maybe Mr. Dutton will forget that the book is hidden in his Bible and ask a boy to read from the book on his desk. Maybe Mr. Dutton will begin laughing at what he has read, forgetting he is supposed to be studying the Bible. When the Head enters the classroom, the reader's attention has been diverted by the inky dart, so when the Head goes unerringly to Mr. Dutton's desk and finds the offending book the laugh is redoubled in the relief that David has not been caught. Furthermore, even if logic tells us that if the Head has been looking through the window and seen the dart, he has also seen the hidden novel, the fact that he has most probably mentioned the book being open to page 56 as proof that Mr Dutton has been reading, that fact is also lost in the comedy of the reader knowing that the page concerns the 'misfortunes that happen to Mademoiselle Fifi,' and so it appears that the Head knows the content of the book as well. Nevertheless, the Head's rage and utterly unprofessional behaviour towards his teacher cuts across the comedy and makes a serious attack on heterosexual desire: if the boys knew about it their inviolable innocence would be lost.

But the Head has not finished denouncing sex in the attack on Maupassant. Although I would not want to read the inky dart, which left its mark on David's mouth, as a Freudian phallus delivering an oral load, the punishment the Head imposes upon Bags and David nevertheless denounces homoeroticism.

> "I infer that the ink on Blaize's lips was made by this weapon," he said. "That is so? Then you will now beg Blaize's pardon, and as soon as Catechism and Bible-class is over, you will fetch a basin of water and bathe Blaize's mouth with your own sponge, until it is pronounced clean by your matron."[3]

Literally to wash the mouth of his friend in front of the matron is to be told to perform an intimate homoerotic act in public, since English men (and boys) have no socially acceptable way to touch one another's faces. That Bags has to use his own sponge adds another frisson to the eroticism of the act. But at the same time, the boys' inviolable innocence is maintained as the eroticism is defused in the public nature of the act: it is watched over by the matron.

The two parts of the Head's denunciation of sex, draws out the main message of the book: that to maintain inviolable innocence, one should live in private as though one was living in public, and

3. Benson, *David Blaize*, p. 12.

that all one's private sexual actions are watched over by a superior. As with the Head revealing Mr Dutton's pornographic book, which hides the words of the Bible from him, the superior who watches all private life and thoughts is, of course, God.

Returning to the denouement of the first scene, the Head makes the religious aspect of his message clear. After meting out the punishments, he repeats the Catechism and Bible story lesson, which Mr Dutton is supposed to have taught, whence:

> Boys who had got full marks earlier in the afternoon found themselves unable, when facing the grim mood of the Head's, to repeat their duty towards anything. The ground already covered was taken again, in order to give them a fresh start, and now the Creed itself presented pitfalls and stumbling-blocks.[4]

Under the relaxed regime of Dutton, where sensuality in the guise of the Maupassant novel occludes the message of the Bible, the boys recite their lessons perfectly but by rote. But this is not the way to true knowledge, since 'Mr Dutton always consulted the New Testament Maclear … whereas the boys had to shut up that useful volume when they were questioned [by the Head].'[5] Under his watchful eyes, whence they confront the word of God directly, there is no crib sheet by which to understand and obey God's law. Lessons must be learned properly to live a life of inviolable innocence that is acceptable to God.

David learns the same lesson, that he must live his private life as though he is living in public, from his father, and once again the method of telling it is comedy, and once again thwarted sensuality is bound up with the lesson. Father and son have nothing in common, and when writing the letter, which began the novel, we learn that,

> It was really difficult for him to know what to say to his dear papa, for all the events of the past week were completely thrown into shadow by the one sunlit fact that he had got his school colours for cricket, and had made twenty-four runs in the last match. But, as he knew perfectly well, his father cared as little for cricket as he did for football; indeed David ironically doubted if he knew the difference between them, and that deplorable fact restricted the zone of interests common to them.[6]

4. Benson, *David Blaize*, p. 14.
5. Benson, *David Blaize*, p. 14.
6. Benson, *David Blaize*, p. 5.

Later the same evening, after the Head's tough lesson, the other boys taunt David with the idea that religious lessons are painful:

> "Anyhow, I'm glad my father isn't a clergyman, like Blaize's. Do you do divinity with him in the study on Sunday afternoon in the holidays." Whack, whack. "There my boy!" "Oh, papa, don't hit me!" Whack, whack! "Oh, papa!" Squeaked Sharpe Major.[7]

The letter writing and the taunt are incomprehensible on their own, but come together to make the lesson clear later in the book when David's father visits the school to attend a cricket match and preach a sermon in chapel. The Archdeacon is the very 'parody of a parent.'[8] He bowls into the wrong net, he is wearing a Jaeger vest visible under his brown flannel shirt, he even kisses David in front of the other boys, but worst of all, he calls out David's first name during the game. At private school, first names are so secret that they are the last token of friendship between two boys, and never to be revealed in public. The public declaration of his name so spoils David's concentration that he gets out – losing the most important cricket match of the year to the opposing team.

The revealing of David's name repeats the gesture of the Head taking the Maupassant novel off Mr. Dutton's Bible, and once again sensuality is the victim of spirituality. After the Archdeacon's gaffe, Bags initially wants to demonstrate his friendship with David (whose first name he knows as they are so close) by having his name revealed in the same way, but he withdraws his desire at the moment that it might become public. In *David of King's*, Bags will be the vehicle for David to get closest to being initiated into heterosexual sensuality, but at this stage his sensuality is homosexual, and directed at David, whom he thinks

> … such an awfully fetching chap. He had all that one boy admires in another: he was quick and ready of laughter, he was in the eleven, which was an attraction, he was very good looking, which was another, and in point of fact, at that portentous moment when it was made common knowledge that his name was David, Bags would have rather liked it if someone had proclaimed that his own name was Jonathan. But as it was only George, it might remain a secret.[9]

7. Benson, *David Blaize*, p. 19.
8. Benson, *David Blaize*, p. 62.
9. Benson, *David Blaize*, p. 68.

I would suggest that Bags's desire for his name to be known is stifled and thereby the friendship becomes at once platonic because he has learned from the first incident of the book that he must maintain his inviolable innocence. He realizes the implication of the name Jonathan links him sensually with David, and instead, he gives David mild support by remarking 'It must be jolly difficult to play cricket if your pater is making an ass of himself.'[10] The comment demonstrates the lesson of the school museum, that everything must be both publicly and privately acceptable, acceptable to God, and to the rest of the world: in order for him to be inviolably innocent.

But the fact of Bags's private desire for David remains, unaccounted for and unaccountable, since Bags becomes an inveterate womanizer while still at school. Once again, an early incident, this time with stag beetles, explores the question of whether it is possible to keep private thoughts to oneself, and once again sexuality is involved, although indirectly. David's most prized possession is a matchbox containing a male and female stag beetle. While they are somewhat typical of a schoolboy's possessions E.F.B. suggests that he keeps them to find out about the mysteries of sex.

> They were male and female, as the lady's absence of horns testified, and it was hoped that even in confinement [in David's box] she might some day be confined. Indeed there were several bets on, as to which form the babies would take – whether they would be eggs, or some sort of caterpillar, or minute but fully developed stag beetles.[11]

Albeit that the bets are naïve, they demonstrate that David has a rudimentary knowledge of reproduction. Nor do the boys bet on the method of copulation, just the product of birth. Nevertheless, sex is once again at the heart of this second lesson about private thoughts, for Bags steals the matchbox in an act of revenge after he has had to wash David's mouth. Immediately, his bad conscience requires that he secretly put the box back on David's bed, though not before a long search for the lost treasure. What is important here, is that although Bags has returned David's beetles in secret, David knows it was his best friend who took them in the first place, for as he says 'I saw you had a bad conscience.'[12]

10. Benson, *David Blaize*, p. 68.
11. Benson, *David Blaize*, p. 20.
12. Benson, *David Blaize*, p. 57.

The lesson which David learns from this incident is that there is no possibility of having private thoughts: the guilt is written all over his friend's face, so maintaining inviolable innocence cannot be a superficial matter. From the beetle incident, David also learns a method of getting over unhappy feelings towards a friend: to acknowledge them and forgive them. Bags craves forgiveness:

> Whatever Bags had done ... he ... blurted out that "he liked him [David] awfully."[13]

The sincere declaration of friendship marks the theft as an aberration in the relationship between the two boys, brought on by the humiliation of the public mouth washing. Forgiveness is therefore possible:

> What Bags had said in all sincerity took rank over anything Bags might have done. And with that he wiped the whole affair clean off his mind and held out a grubby hand.[14]

What is important about this is that when the private thought –in this case guilt – is 'sincerely' out in the open, forgiveness is possible, and the two boys can get on with their friendship without let or hindrance. But it is a fatal lesson, and when the process is repeated in David's Public School towards Frank, it marks the end of his inviolable innocence and the beginning of his phase of knowing innocence.

David learns two more lessons at his Private School before the demands of growing up take his inviolable innocence to its limit in his desire for Frank. The first helps him to realize that he can dismiss females as a source of sexual interest, the second illuminates an acceptable form of sensuality, since though he may resist women, he will not be able resist the 'almost infinitely strong' desire for his own sex, unless he has a viable substitute.

While in chapel service, David contemplates the two daughters of the Head sitting on the organ bench.

> These two female figures, with plump backs turned to him, afforded David plenty of rather acid reflection. Goggles (so called for obvious reasons, but addressed as Miss Mabel) was the elder, and wasn't so bad, though she had a woeful tendency to improve and console the occasions when any boys got into trouble, and was a kind of official dove with an olive branch after the deluge.

13. Benson, *David Blaize*, p. 57
14. Benson, *David Blaize*, p. 57.

> But Carrots (this otherwise concerned her hair, which otherwise
> belonged to Miss Edith) had lately shown herself altogether too
> beastly.[15]

It can be no surprise that the two girls represent, by synecdoche, the
virgin and whore dichotomy. Mabel represents the caring, soothing
and curing aspect of femininity, and Edith the sexual, with her
association with the words 'beastly' and 'beastliness.' Although repre-
senting opposed aspects of femininity, both women are to be treated
with caution. Mabel's caring, her olive branch, is proffered only after
the boys have got into trouble and is not given freely out of kindness.
Edith's present beastliness is due to her telling her father that a boy
has been out of bounds and getting him into trouble – presumably
so Mabel can care for him after his punishment. Women entice but
let men down.

David has no mother, and there are no developed female characters
in the plot of the trilogy. Women are therefore unmapped territory,
and when, as we shall see at the end of *David Blaize*, David has a
grand passion on Violet Gray, his emotional response to her is no
more developed than that he has here towards Mabel and Edith.
Women 'pretended to be friends' but had 'treacherous smiles' and
relationships with them got in the way of friendships with other
boys.[16] When Goggles offers David a visit to the strawberry beds[17]
to congratulate him on his innings of 24, he refuses so as to maintain
his good relationships with his school chums who have decided to
cut the girls for telling on one of them. Like Adonis in Shakespeare's
Venus and Adonis, time spent with his friends is more important than
having pleasure with a woman.

But if the sensual enticements of girls can be shrugged off so easily,
sensuality is not so easy to avoid, and arises in the most unexpected
places. At the same service, the Head is giving the sermon, when:

> ... [his] voice shook and grew lower yet, reminding David of
> something he had felt once when he woke early and heard the
> chirruping of the birds before daybreak ...
> "So prepare to be men," he said, " and when manhood dawns
> on you, let it dawn on you as on the clean dewy grass, with birds

15. Benson, *David Blaize*, p. 24.
16. Benson, *David Blaize*, p. 24.
17. The sexual connotations of that fruit had recently been made clear in
Thomas Hardy's *Tess of the D'Urbervilles* (1891).

singing in your hearts and innocence still looking from your eyes. Never contemplate evil, and the desire of it will fade from you. Run away from it, if by staying near it you would yield, and "Whatsoever things are lovely, whatsoever things are of good report, think on those things,"'

David gave a little gulp; not only were these beautiful words, but they meant something …[18]

The rumbling of David's growing manhood will, the Head argues, begin with a rise of sensuality, and sensuality can lead either towards good or evil. The metaphor about manhood dawning like 'the clean dewy grass' suggests that it should, like dew, just appear without apparent cause. Considering the physiology of boys becoming men, the suggestion seems to be that David and the other boys should allow their semen to flow by itself as a wet dream, rather than to entice it by masturbation. But David does not hear the meaning behind the metaphor, he hears the words, and realizes that there is another level on which they mean, because they are poetry. When the Head speaks and his 'voice shook and grew lower yet, reminding David of something he had felt once when he woke early and heard the chirruping of the birds before daybreak,' the words have nothing to do with the transitory pleasures of early-morning emissions, and everything to do with the longer lasting sensuality wrought by the proper associations with nature that are at the heart of Romantic poetry. From the Head's sermon, David learns that there is a sensuality that is acceptable: poetry and its appreciation of the aesthetics of nature. The lines the Head uses as a guide are from Philippians 4:8:

Finally, brethren, whatsoever things are true, whatsoever things are honest, whatsoever things are just, whatsoever things are pure, whatsoever things are lovely, whatsoever things are of good report; if there be any virtue, and if there be any praise, think on these things.

The true, honest, just, pure, lovely and of good report will soon lead David to the Romantic poetry of John Keats. And at present, David remains innocent of 'evil' sensuality. He notices that there are two types of information, facts such as those of history, and:

… music and poetry [which] were entirely different: they meant to you what you were capable of finding in them.[19]

18. Benson, *David Blaize*, pp. 30–31.
19. Benson, *David Blaize*, p. 96.

Facts might refer to the physiology of his body and what it did as it changed will-he nill-he to adulthood, but he could manipulate poetry and music so that they moved him in a way he could control. This is the final stage of the method E.F.B. offers in answer to A.C.B.'s hard determinism about sexual desire. Physiology may be pre-determined, and nothing can be done about it and the ways the body seeks sensual fulfilment. But with art, one is in dialogue, and one can therefore control its direction and affect. The first sensuality, as it is uncontrolled, is 'evil' and the second, as it may be controlled is 'good'.

The lessons about inviolable innocence come together in the final meeting David has with the Head of his Private School. Two boys have just been expelled for an unnamed crime that will 'spoil the rest of their lives', but when the Head confronts David with the possibility that it might be homosexuality, we learn that David does not understand.

> "But you will find," continued the Head, "that there are worse things than smoking, and all the misdeeds you may or may not have been punished for, and you will find out that there are even worse things than stealing, and that many quite good chaps, as you would say, don't think there is any harm in them. Do you know what I mean?"
> David looked up in quite genuine bewilderment.
> "No, sir," he said.
> "Thank God for it, then," said the Head.[20]

That 'many quite good chaps' might not think there is any harm in it, and that two boys have been expelled, suggests this is not the 'sin' of masturbation, but the 'crime' of mutual masturbation. The fact that David is ignorant of what the Head is talking about, in turn, suggests that he has learned all the lessons of inviolable innocence, and lives his private life as though in public. His body is sexually untainted inside and out, the Head has succeeded in his 'education.'

At Public School – Maintaining the Right Kind of Sensuality

However untainted David might be as a child, he will and does mature and take on secondary sexual characteristics, and his purity comes under assault from his attraction to Frank Maddox, whom he meets on his first visit to his Public School. The attraction he feels

20. Benson, *David Blaize*, p. 115.

for Maddox is similar to that instantaneous empathy felt by Arthur Hamilton for Edward Bruce, and by Bags for David at their Private School.

Since David is defined by his inviolable innocence, his infatuation with another boy cannot consciously manifest itself in 'evil' sensuality, as it has in the other two cases (albeit as proof that he will not succumb again in the case of A.C.B., and momentarily in the case of Bags), so it is initially displaced and becomes internalized, not as love or lust, but as David's vow to give up smoking because Maddox says it is 'scuggy', and that none of the chaps do it at Marchester.

A reason for the displacement of his infatuation with Maddox may be seen in the delight he finds in the common room of Adams's house:

> Never in all his day-dreams had he conceived that Adams's would be like this. It was not like a school, it was like some new and entrancing kind of home, with the jolliest man he had ever seen as a master and father, and for family these friendly boys, and the black-haired girl, Adams's daughter, whom everybody called by her Christian name.[21]

The idea that a school house might be like a family home, with the Master as father is not at all far fetched. My own school house was built so that the House Master's office on the ground floor and his bedroom on the first, abutted respectively onto the boys' work room and dormitory, each with an unlocked interconnecting door between Master and pupils so any boy could call upon John Brooksmith at any time, day or night, as a child might call upon his own father. With Frank as a brother to David in such a family, sibling affection is offered as a way to displace sexual desire. David's real sister Margery, however, understands things differently, though she is not sure what is happening to her brother.

Home again for the last time from his Private School, David is bored with the childishly ghoulish games he has hitherto played with Margery in the attics of the Archdeacon's house, and is listless. Sad that he no longer plays with her, Margery analyses David:

> You've dropped one lot of things and haven't got the next lot yet. Then there's this. Do you remember that green snake you used to keep, and how when it was changing its skin, it used to lie quite

21. Benson, *David Blaize*, p. 107.

still, not eating or drinking, and seemed awfully depressed? I expect that sort of thing is happening to you. I shouldn't a bit wonder if our minds changed their skins now and then, just like snakes ... Oh David , do be quick about changing your skin, and let me see the new one ...[22]

The change Margery has noticed may be accounted for in his coming to sexual maturity, but it works on at least two other levels as well. On one level David is moving from his real family home to the grown-up family home of the school house, from which halfway stage he might be expected to become a man and set up his own family home. On another level, David is coming to the realization that the grown-up home of the school house represents an alternate adulthood, where he will not know women other than as sisters.[23] Adams's daughter has a first name and can be trusted, like Margery, and not a nickname like the sensual but untrustworthy Carrots and Goggles.

David's decision about women seems to be confirmed by his developing close association with Frank Maddox, which is choreographed around a second edition of Keats's poetry: representative of 'good' sensuality. His desire for his hero is introduced as asexual, poetic rather than carnal, and his sister plays the role of cupid, bringing the two boys together as siblings.

David and Margery are looking in a bookshop near a Cathedral Close, when she finds a copy of a second edition of Keats's poetry. She and her brother buy it, and when they are on their way home they meet Frank Maddox. Confirming their status as near relations is the fact that Frank's uncle is the bishop, while of course their father is archdeacon, and that Frank calls David by his first name. As a sibling, they are free to invite Frank for tea: he is not a dark stranger who might wreak sexual havoc in the Blaize household. Frank's status as older brother or cousin becomes clear when he translates Latin on a sundial in their garden, a task neither David nor Margery are educated to do. And although David sees him as 'The Fairy Prince'[24] and 'The Idol'[25] Frank's skill in Latin suggests the same way the Head of his Private School did for David to get over his listlessness and

22. Benson, *David Blaize*, p. 125.

23. In fact, David's delight with Adams's house suggests that it is 'heavenly', where all shall be brothers and sisters in Christ.

24. Benson, *David Blaize*, p. 135.

25. Benson, *David Blaize*, p. 138.

boredom: literature, good sensuality. The alternate way of spending the long summer days, in evil sensual pleasure, is foreclosed by their status as siblings.

David feels that he needs to show gratitude to Frank for the lesson, and offers him, significantly of 'good' sensuality, the second edition of Keats. Frank refuses the gift but wants to look through the rest of the shop to see if they can find anything else that might be good, confirming, at least for the present, his affiliation with 'good' sensuality. David can now see how he will best fit in with the Marchester family, so takes a backward step emotionally when he resuscitates the games with his sister in the attic. The fact that they begin again to play their gothic games because Frank likes ghost stories demonstrates David's regression to childhood is necessary for his management of his feelings for the older boy: he must not move forward to 'evil' sensuality and be guided by his secondary sexual characteristics, but he can remain in the 'good' sensual world of literature which, for the moment, directs his childish games.[26]

At this point it is worth remembering A.C.B.'s determinist dictum, since the next important incident between Frank and David was edited at A.C.B.'s suggestion. In A.C.B.'s determinist world, we saw that the acting out of sexual desire was fraught with danger, since:

> if man was created with a free will, he was also created with predispositions which made the acting of that will a matter of mathematical certainty.

Thus, we might expect that Frank and David must necessarily succumb to their mutual attraction, if only that they learn not to do it again, either from their revulsion at themselves or from the help of others who will rescue them. For A.C.B. the mathematical certainty of same-sex desire makes the physical act of sex inescapable, and repentance after the fact the only way to defeat it. From the second meeting with Frank, we see E.F.B. move to counter argument with his brother. The incident, which takes David beyond inviolable innocence into knowing innocence, and which takes the rest of the first volume to negotiate, is a long one, and, as the text is largely unfamiliar to readers, will take a certain amount of description and quotation.

---

26. We shall see the same move in *David of King's*, when David asks his father if he can become a writer at the same time his father has told him to give up masturbation.

One night in the dormitory, an older boy called Hughes, who used to be David's hero in his Private School, is telling dirty stories that his audience does not understand. Hughes sits on David's bed and says he will explain, but Maddox catches wind of the conversation and sends Hughes away. The next day Hughes asks David 'if Maddox had become a saint, and if … [David has] converted him.'[27]

Hughes's question suggests that either Maddox is not innocent about sex and so is being hypocritical in criticizing him, or even that Maddox is trying to have sex with David and Hughes is jealous, being David's former hero. Hughes is a peripheral character, who will return later in the narrative as a practicing homosexual, but for the present, the vehemence with which Maddox chases him away from David suggests that Maddox is already at least a knowing innocent, and that soon David will begin to understand about sex too since references to it surround him on all sides. Maddox's treatment of Hughes also puts an ironic perspective on the foiled sexual encounter between Frank and David, which happens immediately after.

Maddox has been watching David playing squash in the rain, seeing him as:

> … a completely dishevelled and yet a very jolly object … quite altogether wet, his knickerbockers clinging like tights to his thighs, the skin of which showed pink through them, while the water trickled steadily down his bare calves into the dejected socks that lay limply round the tops of his shoes. They and his legs were stained with splashes of watery gravel, his shirt, open at the neck and slightly torn across the shoulder, lay like a wet bag glued to his back, and his hair was a mere yellow plaster from which the water could have been wrung in pints.[28]

The description is a mixture of erotica and humour, with the visible pink flesh juxtaposed with the wet socks and hair. When David sees him watching, he allows the older boy to intervene in the game, and to coach him as an older brother should. But very soon, Frank allows his knowing innocence, which Hughes has pointed out to David, to open up the possibility of 'evil' sensuality.

After the game, David has been luxuriating in a hot bath, and has forgotten it is time to fill Maddox's kettle and make his tea. Maddox comes into the bathroom, and holds up the empty kettle while David

27. Benson, *David Blaize*, p. 144.
28. Benson, *David Blaize*, p. 144.

is drying his hair. When David sees Frank, he tries to take the kettle, but Maddox won't let him, saying he will make tea himself. The fact that David is drying his hair suggests that he is naked and vulnerable in front of the older boy, whose play with the kettle means that David must press his naked body against Frank's. This might be read as horseplay, the two boys being used to bodily contact from rugby, but without warning the incident turns sexual.

> "Oh it [the tea] doesn't matter," he [Frank] said. "Just having a bath, were you?"
>
> David paused. There was Maddox only looking at him, only smiling. But instantly he had some sense of choking discomfort. He looked back at him, frowning and puzzled, and his sense of discomfort hugely increased. He merely wanted to get away.
>
> "Oh then I'll go and dress," he said hurriedly, and, picking up his sponge, left the room and ran away down the dark passage to his dormitory.
>
> David sat down on his bed for a minute, feeling as if he had escaped from some distant nightmare that had vaguely threatened to come near him. Then, very sensibly, running away from it instead of thinking about it, he began to dress in a great hurry.[29]

The theme of the nightmare and running away from sexuality is discussed in detail in *David Blaize and the Blue Door*. But in a boys' school, where David is Frank's fag, there is nowhere to escape, so the nightmare has to be negotiated, and David begins to understand his inevitable move from inviolable innocence to knowing innocence.

All that has happened is a look between the two friends, similar to that earlier on the squash court, after which Frank has done what an older brother should. But this time, David has felt sexual longings 'some distant nightmare' in himself that he feels to be wrong. Significantly he washes his hands again and again, and rubs his hair, acting out the ridding himself of the feeling, as though it were contaminating him and was all Frank's, and not his as well. David is then baselessly angry with his friend Bags, who, it will be remembered had momentarily a similar feeling for David, and who, as another close friend, might give rise to further feelings in David of the same unwanted kind. David decides he does not want to see Frank for a while, but his anger with his friend is inchoate because on some level he recognizes that the desire is his as well as Frank's.

---

29. Benson, *David Blaize*, p. 146.

As for Frank, who we know understands sexuality from his reaction to Hughes the previous day, he is all too willing to blame himself for everything that has happened, and to believe that David is still inviolably innocent.

> Maddox had gone straight back from the bathroom to his study, without filling the kettle. He sat for ten momentous minutes in front of his fire without doing anything, without thinking even, but looking with open eyes, so to speak, on himself. All these weeks that intense friendship which was springing up between himself and David had been splendidly growing, and till now his influence over him had been exerted entirely for David's good. He constantly shielded him, as on the night he found Hughes sitting on his bed, from all that could sully him, he had checked any hint of foul talk in David's presence, for, of all his loveable qualities, there was none so nobly potent to the elder boy than David's white innocence, his utter want of curiosity about all that is filthy. It didn't exist for him, but the danger of it (though thank God it had passed) he knew that he himself had brought near to him ... Then he got up and looked at himself in the mirror above the mantelpiece, hating himself.
> "You damned beast," he said. "You deserve to be shot."[30]

Frank's feeling of responsibility is fully understandable as being derived from the hierarchy of the school house in which the two live, where the older pupils are charged with the moral care of the younger, while the younger do the chores of the older. And his responsibility is also understandable from his sense of being a knowing innocent in charge of an inviolable innocent. But his reaction is also understandable in relation to contemporary understanding of homosexuality,[31] where the heterosexual model of the active male and passive female dyad was substituted for active older and passive younger partners. That this is also the Greek model of 'erastes' and 'eromenos' will become clearer later in the novel, in terms of a platonic ideal of knowing innocence, in which the sexual has been sublimated and *The Symposium* ignored. However, this is a step that David is not yet able to believe he has taken. For now, he attempts to negotiate what has happened by a process of forgetting and regression once again to the childish state of purity and inviolable innocence:

30. Benson, *David Blaize*, p. 148.
31. Of Havelock-Ellis for example, in *Sexual Inversion* (1897), where seven of his 21 examples of homosexuality are intergenerational.

Vaguely, perhaps David had guessed something of the nature of that muddy place, and had got clean-footed from it. With much greater sureness Maddox saw that, if their friendship was to continue, he must turn his back on it too, and convince David that he had done so. He was ashamed: he hated himself.[32]

In order for him to negotiate what has happened, Frank must take responsibility for the look, and David must believe he was not looking back. Worrying about what to do in the aftermath is Frank's role as he is already a knowing innocent, and 'erastes.' It is therefore no surprise that Maddox, as the active partner, calls David to his room and apologizes, but David leaves without really accepting it. As the passive partner, David ought to be able to blame Frank as though the suspect look was all one way, so as to absolve himself of any guilt and become an inviolable innocent again. As an inviolable innocent, David cannot have done anything he might be ashamed of. The problem is, and as his next action shows, he is beginning to realize that he was as much to blame as Maddox.

> All his love and his loyalty insisted he was wrong not to trust the regret and the assurance that had been given him [by Frank], that he was doing a mean and a cowardly thing to retreat like this. But the talk he had had with the Head on his last day at Helmsworth was very vivid in his mind … But the Head had [also] told him never to turn his back on a friend, or to refuse to trust that which his heart knew was sincere. And so once more from inside Maddox heard a familiar step return and once more David tapped and entered.
>
> "I don't know why I went away," he said, "or why I was frightened when you said I needn't be. So-so I came back."
>
> Then he had the instant reward of his confidence. He saw Maddox look up at him with unshadowed eyes of affection. He came and stood close to him.
>
> "It's bang all right," he said. "I'm-I'm awfully glad it's all right."
>
> Then a positive inspiration seized him. There was nothing more to be said on the subject, and the sooner it was dismissed the better. He instantly became Maddox's fag again.
>
> "I say, you're awfully late having tea," he said. "Why your kettle's not boiling any longer."[33]

32. Benson, *David Blaize*, p. 150.
33. Benson, *David Blaize*, p. 151.

It is not David's inviolable innocence, the lessons learned at his Private School to live as though he is always under the matron's or God's surveillance, that enables him to regress to childhood once again to be able to become Maddox's fag. David's internal debate about what he should do, and his decision to stay close (and in the quote above also to get physically close) to his friend demonstrates his knowledge that he wants exactly the same as the older boy. The look went both ways, and his attraction (whatever it meant, and as yet David is unsure) was more important than the fact that it might lead to 'evil' sensuality. Although his being Maddox's fag again requires that he is an inviolable innocent, he is, in fact, becoming a knowing innocent. In forgiving Frank, as he had forgiven Bags, for his 'sincerity,' he puts himself into what will quickly become an impossible position, which will require his acceptance of himself as a knowing innocent and begin his journey through solo masturbation to asexual marriage.

The beginning of David's testing of his gift of continency might be understood as the playing out of A.C.B.'s 'mathematical certainty' that same sex desire will be expressed, so that it may be regretted and transcended. And this is why it is important to note that E.F.B. had originally written a kiss between Frank and David in the bathroom scene. Although perhaps only a small indication of 'evil' sensuality, E.F.B. would nevertheless have been following his brother's suggestion in *Arthur Hamilton*: the kiss was necessary for the decision not to partake further in same-sex sexual activity. But with no kiss, E.F.B. is free to offer his way to avoid same-sex sexuality and in particular to avoid remorse completely, which is first to become a knowing innocent.

E.F.B. begins with shutting sexuality away and pretending it does not exist, to pretend to regress to childhood and remain an inviolable innocent, here, David becoming Frank's fag again. But the impossibility of the logic of shutting away appears while David is musing on his life at school:

> Public-school life began with his installation as fag, and there hero-worship had soared like a flame day by day, until that afternoon when, after playing squash with Bags in the rain, he had gone back to the house for a bath. David had always avoided the thought of that; it remained a moment quite sundered from the rest of his intercourse with Frank, embarrassing, and to be forgotten, like the momentary opening of a cupboard where nightmare dwelt.

Anyhow, it had been locked again instantly and the key thrown away. Never a sound had again issued therefrom.[34]

Like a criticism of Freud's idea of the unconscious, E.F.B.'s cupboard of nightmares is defined by remembering what is locked away. Almost ironically, the idea is an old school masters' trick for teaching spelling.[35] Boys are told to learn their spellings in the evening, and the following morning when they come to lessons, they are told they must forget the spellings they learned the night before. The joke is, that in order to forget how to spell 'miniature' you have to spell the word out for yourself, and so you remember it. And it is the same with sexuality. Once sexuality has been thought of it cannot willingly be forgotten, and innocence can never be inviolable again. David's recognition of the look that passed between him and Frank means he is a knowing innocent no matter how much he might want it otherwise.

Pandora's Box

We discover David's status as knowing innocent while he and Frank are on a golfing holiday together in the summer, when one afternoon the post brings a letter from Mr. Adams, the House Master, news that renders Frank silent.

"I've heard from Adams," he said at length. "There's been a row. Some letter has been found, and Hughes isn't to be allowed to come back in September." "Why? What sort of letter!" asked David. Then, as Frank was still silent: "Oh, something beastly, is it?" he asked. "What an ass Hughes is! He was such a nice chap, too, at my other school."

The very fact that Adams has written the letter to Frank must make us pause. There seems no reason for Frank to know that Hughes is not allowed back in September, except that Adams is warning *him* to be careful about how he acts towards David with whom he is on holiday. What follows in their discussion seems to confirm Adams's suspicions:

Frank had finished reading, and was looking out over the Surrey garden, biting his lip.

34. Benson, *David Blaize*, p. 184.
35. At least it was the trick that Chris Bower used to teach me spellings at my private school.

"I say, Frank, what's wrong with you?" said David.

Frank gave Adams's letter to him. "Read it," he said.

David took it. It spoke of the letter written by Hughes to a boy in the house, a letter disgusting and conclusive. Then it spoke of the disgrace Hughes had brought on himself, and the misery he had brought on his father and mother.[36]

As with the bathroom episode, the scene is deceptively simple. An intercepted letter between Hughes and another boy gives evidence that they have indulged in same-sex sexual activity, and Hughes is expelled from school. The incident is the same that resulted in two boys being expelled from David's Private School, but in that situation, David's inviolable innocence was intact and he did not understand what had happened. After the incident in the bathroom, things have changed. The fact that Frank gives Adams's letter to David to read demonstrates how complex their relationship has become. Frank cannot withhold the letter from David, as he is a friend from whom he can have no secrets, as he knows that David can read his inner thoughts from the look on his face. But since the letter reveals that Hughes has done with another boy what Frank wanted to do with David in the bathroom, showing the letter demonstrates that Frank no longer feels he has to protect David from same-sex sexuality, as he had decided to do immediately after. David is older, to be sure, however, giving the letter to David to read may suggest less that Frank is treating David as a grown up, and more that Frank wants him to know that Adams was correct, and he did really want to test David once more to see if he will turn from the 'good' sensuality of healthy sports to consider 'evil' sensuality as a way to pass the long summer holiday. What happens in the next interchange is very ambiguous. David, of course, notices the change in Frank's face when he has read the letter, but when questioned, Frank claims that he has tried to become an inviolable innocent following David's example, however, Frank makes the declaration with his face hidden:

"What's up?" he [David] asked.

Maddox turned over on to his back, and tilted his hat over his eyes till his face was invisible.

"I might have been Hughes," he said.

Again the memory of what David always turned his face from came into his mind.

36. Benson, *David Blaize*, p. 189.

"Oh rot," he said lamely, hating the subject.

Maddox remained silent a moment.

"Tisn't quite rot," he said. "But then there came a thing, which I dare say you've forgotten, only I haven't. You came in from playing squash one wet afternoon. And you and your innocence made me see what a beast I was."

David could not help giving a shudder, but the moment after he was ashamed of it.

"I don't care what you were like before," he said. "But what I'm perfectly sure of is that since then – I remember it very well – you've been all right."

"Yes."

"There you are then!" said David.

Frank was still lying with his hat over his face, but now he pushed it back and looked at David.

"It's all serene for you," he said, "because you've always been a straight chap. But it's difficult for me. I feel just rotten."

David scratched his head in some perplexity. The whole matter was vague and repugnant to him, and he did not want to hear more or know more. There were heaps of jolly proper things in the world to be interested and curious about. But he understood without any vagueness at all and with the very opposite of repulsion, that his friend was in trouble, and that he wanted sympathy with that. So the whole of his devoted heart went out there. It was bad trouble too, the worst trouble a fellow could have.

"It must be perfectly beastly for you," he said, "and I'm sorry as I can be, but you're sorry yourself, and what more can a chap do? If you weren't sorry that would be different. There's another thing too, to set against what you've done. And that's how you've behaved to me. You've been an absolute brick to me. You've kept that sort of filth away from me: I know you have."

...

Frank had kept nasty things away from him; here was atonement.

...

"Then let's chuck the whole subject," said David.

"In a moment. I just want to tell you: I have tried instead of corrupting you to uncorrupt myself. But it was all your doing. You made me ashamed."

David gave a shy little wriggle towards him.

"I have never heard of anything so ripping," he said. "Though it sounds rather cheek."

Maddox sat up.

"That's what you've done, and the other name of it is salvation."

There was silence a moment, and probably David had never known such intense happiness as he tasted then. And just because he was feeling so deeply, the idea of anything approaching sentiment was impossible. It had been said, and a harvest was garnered.[37]

E.F.B. draws our attention to the question of faces with the descriptive clause about 'evil' sensuality, which David uses: 'the memory of what David always turned his face from came into his mind'. Spoken with full face, words are 'sincere', as was Bags's apology for stealing the stag beetles. Frank's covering his face suggests his words are less than brutally honest. This is the first time they have discussed what happened in the bathroom, and there is nothing very discursive about it. Nevertheless, while on one level, the passage suggests that Frank really has regressed to inviolable innocent, and that David has saved him, Frank's bland 'Yes' spoken into his hat in reply to David's assertion that he has been alright sounds less like schoolboy inarticulacy and more like a lie. He cannot face David as Bags did when owning up to stealing the beetles, but he knows he cannot do what he was planning because Adams has challenged him not to. Therefore on another level, David's comment 'but you're sorry yourself, and what more can a chap do? If you weren't sorry that would be different' throws out a challenge to Frank, since his words imply that he too knows that Frank is not sorry for what he did. And furthermore, David's 'making a shy wriggle' towards Frank, repeats the gesture of getting physically closer to his friend, as he did when they were making up after the bathroom scene, which suggests once again that David is not as inviolably innocent as he would like to think he is. The boys' actions say one thing, and their words another. Frank's speaking into his hat suggests he is lying, but when he takes his hat off his face, this is the very moment in which he is telling David that he *does* harbour sexual feelings for him. 'It's all serene for you,' he said, 'because you've always been a straight chap. But it's difficult for me. I feel just rotten.' David manages to forgive Frank once again for his sincerity about his feelings, but this has become yet another test of his gift of continency, which has resulted in another shutting of the door on the cupboard of nightmares, with its counter-logical

37. Benson, *David Blaize*, p. 192.

'willing forgetfulness,' rather than a removal of the possibility of 'evil' sensuality:

> But, in spite of the intimate nature of all that had passed between the two so few minutes before, their unbroken solitude together did not produce in either of them the least wish to reopen the subject. It had been closed; a door had been triumphantly slammed on it, so that even if golf had not been so absorbing, they would neither of them have mentioned it again. And yet, deep down in each, and unknown to them, all that had passed had taken root, and was silently germinating, making fibre in their unconscious minds, building up the stem on which character bursts into blossom. Many words were consciously spoken, and many thoughts were thought, and all the words and all the thoughts did not stray beyond the fortunes of the little white India-rubber balls.[38]

Character building it might be, to deny what you know you want to do, but it is not in the pretended forgetting of the unconscious that character is made. All the 'triumphant' shutting of the door has done is to allow Frank temporarily to avoid remorse, and to turn back to the healthy pursuit of golf balls.

> … absorbed in their game and yet absorbed in their boy-love, hot as fire and clean as the trickle of ice-water on a glacier. The knowledge of their talk had made Frank able to turn himself away from Adams's letter, and instead of brooding on the irremediable worst of himself, he took hold of the best. And by his side was David, the friend of friends, now with his arm linked in his, now excitedly addressing a cupped ball with his largest driver …[39]

The fact that he has an 'irremediable worst of himself' may temporarily be forgotten but it will not go away. Furthermore, since reading the letter, it is now assumed between them that both Frank and David are knowing innocents, and that same-sex sexuality will return again and again, and will require more and more complex strategies to avoid, particularly since David may now choose whether or not to forgive his friend. The nightmare being named in David's mind has come out of its cupboard, and cannot be kept hidden away as though it never existed: like Pandora's box, when it has been opened, it can never be closed again.

38. Benson, *David Blaize*, p. 198.
39. Benson, *David Blaize*, p. 201.

We see this when, almost as soon as they have returned to school from the holiday, in a fit of temper, David opens the door of the cupboard of nightmares himself. David has been caned by the Head for a trivial offence, but really because he is becoming generally unruly and is not responding to the usual punishments. Frank has been to Cambridge taking scholarship exams, and returns to find his friend in a foul mood.

"Just been swished," said David.

"What for?"

"Accumulations, so that blasted Head told me. Throwing a snowball finished it."

"Oh you infernal ass, " said Maddox. "You jolly well deserved it."

At that a devil, no less, entered into David.

"Anyhow, I never deserved being expelled," he said very evilly.

Frank looked at him for a moment; then, without a word, left the room.

For a few seconds David was not in the least sorry for that speech. He was smarting himself, and if all Frank had to say was that he deserved it, he was glad to have made Frank smart too … And then with a sudden sense of sick regret, he remembered who Frank was, and all that Frank had been to him. And on the moment he was out of his study, and off down the passage to Frank's. He went in without knocking.

"I say, I'm a damnable chap," he said. "I'm frightfully sorry. I don't know if you can forgive me."

He held out a rather timid hand. Instantly it was clasped and held.

"I didn't mean it," he said. "I felt mad."

"David old chap," said Frank.

They stood there for a minute in silence, for really there was nothing to be said. Then David smiled.

"I think I'd better not make an ass of myself any more," he said.

"Beastly good idea," said Frank.[40]

David's accusation of Frank marks the end of all pretence of inviolable innocence in either of them. David knows that Frank has sexual feelings for him, and Frank cannot pretend he has been able to put his feelings aside since at the golf course he said it was impossible for him

40. Benson, *David Blaize*, p. 230.

to do. But nor can David pretend he does not harbour sexual feelings for Frank, since when making up it is always he who returns to and gets physically close to Frank: he knows that he cannot live without Frank near him. However, the state of knowing innocence has, by David's accusation, been shown to be precarious. David was not sure he'd be forgiven; and neither boy knew what to say, because neither could claim even to want to regress once more to inviolable innocence. They need a new strategy to negotiate their sexual attraction for one another, and they try three before the end of the novel: platonic love, courtly love and comrade love. All are forms of knowing innocence, and neither is ultimately fulfilling, which is why two further volumes of David Blaize stories were needed.

A Platonic Paradise?

Frank first introduces the idea of a future together for the two boys, after they have left school. Classical studies and construing Latin and Greek, is the major way Frank and David can be physically close together, poring over a book, while seeming to be doing something that is not sexual. But after a lesson with the Head, now they are both knowing innocents, homoerotic Hellenism moves to the fore as the solution to their being able to continue to be together:

> "We had a Plato lesson with him [the Head], but instead of going through a single line of it, something set him off, and he talked to us for the whole hour about Athens and the life they led there. You never heard anything so splendid. You could go up to the Acropolis in the morning, and look at the frieze Pheidias had put up in the Parthenon, a procession of horses and boys riding to the temple on Athene's birthday. He showed us pictures of it; some were mounted, – oh Lord, they had good seats – and others were still putting their horses' bridles on, and one horse was rubbing its foreleg with its nose, or t'other way round,"
>
> "Pheidias?" asked David.
>
> "Yes, the biggest sculptor there's ever been, far ahead of Michaelangelo or Rodin or any one. And when you had seen that, you and your friend – you and me, that is – would sit on the wall of the Acropolis looking over the town out of the mountains, the purple crown of mountains, as they call them, Hymettus where the honey came from, and Pentelicus where they got the marble for the Parthenon, and another one – what's its name? Oh Parnes. Then to the south you would look over the sea, all blue and dim,

out towards Salamis which, as the Head said, was the Trafalgar
of Athens, where they beat those stinking Persians; and then we
should have lunch off grapes and figs, and cheese wrapped up in
vine leaves, and yellow wine, and go down to the theatre just below
to hear perhaps this very play by Sophocles, first performance,
and no end of excitement. Then perhaps we should see Pericles,
awfully handsome chap. And the biggest Prime Minister there
ever was, and a queer ugly fellow would go by, who would be
Socrates. And all the boys and young men were fearfully keen
about games, quite as keen as we are, because they used to date
the year by the Olympic games, same as we use A.D. or B.C. ...
In everything, so the Head told us, the Athenians of the great
age were the type of the perfect physical and intellectual life. Oh,
David, let's save up and go to Athens."[41]

It would be easy to make a link between Oscar Wilde, turn of the
century Hellenism and the undoubted homoeroticism of this passage,
to draw the conclusion that this is simply an encodation of homosexual
desire between Frank and David. However, it must be born in mind
that E.F.B. took a first in classics at Cambridge, which suggests that
we might take the references to Pheidias, Pericles and Socrates, as
more than a creator of beautiful statues, a beautiful ruler and an ugly
philosopher. Nor should we suggest that the references to the riders'
'good seats', to Pericles' beauty and to Socrates as statements made
in the chasteness of Platonic love. The attribution of asexuality to
Platonic love was not made until the fifteenth century, whereas in *The
Symposium*,[42] in which Plato discusses love, homosexual love is taken
as the given, and the relationship between Socrates and Alcibiades
too complex to be reduced simply to foregoing sexual activity.

The descriptions, given from each partner's perspective, of the
relationship between Socrates and Alcibiades, are preceded by six
general descriptions of love. When at last we hear the lovers discuss
their relationship, for once, Socrates does not get the last word, and
his interchange with Alcibiades explores a homosexual relationship
in which one party finds sexual fulfilment outside the dyad: an
arrangement which might be argued to be a development of that
between Frank and David, as discussed on the golf course, which
will allow Frank to fulfil his desire without violating David. The fact

41. Benson, *David Blaize*, p. 250.
42. References to *The Symposium* are not footnoted as the text was read to
me electronically, so has no page numbers.

that Frank has an 'irremediable worst of himself' need no longer be temporarily forgotten, or locked in the 'cupboard of nightmares', he can find the sexual fulfilment he needs wherever he wants, and face his own remorse if he has any, while at the same time he can continue his loving relationship with David without demanding sexual favours from him. The problem with the arrangement, as we shall see, is that Frank's status as 'erastes' means that he should play the role of Socrates, while his demand for sexual fulfilment from David places him in Alcibiades' position as 'eromenos'. The inversion of their relationship comes at the time when David is himself testing the boundaries of his knowing innocence, and we discover that his apparent chasteness does not appear to be as absolute as Socrates'. When he finds himself promoted to the 'erastes' role with his own fag, Jevons, his behaviour is uncannily like that of Frank's towards him. The easy negotiation of their sexuality that has gone on before is no longer possible. Knowing innocence brings with it new dangers and new demands for which new solutions must be found. So much so that David puts on a heterosexual mask for a while in courting Violet Gray to deflect the house master's suspicion of his feelings for the younger boy.

Phaedrus, Pausanias, Erixsymachus, Aristophanes and Agathon give the first five general descriptions of love at the start of *The Symposium*. Phaedrus claims love is the eldest of the gods as it is represented by our wanting to look good and noble before our beloved. Pausanias finds that there are two kinds of love, derived from the two types of Aphrodite: as daughter of Uranus and as daughter of Zeus. These types are sexual love and noble love, where the latter is defined by the casually homosexual epithet 'they love not boys but intelligence.' The reason for the value judgement against sexual love is that 'Love of the noble disposition is life long.' It is this point to which Socrates and Alcibiades return in their interchange at the end, which suggests that Socrates' discussion of Love is not the final position.

Erixsymachus, the physician, also believes there are two types of love, but he restricts their location to the body, though they are still defined as good and bad. He argues that the body has desires, and good desires have to be nurtured while bad desires have to be transformed into the good. In the context of Pausanias' argument that good and bad love are discerned by their relation to intelligence, the reduction of good and bad physical desires to hetero and homosexuality, is an unlikely interpretation. Aristophanes' joyous and experiential tale glosses my interpretation of the idea of good and bad love, telling that love is the finding of the two separated halves of one person. We know it is love whether it is a man or a woman whom we love, since we know it is good that we have found our other half.

Lastly comes Agathon's exploration of love, which sets up the complex situation between Socrates and Alcibiades. He tells us that love is a new and young and tender thing, rather than the oldest of things. Love is beautiful and requires the greatest beauty of body. Love is just and can do no wrong. Love is a poet, and makes poets of those in love. We have to wait until Alcibiades comes into the dinner party to crown Agathon and embrace him, to understand that his description of love is based on his new relationship with Socrates' lover. But first Socrates rehearses his dialogue, which significantly is a reported dialogue with an absent woman: Diotema.

Socrates begins by defining what love is, and is the first to emphasize its transitive nature. Love is of something: he who desires does not have the thing he desires, so he who loves must be in possession of something. Socrates tells us that love makes what it wants into the beautiful, and love makes what it wants into the good. But then he asks, how can love be sure that what it wants is beautiful and good, if it transforms its desired object into the beautiful and the good?

The reported dialogue with Diotema answers Socrates' question: love is a daimon, a mediating spirit between the human and divine, and in it (the daimon) both are bound together.

> "[Love] interprets," she [Diotema] replied, "between gods and men, conveying and taking across to the gods the prayers and sacrifices of men, and to men the commands and replies of the gods; he is the mediator who spans the chasm which divides them, and therefore in him all is bound together, and through him the arts of the prophet and the priest, their sacrifices and mysteries and charms, and all, prophecy and incantation, find their way. For God mingles not with man; but through Love."

Diotema expounds a method of surmounting the problem of love being founded on desire, which may or may not be truly fulfilled, since it makes the desired object into the good and the beautiful, even if it is foul and ugly. For she suggests that love must bring the divine into the human dyad as judge of the goodness and beauty of the desired person. Since this is not a Christian dialogue, the divine to which Plato refers is not the Father, Son and Holy Spirit, it is the Ideal Form of Beauty, which is reflected in earthly things, but which is not of earthly things, and which should lead us away from contemplation of the ephemeral and lead us to the eternal.

At this serious note, there is a commotion outside Agathon's house, and Alcibiades enters, very drunk and makes lascivious approaches to the host of the party. Since he holds before him the ivy and ribbons he has brought to crown Agathon, 'this fairest and wisest of men', he does not see that Socrates is lying beside him, so following the rules of comedy, Alcibiades unwittingly reveals to the man who is supposed to be his lover, the desire he has for another man. Again, following the rules of comedy, it is at the very moment of his revelation that Alcibiades notices who is next to him at the party, and Socrates, playing the part of the comic cuckold, declares that Alcibiades is jealous if *he* looks at anyone else, implying that he, Socrates is more justified in his jealousy because Alcibiades has just made up to Agathon.

Alcibiades counters that it is not he who attacks Socrates when Socrates looks at another man, but Socrates who attacks him when *he* looks at another man, which he has just done. Erixymachus breaks into the argument and suggests that Alcibiades tell his tale of love, and that then as a new party game, they should each ask the person on their right to do their bidding. Because Alcibiades is reclining between Agathon and Socrates, it will be Socrates who has to do Alcibiades' bidding after his tale.

Alcibiades' tale is interesting since he neither gives a general account of love, as did the first five, nor does he present a dialogue as Socrates had, he gives the personal details of his affair with Socrates. The tale has also been set up as a riposte to Socrates' accusation about his infidelity, and a justification of the comic scene that has just been played out with Agathon. The purpose of the story is to point out that Socrates is so bound up with communing with divine Ideal Forms that he has lost touch with the world and the people in it.

Alcibiades compares Socrates to a bust of a satyr that opens up and has the image of a god inside. He also compares Socrates speaking to Marsyas' flute playing, which affects so deeply the people who hear him. Socrates' words can make Alcibiades confess that he should not live like he wants to, as he is the only person who can make him feel ashamed, since there is no answering him. But this paean to

Socrates, which accounts for Alcibiades falling in love with so great a philosopher, is juxtaposed with a blow-by-blow account of their physical life together, which has resulted in Alcibiades crowning Agathon that evening.

Alcibiades has tried to seduce Socrates because he believes himself to be the most beautiful young man (eromenos) and Socrates to be the most worthy and intelligent older man (erastes). But try as he might nothing sexual has happened. They have even wrestled naked together, dined together repeatedly, and slept together, but they have never had sex. Alcibiades claims to have been bitten by philosophy, which was why he wanted to seduce Socrates, the greatest of all philosophers. But Socrates always refused his advances, and offered him only the truth of Ideal Forms, rather than his body.

In the light of the lovers' tiff that marked the beginning of the section, Alcibiades' next move, of listing Socrates' good qualities appears a little odd. Why should he praise the man who has resisted his sexual favours? In the economy of Greek thought, Socrates should receive the gift of Alcibiades' body in recompense for the knowledge he passes on. Nevertheless, we hear that Socrates is capable of suffering hardships in the army, and how good he is in a siege since he can go for long periods without food. Alcibiades also tells a story which demonstrates how determined Socrates is in thought, standing still for a day and a night working out a problem. Socrates might appear to be something of a superhuman from the manly attributes he is reported to bear, but we must be careful simply to accept the fact that he does not respond sexually to Alcibiades as another aspect of his superhuman nature, since it is against the expectations of Greek society. What is more, coming from the lips of the drunken Alcibiades, it sounds just as likely to be an accusation of impotence and a justification for the attention he has just paid to Agathon, than praise for the powers that Socrates has to resist him. Furthermore, after the accusation, Socrates asks Agathon to change places with him so he does not have to perform whatever Alcibiades asks him in the game suggested by Erixymachus, which may be a demand for sexual gratification, given that Alcibiades has drunk a quart of wine before telling his story.

However true to the text my reading of the final scene may be, there seem to be grounds enough to believe that Plato is not simply heaping more praise upon Socrates in the guise of his sexual abstinence. The comedy of the section appears intended to tease out Socrates' divine thoughts about love of Ideal Forms, and bring them back to real people who live and love physically, and to point out the extreme difficulty of asexual love for a young and sexually active man like Alcibiades. Socrates might be capable of resisting beautiful young men, but his fellow philosophers are not. In all, the *Symposium*, does not present, nor does it seem intended to present an unequivocal account of love as the seeking for Ideal Forms. Alcibiades' has undercut Socrates with his reminder that physical desire may still need to be satisfied.

In the light of this, it is unlikely that as a classical scholar, E.F.B. would have meant Frank's description to suggest unequivocally that Athens represented a perfectly asexual destination to which the two boys might escape. The place of manly beauty and sporting prowess has but one ugly inhabitant, Socrates, of whom it might be thought that only love could make him appear beautiful. The point seems to suggest that asexuality is a difficult option, and one that needs a great amount of devotion to maintain, particularly when such beautiful men surround one. The memory of Alcibiades' physical need turning him away from Socrates because of his lover's refusal to engage in sexual activity, might even suggest that Frank was considering Athens the place to go to do the same, faced with David's continued refusal. The fact that this occurs shortly before Frank leaves Marchester to go to Cambridge, and the boys will be separated for a year, might even equate Athens with Cambridge as the place Frank is hoping to begin his life of sexual gratification. Cambridge, and King's College in particular, was known for its associations with homoeroticism, and A.C.B. had been a member of the Apostles, a group of homoerotic Hellenists, though when E.F.B. had gone up, he did not join them. It would seem from the inversion of sexual roles (Frank to eromenos and David to erastes) that Frank is moving beyond knowing innocence to sexual maturity, and has decided to engage in sexual activity. However, David's status as knowing innocent means that his sexuality also comes under pressure.

As David moves into the sixth, he has a fag to do his chores for him, as he had done for Frank. Jevons in this sense becomes Alcibiades to *his* Socrates, but when he moves properly into the role of 'erastes', rather in the inverted sense, his role model is Frank, rather than the asexual Socrates. David describes being in charge of Jevons as 'good sport', but every aspect of his description of what he does are the same as those Frank did to him, including the fact that Adams, the house master, has noticed that he is a bit too keen on Jevons:

> "... Adams said I was fussing over him too much, and tying a string to his leg, and clipping his wings, when it was time for him to fly about as he dam pleased ... But, you see, he's turning out rather a fetching kid – good-looking, you know, and all that, and I'm not going to have him taken up by some brute and spoiled. However, any one who tries will have a nasty time with me first. But I suppose Adams is right: Jev's got to begin looking after himself. I am rather sorry in a way, though. It was good sport looking after a kid like that, and seeing it doesn't come to any harm. He's an affectionate little beggar, too, and I believe he knows it would make me pretty sick if he got into beastly ways ..."[43]

David may think that he does not want 'to have him taken up by some brute and spoiled' in the sense that he is repeating for Jevons the protective role Frank acted out for him against Hughes, but the fact that he also calls Jevons 'a fetching kid – good looking, you know' and 'an affectionate little beggar' suggests that he feels something more akin to Frank's 'irremediable worst of himself' than Pausanias' 'noble love'. If this remained between the boys, they could probably contain it within the 'cupboard of nightmares', but since Adams has noticed it too, and told David to leave Jevons alone, it requires a more visible show of heteronormal behaviour. In the twentieth century we might call it sexual experimentation, or even 'trans' behaviour but I would argue, that for David, it is another test of his gift of continency, in the face of his falling too readily into the patterns of behaviour he has learned from Frank.

Violet Gray – Courtly Love

E.F.B. follows the rules of comedy once more to make David's first heterosexual love affair excruciatingly embarrassing. Like Romeo, David sees and is immediately in love with the daughter of one of the dons, at a cricket match. The relative value of cricket and Violet Gray will, therefore, become important as he is finally made to decide between her and his favourite sport. Nevertheless, though his feelings for her are coltish to say the least, he believes they are genuine and they turn away suspicion that he is still pursuing Jevons, but, I would

---

43. Benson, *David Blaize*, p. 293.

argue, they are no more than that. Without rehearsing the twists and turns of David's feelings for the girl, who, like Frank, is older than he, and therefore conveniently out of reach,[44] it is probably best in the space available to explore the only discussion he has about Violet with his old friend Bags:

> "Look here: [Bags said] supposing you might either kiss Violet Gray, twice, we'll say, or see the Oxford and Cambridge match, which would you choose?"
>
> "Depends on the match," said David. "Of course if Frank was going to make a century, and I were to see him do that, I don't know what else I'd choose. O Lord, but fancy kissing her, though! I wish you wouldn't ask such stumpers. But I just can't! I-I feel like a dog which is being whistled to from opposite directions by two fellows it loves. Doesn't know which way to go."
>
> Bags sniffed scornfully.
>
> "Oh, you've not got it so desperately, if you only feel like that," he said.
>
> David shut his eyes and made his mouth tight with an air of martyr-like determination.
>
> "I should choose kissing her," he said, "because Frank could tell me all about the match afterwards, and besides, it would all be reported in the *Sportsman*, and I could read about it. But I couldn't read about kissing her in the paper; at least, I don't know in which. Oh Lord, but fancy missing seeing Frank putting perfectly straight balls away to the leg boundary in the Varsity match, and then scratching his ear as he always does when he hits a boundary, as if wondering what happened to the ball. I don't know which I would choose. I don't know."

David's first response to Bags' request for information about the importance of the cricket match before he makes his decision is the sort of thing that would be said by William in a Richmal Crompton story. It is formally comic. However, David's immediate reference to Frank playing in the match alerts the heterosexually minded Bags, and leads to his scornful denial that David 'has got it so desperately'. What David has said has demonstrated that cricket is associated synecdochically with Frank, and though originally a healthy sport, it

---

44. As we shall see in *David of King's*, the next time David attempts heterosexuality, he is careful to buy drinks for a prostitute who is old enough to be his (long dead) mother, while he looks longingly at another, knowing that he feels that he ought to have felt sexually attracted to her, since she was not 'out of the question'.

has now become associated with 'evil' sensuality. Bags's question has cut through his friend's subterfuge, and no matter how much David may complain he ends his deliberation with a tender observation about Frank rather than a definite shift to heterosexuality. It takes 'martyr-like determination' to say that he would rather kiss Violet. But this comic scene is immediately followed by a gloss, which returns David to the path of continency, if not to Violet.

What is important for understanding David's viewpoint on his sexuality is that in bringing him to make a decision about which is preferable, Bags has only weighed two kisses in the balance against a single game of cricket. David is clever enough to know his first answer has caught him out, so follows his bumbling indecisiveness with a Socratic answer to his friend, deliberating upon the relative values of the transitory pleasure of the two kisses and the long lasting friendship he has with Frank. In effect, David turns the question about his sexuality into a symposium on love, and having learned from Socrates, he knows that the divine can win out over the physical if he has faith in his gift of continency.

> David looked mournfully round for inspiration and lay down again.
>
> "After all, I wonder whether it's worth while doing anything or getting anything," he said with a sudden lugubrious accent. "I tried to think it would be a damn fine thing to get into the sixth, and yet before a month was out we both got absolutely accustomed to it. It's been just the same about getting into the school eleven – oh, well, not quite, because I do enjoy that most awfully still. But I dare say it won't last. Why a year ago, if I had been told that I might have any two things I wanted, I should have chosen to get into the sixth and the eleven. It didn't seem that there was anything more to want."
>
> "I should have thought you would have chosen that Maddox shouldn't leave," remarked Bags.
>
> "No use wishing that: he had to. Besides if he hadn't he wouldn't be in the Cambridge eleven now. And you can't choose anything that clips your pal's wings. ..."[45]

After David's dismissal of the evanescent pleasure of sensual fulfilment, Bags's comment that David might have desired that Frank had not left Marchester has been turned from an inference of

45. Benson, *David Blaize*, p. 291.

sexual desire to a childish way of keeping a friendship by remaining forever in the same place, a return to inviolable innocence. But, as David's response demonstrates, he has moved beyond that, learning from Adams's intervention in his treatment of Jevons, that for friendship to work, it cannot tie the friend down, for if it does, it is not friendship, it is control. David has given back Bags his own question, and told the boy that an obsession with kissing girls is of less value than a friendship with a male friend if he wants only the best for his friend.

Furthermore, from the combination of the two parts of his argument, David convinces himself that since he is able to maintain his feelings for Frank at a distance, they cannot be based in 'evil' sensuality. Bags has tested his gift of continency and David has found it to be intact. Bags, the heterosexual devil on David's shoulder casting aspersions upon his sexuality, has been seen off, and what is more, it has not cost David much effort. By simply having faith that he has the gift of continency, he has come up with an answer that will suffice. Violet Gray's marriage to a cousin is, therefore, no more than an aside in David's life, but this makes E.F.B.'s rare authorial intervention about David falling in love for the first time, with Violet, the more interesting.

> There are exactly as many ways of falling in love as there are different natures in the world, and since every boy or man, girl or woman, falls in love off the same carpet, so to speak, on which he transacts the other affairs of life, it followed that David's first excursion into the enchanted country was made with enthusiasm and gaiety and innocence, and with that forgetfulness of himself that characterised his other ways and works.[46]

Taken in the light of what has happened before, with what follows and especially with what will be said about David's relationship with Frank before this volume ends, it is obvious to the reader, even if it does not seem to be to the author, that David's infatuation with Violet is not the first time he has fallen in love. But if E.F.B. is either unaware or is merely trying to disguise his creation's feelings, he is careful here to let his readers know about David's ability to 'forget himself' in his interactions with other people. The discussion with Bags has shown us that David can do just that with both men and women: but only by keeping a safe distance from men. However, when David

---

46. Benson, *David Blaize*, p. 301.

is wounded and near death, his need for Frank's physical presence emerges again, and their love is spoken of with approval, by, of all people, the Head. What is more, this time it is Frank who comes to David's side, though it is David who wants to touch his friend.

Comrade Love

I would argue that the publication date of the novel, 1916, is important for understanding how the final section of *David Blaize* works. Palmer and Lloyd's biography notes that many young soldiers wrote to E.F.B. about the book pleased that he had not allowed David to die from his injuries when a cart ran him over. How much E.F.B. knew of the depravities of the trenches at so early a stage of the war, or yet whether he had heard of the close relationships between the soldiers who lived in such conditions, cannot be certain. He was in a literary set in London, and may have met younger soldier poets such as Sassoon, Owen or Brooke when they were on leave. We know that Wilfred Owen met Robbie Ross, who had introduced E.F.B. to Wilde, but I have found no documentary evidence that E.F.B. had also met Owen, though the two lived only a few hundred yards from one another.[47] However, there is no doubt from reading *David Blaize* that E.F.B. understood that caring for a friend near death sanctioned the expression of the deepest of emotions between men. Such emotionality is the sort of comrade love discussed in the chapter on Edward Carpenter, with its sentimental association between men that may or may not end up in physical expression, a love that would seem to have found its apogee in the trenches of the battlefields of the Great War. Since comrade love did not inevitably end up in physical expression, the confusion that surrounds the sexuality of the men who attended the Eagle Street College in Bolton, the same confusion that for many years surrounded Walt Whitman, and which still surrounds E.F.B. is not erased from the sentimental ending of *David Blaize*. The fact that it is sentimental rather than aesthetic (or Wildean) may be seen to demonstrate that E.F.B., as Palmer and Lloyd suggest, 'retired to the sidelines' of the homosexual world. But if that were so, the following two volumes of David Blaize stories suggest that the withdrawal was difficult, and the final scene of this first volume suggests that their love does reach a physical climax of an oblique kind.

47. Ross in Piccadilly, and E.F.B. in Oxford Street.

David has been seriously injured in an accident with a cart, and is in the sanatorium. Frank comes to Marchester at the Head's instigation, since David is near death. The scene that follows allows them to have intimate conversation and to touch tenderly in public, and, oddly, although it is introduced by Frank trying desperately to claim that they are still inviolable innocents, nevertheless, the Head blesses their relationship, as though in some sort of marriage:

> "He's quite the best chap in the world, sir," [Frank] said. "He saved me, you know. Just saved me."
>
> The Head pressed his arm.
>
> "Ah, that's between you and David," he said. "It's not for me to hear. But I know you love him, which is the only point ..."[48]

At the moment of imminent death, Frank's friendship can be acknowledged for what it is: love. In the same way that the Elegy[49] can 'openly' disguise feelings between men, which cannot be spoken while both are alive, so Frank is told his feelings for David are allowed to remain 'between you and David.' The Head's demand for silence condones any sexual activity that may have already happened between the lovers; at least they did not let it be known, as did Hughes. The 'point' of Frank coming to be by David's side is that their love might bring David back from death's door, which the Head's mere allowing Frank to come demonstrates he feels is more important than condemning same-sex sexual activity. When Frank reaches David's bedside, they are allowed to share their first night together acknowledged as lovers, and acknowledging each other as lovers.

> "I say, would it bore you awfully to hold my hand?" [David] said. "You are strong and fit and quiet. I might get some [sleep]. I don't know. Am I talking rot?"[50]

At key moments of high stress in the novel we have seen David trying to get physically close to Frank, most significantly after the bathroom scene, on the golfing holiday and after David's denunciation of Frank. By asking to hold Frank's hand, he acknowledges to himself the importance of bridging the gap between them. Frank's

48. Benson, *David Blaize*, p. 313.

49. See, for example, Chris Mounsey, 'Persona, Elegy and Desire', in *Studies in English Literature 1500–1900*, Vol. 46.3 (Summer 2006): pp. 601–18. Available at: http://muse.jhu.edu/journals/studies_in_english_literature/toc/sel46.3.html

50. Benson, *David Blaize*, p. 313.

touch keeps him alive, it always has, and it always will. As with the Head's acknowledgement of their love, and forgiveness of any sexual activity they may have indulged in, so David acknowledges his desire for Frank, when it can no longer lead to sex. His life of continency cannot be sullied because it seems nearly to be over. What is perhaps more astounding is that the school doctor realizes that Frank's touch might heal David, and prescribes Frank as David's medicine. And this draws out a tension in the lessons David has learned and is still learning about his sexuality.

> David's eyelids dropped again, and the doctor came round to Maddox's side.
>
> "Sit quite still," he whispered, "and don't speak to him again."
>
> "Sure it doesn't bore you?" asked David once more.
>
> Again there was silence, and the two, the friends and the doctor, remained absolutely still for some five minutes. Then from the bed came a long sigh. David's head rolled sideways on the pillow, and after that came the quiet, regular breathing. Then the doctor whispered once more to Maddox.
>
> "You may have to sit like that with your arm out for hours," he said. "We'll try to make you comfortable presently. Can you manage it?"
>
> "Why, yes," said he.[51]

The Head of David's first school, like the God of the Old Testament who made rules based in the negative, taught him that he must live all his life as though he was being watched, and that indulging in same sex sexuality will bring shame onto his parents and spoil the rest of his life. The Head of Marchester, like the God of the New Testament who forgives human failings, now tells Frank that he knows of the love between the two boys and blesses it, whether or not it has been physical, so long as he does not hear about it. For him, some sins are less than mortal, and love is worth more than life itself, no matter who is in love, or from which carpet they have fallen. Likewise the doctor absolves David and Frank of the guilt of their sexuality, and, like Erixymachus brings their hands together with the excuse that it will encourage David to sleep, turning bad physicality good. If this were all, then after David has fallen asleep, Frank might sleep beside his friend in a chair in case David wakes in the night, but

51. Benson, *David Blaize*, pp. 313–14.

the doctor's prescription is for constant physical contact all night, like Socrates and Alcibiades. In this sense, while the Head blesses the marriage, the doctor furnishes the wedding bed, after which he leaves the two alone.

> "I'm going to get a bit of sleep now," [the doctor] whispered to Frank, "but I'm afraid you won't. You must stop just as you are. If he lets go of your hand you must still sit there in case he wakes and asks and asks for you. If he says anything, answer him as if he was in the dormitory, and you in the bed next to him. You're in charge."

A wholly opposed way of reading this scene is that when the doctor goes to bed and David is left entirely in Frank's power, the fact that Frank does not take advantage of him demonstrates that he is an inviolable innocent as he claimed to the Head. However, I would argue that this is a misprision of what is happening. Frank is not only allowed to touch David, but David has asked to be touched. The contact of their hands is healing because he has finally been able to ask for what he wants, knowing that in that moment, his friend will not take advantage of him. The touch is so slight, and as hand-to-hand touch between men is sanctioned, it would never be classed as sexual activity. But the love that passes in the touch from Frank to David is stimulating, and David lives. E.F.B. even calls it 'the tie of their love', and with the acknowledgement of that love, their roles of 'erastes' and 'eromenos' are reinstated:

> All that morning Maddox sat by David's bed as he slept. It was he who had brought to him, through the tie of their love, and David's instinctive obedience to his suggestion, the sleep that had been so imperative a need, and the sunny morning grew broad and hot as he dozed sometimes, but oftener watched, filled with a huge and humble exultation of happiness that he had been able to help David. And when David woke, a little after noon, it was the best of all. For even while his eyes were yet scarcely unclosed, he spoke just one word – Frank's name, still sleepily.[52]

Frank as 'erastes' has given David the sleep that has kept him alive, and David as 'eromenos' has obeyed his master and gone to sleep. But afterwards their relationship becomes much more complicated. Despite the sunny morning that ought to herald chaste manhood

---

52. Benson, *David Blaize*, p. 315.

according to the first Head's injunction, David has just slept with Frank, and wakes calling Frank's name.

The scene is couched in giving and taking away, banning and sanctioning friendship, love and sexuality, so that it becomes, not an end, but a further negotiation of David's and Frank's love in the society in which they find themselves. The final moments of the novel do not give us a transcendental place of abstinence, as in A.C.B.'s *Arthur Hamilton*. The sentimentality of comrade love at death's door has allowed their feelings for one another to be acknowledged, and allowed them to sleep touching one another, but however far they feel they may go that way, they withdraw from giving themselves the fulfilment of the physical passion for one another that has been hinted at. It is as though the messages of the first and second Heads, like the Old and New Testaments, are opposed, the second fulfilling the first, while at the same time 'one jot or one tittle has in no wise passed from the law'.[53]

One might also read the ending as David coming to the knowledge that he has reached sexual maturity, and will go on to explore the physical side of his sexuality, as though the trilogy were a bildungsroman. However, while *David Blaize and the Blue Door* explores physical sexuality, it does so from the point of view of an eight-year-old boy, and ends envisioning only solo masturbation. When we arrive at the final volume, *David of King's*, even that pleasure must be put aside as a childish thing, in order that David and Frank's asexual relationship continue to develop to maturity.

53. Matthew 5: 18.

Chapter 4

E.F. BENSON: THE *DAVID BLAIZE* TRILOGY, A SEXUALITY
FIT FOR MY LORD – THE RELEASE OF MASTURBATION

The end of *David Blaize* left us with David apparently asking
Frank for a physical expression of the sexuality underlying their
friendship. The special circumstances that sanctioned the request
fitted the context of writing the book: the sentimentality of comrade
love in the trenches of the Great War. The act itself was so slight
that though E.F.B. called it 'the tie of their love', it might hardly be
termed sexual. At the same time, it was significant that continued
touch from his lover kept David alive, which furthermore, was
acknowledged by the Head and the doctor as a physical sign of
the love between the two boys, and possibly one sign among
many. Frank holding David's hand all night and for the following
morning must also be set in context of his having nearly acted on
his physical desire for David in the bathroom at school, and his
later admission that he still found it difficult not to ask David for
sexual favours when they were on a golfing holiday. Now that
David has apparently recognized his reciprocal desire for physical
closeness with Frank, (a desire that has been hinted at throughout
the first volume of the trilogy) no matter what the circumstances
the request was made, Pandora's box has been opened, which can
never be closed: David's sexual maturity with its concomitant sexual
activity with others. This chapter will argue that *David Blaize and the
Blue Door* offers the first attempt E.F.B. made to close that box, by
suggesting imaginative sexual fantasy accompanying masturbation
lies within the compass of the gift of continency, and the blessing
of the church. Furthermore, the book gives an account of David's
rejection of heterosexual and homosexual love.

It is therefore noteworthy that the first proper description we get
of David Blaize in *David Blaize and the Blue Door* tells us that as a
child he acted first and irresponsibly and reckons the consequences
afterwards.

> Now David was the sort of boy who often wanted to do some-
> thing chiefly because he was told not to, in order to see what
> happened ...[1]

This is said of the eight year-old David, whom we have just left ten
years later spending the night holding his lover Frank's hand. David,
we now learn, has a past in which such impulsive actions are not
uncommon. In this way, the second volume sets itself up as being
an explanation of how he sorts out the difficulties which knowing
innocence has got him into at the end of the first volume.

That said, *David Blaize and the Blue Door* is also a book of nonsense
that is called reality. David goes to bed in his nursery, finds a blue
door beneath his pillow, goes through it, and has adventures with
his now animated toys, and with the characters from his books. Thus,
the book works by dream logic, or rather, as it claims, child logic set
against adult logic, expressed in glossolalia, or the pure joy of playing
with the tongue and lips to make sound. Such baby language belies
the content: adult sexuality, heterosexual and homosexual, as well
as autoerotic. However, since it will be argued that David's decision
in the book is to reject both hetero and homosexuality, and to engage
only in fantasy-led masturbation, it must be remembered that any
book written in 1916 must necessarily address its subject matter in
some form of disguise, and glossolalia with child logic is as good a
disguise as any. Furthermore, while it might be argued that a decision
to withdraw from sexual activity with others was juvenile and so
this volume is about his pre-school sexuality, I would argue that the
book gives us David as a boy, since in *David of King's*, his father tells
him to give up masturbation in return for giving his blessing that
David becomes a writer rather than entering the church. As such even
masturbation has to be overcome in order to maintain the state of
continency, and is put away as a childish thing: When I was a child, I
spake as a child, I understood as a child, I thought as a child: but when
I became a man, I put away childish things.[2] For David, ultimately,
asexuality is manly, and asexual love is manly love. When 'manly
love' is discussed at the end of *David of King's*, Frank is under the
misapprehension that David might fall in love with a woman. What
he does not know is that David's attempts to find women sexually

1. E.F. Benson, *David Blaize and the Blue Door* (London: Hodder & Stoughton,
1918), p. 38.
2. Corinthians 13: 11.

alluring earlier in the same volume have all come to nothing, and in *David Blaize and the Blue Door* we discover that David has always found women of all ages unappealing sexually, and men frightening sexually. Thus, *David Blaize and the Blue Door* takes a pivotal position in the David Blaize trilogy, if the sexual reading is acceptable.

Heterosexuality Denied Three Times

Continuing the biblical theme, the fact that *David Blaize and the Blue Door* is a dream, means that David denies heterosexuality three times before cockcrow. This densely packed metaphor of David as St. Peter and therefore the church,[3] and Jesus as marriage, returns us to the Book of Common Prayer (1662) marriage service, where Jesus, and those with the gift of continency are said to be married to the church through their abstinence, which is a greater gift than procreation. As it states in the marriage service:

> … holy Matrimony; which is an honourable estate, instituted of God in the time of man's innocency, signifying unto us the mystical union that is betwixt Christ and his Church; which holy estate Christ adorned and beautified with his presence.

When we meet the females, in turn, Miss Muffet, a giggling giraffe and Miss Bones, the butcher's daughter, they represent respectively, routine sexual activity within marriage, wanton sexual activity and the expectation of heterosexual marriage for all. Each female is unattractive to David in her own way, and it is therefore unsurprising that it is not obvious to him that all want to marry him, though they will claim they did later in the novel. The only clue to their intention that he does pick up on is the extended section on the card game Happy Families.

David enters a large room, where he is introduced to Miss Muffet by her butler. She screams, falls off her tuffet, and knocks David over into the puddle of her spilled curds and whey while the butler repeats over and over 'Miss Muffet David Blaize – David Blaize Miss Muffet.'[4] Miss Muffet is an old lady, and explains herself to David as though she lives perpetually in her nursery rhyme, repeating her fate and always remaining unmarried.

---

3. *Tu es Petrus, et super hanc petram aedificabo ecclesiam meam.*
4. Benson, *Blue Door*, p. 45.

"... And now we know each other, I may be permitted the hope that you didn't expect to find me a little girl?"

"No, I like you best as you are," said David quickly.

"It isn't for want of being asked that I've remained Miss Muffet," said she. "And it isn't from want of being answered. But give me a little pleasant conversation now and then, and one good frightening away every night, and I'm sure I'll have no quarrel with anybody; and I hope nobody's got any with me."[5]

Her speech seems both to represent the drought of the quotidian routine of a long marriage, and aged coquettishness. However, placing her 'frightening away' at night and every night, suggests it may be a metaphor for a voracious sexual appetite. Added to this the fact that she claims to have been 'asked' many times, and with the lack of a spider to do the frightening, we might even extend the rhyme's metaphor to suggest that, like some spiders, Miss Muffet has remained single because she has eaten her male partners after having had sex with them. My reading may seem to be overly suggestive, but in context of the rest of the book, and of the other two females, it might not seem so outrageous.

Having escaped Miss Muffet's clutches, David at once falls foul of another sexually voracious female, a giraffe who demands to dance with him. As he begins to dance, he begins to grow, a sensation that David does not like, whereupon he is told that the only thing that will make him little again is tickling:

"If I began tickling, [said the Giraffe] we should both begin littling. But as long as I don't tickle, we shan't little. There!"

David could bear it no longer, and he instantly thrust his fingers into the giraffe's ribs, and began tickling her. She gave a loud silly cackle, and he felt to his intense joy, that they started to get littler.[6]

The dancing, growing, tickling and 'littling' appear to be references to sexual activity, with foreplay (dancing), erection (growing) and stimulation (tickling) followed by flaccidity (littling). Whereupon, David's 'intense joy' seems not to be at having achieved ejaculation, but rather that the act, which 'he could bear [...] no longer,' is soon to be over. The giraffe's 'silly cackle' seems to echo A.C.B.'s horror that women might engage in sexual activity that we encountered in

5. Benson, *Blue Door*, p. 45.
6. Benson, *Blue Door*, p. 94.

the first chapter on E.F.B., and the now little David escapes to a town centre relieved rather than satisfied.

Unhappy Families

He finds a meeting of Happy Families in a large building which 'had been the girls' school ... . As he stood there, the door was opened a foot or two, and a large mutton bone flew past his head.'[7] A sign over the door proclaims that the building is now 'The Happy Families Institute', and despite the unwelcoming bone, David enters, where he finds:

> a room, dazzlingly bright, with a stage at one end, and rows and rows of chairs, four on one side and four on the other of a gangway that led up the centre. All the chairs were occupied, and all the occupiers had their backs to the stage, and were looking towards the door when he entered. Over each group of four chairs was suspended a banner, which bore the name of the happy family which occupied it. And every member of every happy family looked at him quite steadily.[8]

The card game, Happy Families, is a version of rummy, where players collect families, each of which are made up of a father with a trade, a mother, a son and a daughter. Collecting is done by asking players for a particular card, which when asked for, must be given up, until all the families are made up correctly.[9] The expectation set up by the game is that procreative heterosexual relationships are right for everyone, and that there is someone perfect for each person, if only one will ask.

All of the families at the Institute are looking intently at David, and it soon becomes obvious that they are trying to find out which

7. Benson, *Blue Door*, p. 95.
8. Benson, *Blue Door*, p. 99.
9. The game is played with a special pack of 44 cards depicting the mother, father, son and daughter of 11 families. All the cards are dealt, and the player to dealer's left begins. The player whose turn it is asks another player for a specific card; the asker must already hold at least one card of the same family. If the player asked has the card it must be handed over and the asker continues by asking the same or another player for another card. If the asked player does not have the wanted card they say 'not at home' and the turn passes to them. Completed families are placed face down in front of the owner. When all families are complete, the player with most wins.

family he should fit into. The first family he tries is one invented by E.F.B., the Rhymes, who make up a joint poem about David. Their interchanges emphasize the idea that the family is an expectation and a role rather than an expression of choice:

> "It gives us all the utmost joy," she [Miss Rhyme] said, "to welcome here a human boy. They say your name is David Blaize, but it don't matter what they says. The great thing is to stick to rhyme" –
>
> "And make up verses all the time," interrupted Master Rhyme, who began writing too. "We're very pleased that you have *got* here."
>
> "I've made a blot, and want the blotter," said Miss Rhyme. "Papa, don't jog my elbow so, it stops my inspiration's flow."[10]

The insistence of rhyme and rhythm implies that every situation will always be predictable, so when David encounters Miss Bones, their marriage would seem to be inevitable, no matter how bad her manners.

> Miss Bones was sitting on his thumb. Somehow she looked quite life size, and yet David did not feel any bigger than she. She was still gnawing at her sirloin of beef, and tore off large pieces of gristle with her hands, just dropping them on David's knee, or on the note books of the Rhyme family, who had got a good deal smaller, but were still sitting round him and writing.[11]

The assiduity with which all the cards play increases David's alarm, though he is not sure what he is worried about:

> Hitherto he had always played with the happy families, and now they were playing with him. And they were so fierce and unkind, like wasps.[12]

Even when a claim is made upon him by Mr Funk the Bather, who reminds us of David's father in *David Blaize*, David does not realize the import of his being called 'Master Funk':

> There was a sudden stir among the newer families, and Mr Funk, the bather, ran up to him. He was dressed in a striped bathing dress, and all his teeth chattered.
>
> "I believe you're a Funk," he said. "I believe you belong to my family. I'm collecting you. Come on Master Funk."

10. Benson, *Blue Door*, p. 102.
11. Benson, *Blue Door*, pp. 106–107.
12. Benson, *Blue Door*, p. 108.

A 'funk' is a person who is too frightened to do something, which turns out to be to ask Miss Bones for her hand in marriage:

> ... [Miss Bones] wiped her mouth on the back of her hand, and sidled a little nearer David.
>
> "That's right: it's your turn," she whispered. "Remember you've got me. Don't ask for me."
>
> "I shouldn't think of it," said David. "What I want is a concert. I came here for a concert. I want to sit down and be quiet for a little. Nobody knows all the things I've been doing."[13]

At this stage of the novel, it is still humorous that Miss Bones's insinuation that David 'has her' and so does not need to 'ask for' her is brushed off with an insouciant 'I shouldn't think of it,' from David. Later when she claims he has broken his promise to marry her, the joke turns sour.

Imagination and Masturbation

For the present, David goes off through the town in search of further adventures, which involve his being denied access to a group of homosexuals and discovering masturbation by accident. The former is introduced by a concealed reference in David's speech above. His desire for a 'concert' suggests he thinks himself to be 'musical,' which is an early twentieth century metaphor for homosexuality. When David goes to the train station, a porter cow tries to keep him from entering, and thus, according to his character, he will go in, where he finds a group of eccentric bald men having designs painted on their pates before taking the Bald Express on their adventures to 'Egypt, or London SW'. David is spellbound by the men and we get our first glimpse of him as having homosexual desires. Exactly to what 'London SW' refers is obscure, but the reference to Egypt seems to suggest E.F.B.'s trip down the Nile with Lord Alfred Douglas, Robert Hichens and Reginald Turner, which caused so much gossip about his own sexuality. For David, the idea of all male company seems to be irresistible.

In fact, David is so entranced by the men, that when he is forbidden to get on their train he runs after it and begins to fly. If revelation were needed about David's sexuality, it is in this incident, in all its complexity. Heterosexuality has been denied because none of the

13. Benson, *Blue Door*, p. 109.

women are physically appealing (an idea to which E.F.B. returns in
David of King's), but homosexuality is fascinating even in the image
of older and bald men. So much so that even when David is denied
access to their pleasures, he fantasizes about them, bringing himself
to ecstasy in the metaphor of flying.

> Then his left foot didn't touch the ground at all, and then his right
> foot. He simply found himself running in the air.[14]

Where David's adventures with Miss Muffet, the Giraffe, Miss Bones
and the bald men have been the result of David's doing things that
he has been told not to do, and learning lessons from what happens,
running in the air, he discovers, is not something he has to learn
since he feels he has always known how. Since few boys are taught
to masturbate it is a practice that does seem, when it first happens, to
be an accident and therefore something that one has always known
how to do. But the point here seems to be that even if David has
begun to masturbate, that is, begun his life of sexual maturity, at
the sight of the bald men, masturbation instantaneously becomes
a strategy for avoiding actual homosexual acts, first by religious
sanctioning of masturbation, then by David's learning that he can use
his imagination to take him to sexual ecstasy rather than by looking
at other men.

The religious sanction for masturbation comes from Canon and
Mrs Rook:

> A pair of [rooks] were quarrelling as to which way a particular stick
> ought to be laid, one wanting it laid crossways, the other straight.
> They had lived for years before they came here in a cathedral close,
> and were always known as Canon and Mrs Rook.[15]

Canon Rook becomes David's mentor in the art of flying, and David
asks the first question about masturbation that all boys want to
know: will you be able to do it for ever, or can you do it only a few
times and no more.[16] Of course, all this is done in terms of whether
he will be able to fly and the Canon tells him he will be able to until
he forgets again. The rook's remark foreshadows the Archdeacon
telling David to stop smoking his pipe in *David of King's*, which we

14. Benson, *Blue Door*, p. 136.
15. Benson, *Blue Door*, p. 140.
16. See Thom Gunn, 'Courage: A Tale' in *Jack Straw's Castle* (New York:
Farrar Straus Giroux, 1976).

shall see in the next chapter. For the present, David confirms the religious sanction for his masturbation by winning a certificate of flying from the birds, by performing a series of tricks, following Canon Rook's directions.

> So he put his precious certificate in his pocket and flew off like a swift, without moving his arms or legs and only balancing and turning in the air. You just had to move your head first, and all the rest followed. You *thought* what you wanted to do, and you were doing it.[17]

What David has learned from the birds is that he can use his imagination to bring him to the moment of ecstatic flight. In terms of masturbation, he can think of what he finds attractive and sensual instead of actually having to see it or engage in sexual intercourse. After his first solo flight with his certificate, David lies by a lake, and gets an erection using his imagination as stimulus:

> "... Oh, I'm having the nicest time since I came through the blue door. I am so thirsty too!"
>
> He lay down on the bank, with his head over the edge, and was scarcely surprised to find that the lake tasted of lemonade, with ice and plenty of sugar. Then he lay back in the long grass, and listened to the birds talking, and the sap humming in the growing herbs.[18]

He hears the 'birds talking' which causes the 'sap' to rise and stalks to grow. The link between the stalks and his penis is made after a complicated exploration of imagination and reality. Flying leads him to ecstasy in a place that is both in and out of this world:

> ... he was no longer afraid that he was back in the ordinary world again, though he was in the ordinary places. He had gone through the blue door, and his eyes and ears were opened to thousands of things he had never seen before in those familiar places. All the colours were infinitely brighter than they had ever been, and there were new sounds in the air, and new scents.[19]

David sees his own house on the other side of the lake and flies across to it. It is as though imagination-led masturbation has allowed him to see the real world of home and family in a new way. In his garden

---

17. Benson, *Blue Door*, p. 154.
18. Benson, *Blue Door*, p. 156.
19. Benson, *Blue Door*, p. 157.

he looks at the flowers, whose stiff stalks and moving bells suggest the anatomy of the penis and glans[20] being stimulated:

> Then a breeze came up from the lake, and set the flowers swinging on their stalks. But they did not swing quite in the ordinary way, for the stalks stopped still, and only the flowers themselves swung. Farther and farther they swung, this way and that, and then the sound of bells began to come out of them. The Canterbury bells and the campanulas began, because they were professional bells, but by degrees, everything else joined in, lilies and roses and hollyhocks and lupins, and love-lies-bleeding, and every other flower you can imagine, for they were all in blossom together this morning.[21]

And after masturbation he begins to have an orgasm:

> David listened a long time in a sort of ecstasy of pleasure, and then this peeling got somehow into his bones, and he had to do something joyful too. But as he could not make a bell of himself, he must throw himself into the air, and poised as a hawk hovering, flapping his arms all the time, and stopping in the same place, and then he skimmed away with his arms quite still and stretched out taut, and flew over the house so close that the tips of his fingers touched the chimney-stacks.[22]

I do not feel that it is appropriate to read these scenes in terms of Freud's *Interpretation of Dreams*, which associates dreaming of flying with sex, though it was published in 1915 in an English translation. The references to sexuality in the novel have grown more and more direct, from the vague suggestions of Miss Muffet to the references to flying and ecstasy, and it therefore seems otiose to import a theory to read a text which seems to use its own language of glossolalia to make its point. What is more, the references to sexuality become clearer as the novel reaches its denouement, after a brief interlude that suggests that David is becoming more and more worried about what people think of him now he has begun to masturbate.

The next adventure, which precipitates the frenetic conclusion to the novel, concerns David's treacherous toy soldiers. In the language of child logic, and the language of growing up, the mutinous army seems to represent a growing self-awareness and self-consciousness

20. The slang for which is often given as a 'bell end'.
21. Benson, *Blue Door*, p. 158.
22. Benson, *Blue Door*, p. 159.

concomitant with developing sexuality. It is the feeling that everyone can tell what is going on inside his head, and that he must therefore try to please the others who know his innermost thoughts rather than pleasing himself.

Landing in his garden, David sees his toy soldiers in a line before his house, and, as its Field Marshall, he inspects them. The Brigadier General, whom he has fished out of the lake, along with a pike, takes him to see the maps of the enemy movement. David soon notices that the movements of the enemy are *his*. As we shall see, the pike represents predatory homosexuality, and what worries David is that his soldiers have been able to read his mind and know that he has been imagining the bald old men to bring himself to sexual ecstasy. It is the lesson the first Head teaches David at his Private School: that what he is thinking is written all over his face, so he must live his private life as though he is in public. The mere fact of imagining having sex with other men makes him into a predatory homosexual.

That night, the soldiers put barbed wire about his tent and he overhears them plan to kill him the next morning. During the night, David escapes, and takes refuge in the lake, beneath the glass, which the fish have put up to protect themselves from the Brigadier General who fell in earlier.

Queer Fish

David believes that the soldiers know he is a 'queer fish' because he believes they recognize him as being the same species as the pike, which is the reason why he has become the 'enemy.' Suffice it to say, while David has found the air a natural medium in which to fly, when he climbs under the ice he discovers that water is treacherous and a medium in which he is not at home:

> At once he felt he was not walking any more, for his feet had come off the ground, and he was lying flat a few feet from the floor. This sensation was rather like losing your balance, and he made a sort of wriggle with his feet in order to recover it again. But instead of recovering his footing, he merely darted off at a great speed in a perfectly unexpected direction.[23]

23. Benson, *Blue Door*, p. 187.

Furthermore, the fish are ill-mannered, unlike the birds. David has to teach himself how to swim like a fish, and accidentally bumps into a trout:

> "I'm very sorry," said David. "I didn't mean to hit you."
>
> "Then you did it without meaning," said the trout, with its back to him, "which is worse, because there's no sense in it, if it doesn't mean anything. I wish you would go away. Right away, I mean: none of your hanging about here. Get some low, coarse fish to teach you. I'm busy."[24]

The trout's way of speaking and demeanour readily leads to the appellation of 'queer fish.' It is not long before David's antipathy to the fish and their ways becomes as strong as his dislike of the women whom he met at the start of the novel.

> … even swimming fish-fashion had ceased to amuse him, for he did not want to do anything that fishes did.[25]

However, when he decides to leave the lake, the pike chases him as if to trap him and keep him in the lake where he belongs:

> He had never seen anything so ugly and cruel.
>
> "You beastly fish," he said. "If I had teeth like you I should go to the dentist. I'm not frightened of you."
>
> He was terrified really, but when you are frightened, it is always comforting to say you're not.
>
> "Yes you are," said the pike, snapping his jaws, and shouldering his way up through the shallow water. "You daren't come down into the stream again."
>
> "I don't want to come into your muddy stream," said David. "I should if I wanted to. And for that matter you daren't come up here."
>
> "Yes I dare," said the pike, pushing farther up, till half his horrid body was out of the stream. "And I'm coming too."[26]

The impasse between pike and boy is odd. Where the trout is simply rude, the pike seems to want David, but not for food. Their standoff is one of fear in the boy and desire in the fish. But it is not a desire that David cannot understand, it is simply something he wants to pretend does not exist.

24. Benson, *Blue Door*, p. 190.
25. Benson, *Blue Door*, p. 198.
26. Benson, *Blue Door*, p. 199.

> [David] made himself very dignified, and walked away, trying
> not to hurry till he was out of sight of the stream.[27]

The reason being, that his growing self-awareness can link the subject
of his masturbatory fantasy with the pike:

> It was not quite proper for a bird-boy, and a Field-Marshal to run
> away from a fish, but this was such an awful fish.[28]

The clue to my interpretation lies here in the juxtaposition of
'bird-boy' and 'Field-Marshal.' The bird-boy is the aspect of David
that began his masturbation while chasing the bald men, and the
Field-Marshal is the aspect of David that sees himself as someone
who can be criticized for his desires. Together they make up a sense
of propriety, or in this case, a sense that David knows that the pike
knows that he is a 'queer fish' too, and thus to be feared.

The Marriage Meadow

If all this still sounds a little far fetched, the final scenes of the book
in the Marriage Meadow and the Court give succinct evidence that
the book is about sexuality, and that David wants neither to marry
a woman, nor to live with the queer fish, but needs to keep in touch
with the birds. He wants neither a heterosexual nor homosexual
relationship, but needs solo masturbation to keep him happy.

With touching dream logic, David finds himself in his father's
grounds after he has escaped from the pike, and they at first look
familiar:

> There were two signboards, he knew, in this field, one down by the
> river about fishing, and the other where there was a path across
> it, on which was the notice, "Trespassers will be prosecuted with
> the utmost rigour of the law." He did not mind about that notice
> since both the field and the notice belonged to his father.[29]

Likewise with dream logic, David reads the second sign, and sees,
with terror, that it has changed:

TRESPASSERS WILL BE MARRIED WITH THE UTMOST RIGOUR
OF THE LAW.[30]

27. Benson, *Blue Door*, p. 200.
28. Benson, *Blue Door*, p. 201.
29. Benson, *Blue Door*, p. 201.
30. Benson, *Blue Door*, p. 202.

At the moment of reading the sign, all the pieces of the dream come together and David sees his dilemma. He is trapped between heterosexuality and homosexuality:

> "Oh, what am I to do?" thought poor David. "There's a girl coming into it all. I know she'll spoil everything."
>
> He began running back towards the stream again, for he felt he would rather fight the pike than be married, but then he thought of the savage jaws and those dreadful teeth, and his legs simply would not take him any nearer the stream. They said "No!" just as if they had spoken aloud. Between his mind that said that he had better face any danger sooner than be married, and his legs that said that they would go anywhere except towards the pike, he completely lost his head, and began running in circles round the field, saying to himself in a most determined voice:
>
> "I won't be married, I won't be eaten by the pike, I won't be married to a pike, I won't be eaten by anybody."[31]

Were it just that David was frightened of getting married to a girl 'who would spoil everything' we would be back in the world of Richmal Crompton, where Violet Elizabeth spoils William and his friends' games. But the fact that his body is in revolt against his mind, and he believes his choice lies between fighting the male pike and marriage, though he does not want either, demonstrates that David will not consider the homosocial as the same childish alliance against 'girls' that William is happy with.

Furthermore, when Mr. Noah, another representative of the social pressure to marry, arrests David for his trespass, David's response is to say that it is up to him to choose his own sexuality.

> "Oh it's you Noah!" he panted. "I couldn't remember who you were. Why did you run after me?"
>
> Noah wiped his face with the edge of his ulster.
>
> "To catch you," said he. "What else should I run after you for? The point is: Why did you run away?"
>
> David didn't see why he should tell Noah that his legs were running away from the pike, and his mind from being married ...
>
> "I like running," he said. "I shall walk and run, and fly and swim, just as I choose."
>
> "Hoity-toity!" said Noah. "I expect that'll be as *she* chooses."
>
> "Whom do you mean by 'she'?" asked David ...

31. Benson, *Blue Door*, p. 202.

"I can't tell you yet," said Noah, "but you'll soon know. I'm not certain who we have on the books this morning. Hark! There are the church-bells beginning. That's for you."[32]

Although given as an excuse for his running in the meadow, David's reply to Noah that he will 'walk and run, and fly and swim' has the connotations of all the rest of the novel giving it meaning. Walking is to marry or 'walk out' with a member of the opposite sex. Flying is masturbation, in terms both of the Head of David's first school, and the birds in this volume. And swimming is associated with homosexuality both here, and in a swimming pool in *David of King's* when our hero discovers Oscar Browning, the noted homosexual master of Eton, in a pool in London. And it is this tripartite opposition that choreographs David's decision to masturbate. Under threat that he is to be married that day, David is offered only the pike as an alternative:

> A brilliant idea struck David.
> "I'm not in the marriage meadow now," he said. "How do you intend to prove I was there at all? It was only you who say you saw me, and you are only a person out of my own ark."
> Noah got up, and opened the door into the meadow. David could hear the pike still calling "Coward!" He was coughing violently having been so long in the air.
> "Pike!" shouted Noah. "Come in, pike!"
> David's legs began to want to run somewhere.
> "No! Shut the door," he said. "I was in the marriage-meadow, but I didn't know."[33]

Thinking he has won, Noah tries unsuccessfully to marry David to the giraffe, who asks him 'Can you grow again?'[34] David also refuses Miss Bones the Butcher's daughter, who calls him an upstart while munching on an ox-tail. David is dejected believing himself beaten, and replies that 'I'd sooner be eaten by the pike than see you eat all day and night.'[35] Miss Muffet says she'll let him sit by her on the tuffet, if the spider says there's room. David is baffled, but with the help of the porter cow, he escapes from the court and is chased home to bed through the blue door by all his toys. Only the birds cheer

32. Benson, *Blue Door*, p. 206.
33. Benson, *Blue Door*, p. 210.
34. Benson, *Blue Door*, p. 211.
35. Benson, *Blue Door*, p. 215.

him on, and suddenly he has won, and need neither marry nor be a homosexual. He still has masturbation: 'it was no use to go on if the birds too, were his enemies'.[36]

Thus, *David Blaize and the Blue Door*, represents a provisional way of closing the Pandora's box of the physical expression of sexuality with other people. David chooses to maintain his orgasmic body, but without the help of either a wife or male lover. References to his autoeroticism continue in *David of King's* in the form of pipe smoking, where its being within the compass of continency is suggested by his Meerschaum pipe's name: Perpetua, Virgin and Martyr. But in that novel, David learns he must put away childish things too.

---

36. Benson, *Blue Door*, p. 222.

Chapter 5

E.F. BENSON: THE *DAVID BLAIZE* TRILOGY, A SEXUALITY
FIT FOR MY LORD – FROM BOY LOVE TO MANLY LOVE:
MARRIAGE, MINISTRY AND MAINTAINING THE GIFT OF
CONTINENCY

Queer Fish and Golf Balls

In the introduction to the only modern edition of *David of King's*,
Peter Burton suggests that the character Arthur Gepp is based on
Oscar Browning, known as 'O.B.', the homosexual and pederast
master ejected from Eton who became a fellow of King's College,
Cambridge.[1]

> Browning died in 1923 and it is possible that his death may have
> stirred memories of undergraduate days, which quickly formed
> themselves into *David of King's*.

Doubtless E.F.B. knew the don, since he had been educated in classics
at King's during Browning's tenure as a fellow in classics. Doubtless
he also knew of O.B. and his eccentric as well as his sexually predatory
ways. Doubtless too, Browning's death would have reminded E.F.B.
of his erstwhile teacher. However, another possibility for E.F.B.
returning to the subject of David Blaize after the death of O.B. was
that he could now write about him without fear of a libel trial. You
cannot libel the dead. O.B. had left Eton without facing action from the
family of George Curzon,[2] towards whom (and towards many other
boys in his care) he had been 'overly amorous' and with whom he
had taken a tour of Europe without the Headmaster of Eton's consent.
What E.F.B. thought of O.B. is not known, but A.C.B. thought him
'greedy, vain, foul-minded, grasping, ugly, [and] sensual'.[3]

It is my contention that Arthur Gepp, known in the volume as
'A.G.', is a recognizable portrait of Oscar Browning, and that Oscar

---

1. Peter Burton, Introduction, *David of King's* (Brighton: Millivres, 1991).
The Introduction is unpaginated.
2. Later Viceroy of India.
3. Ian Anstruther, *Oscar Browning* (London: Murray, 1983), p. 174.

Browning is presented as the sort of 'Queer Fish' that David wants to avoid becoming. For this reason, I would suggest that the pike in *David Blaize and the Blue Door* is a less recognizable portrait of Oscar Browning, the predatory homosexual with a taste for young boys, and that A.G. brings O.B. into clearer focus.

In this secondary link, we can discover a reason for E.F.B. returning to the subject of David Blaize some eight years after the first two volumes. We first encounter the charmingly eccentric A.G. in a scene where he and David meet at a party hosted by Bags. Later the same evening A.G. makes his first sexual advance towards David, whom he has read as a homosexual. Since David is not sure whether or not he can bring himself to fulfil his reciprocal desire for the older man, their relationship bumps along through several amusing episodes. After one such, David becomes suddenly aware of what he perceives as the spiritual danger of making the free choice to enter into a homosexual liaison. Therefore, when, the two meet naked in a Turkish Bath, David has already made up his mind that he must reject his own desire, and so re-imagines A.G. as a fat pink devil whose temptations he can resist. A.G. returns one more time, once again when the two are naked, this time in a swimming pool in London, whereupon A.G. tries to seduce David into the world of rich London homosexuals. David sloughs off these final advances expertly, and as some kind of riposte to his homosexual urges, David tries to seduce himself into heterosexual contact with female prostitutes.

As in *David Blaize and the Blue Door*, neither seduction is successful and David rejects both homosexuality and heterosexuality. However, while this aspect of *David of King's* repeats the earlier volume, what is new is the development of the relationship between David and Frank, from one of 'boy love' based on hero worship in *David Blaize* into 'manly love' which seems set to continue throughout their lives in the form of their asexual marriage.

In this sense, I would disagree with Peter Burton that E.F.B.'s 'fiction was a safety valve for his life.' Instead I would argue that for E.F.B., fiction had become his sexual life, in the only form of homosexuality that was acceptable to My Lord. In *David of King's*, imagination is separated from masturbation, and becomes everything that is sexual to David. I would also disagree with Burton's suggestion that the novel is autobiographical, and that that Frank is now the self-portrait, where David had been in *David Blaize*. Burton's suggestion is based on the idea that David will turn from homoeroticism to heterosexuality and leave Frank behind. What we shall see is that this is far from the case. David intends to remain Frank's partner for the rest of his life, though this will incur during the novel, and seems expected to continue to incur, negotiations between them in order that they both remain within the compass of continency.

As if to confirm the suggestion that *David of King's* repeats and develops the action of *David and the Blue Door*, the beginning of the third volume of the trilogy reminds us of the end of the first. Since it was David who, at the end of *David Blaize*, had asked for Frank to be with him when he was ill, his action would seem to have opened the Pandora's box of his mature sexuality. Before Frank had come from Cambridge at David's behest to hold his hand, David had always been the passive party and the sexual desire was all Frank's. Now both know the feelings they hold for the other. In *David Blaize and the Blue Door*, E.F.B. gave us a metaphor of David rejecting Happy Families and Queer Fish, as the sign that David would not act further on his sexual desires with others, female or male, but would give himself the ecstasy of masturbation as a release of his sexual tension. But this was all done in the dream world of his childhood, whereas David himself would have to continue to face growing older, and presumably a real threat to his continency from his continued association with Frank, since now both recognize themselves as the object of each other's affections.

David of King's opens with a scene in which the complexity of the relationship between David and Frank is laid bare. David throws a golf ball over a furniture van, and the ball hits Frank on his right toe. David observes Frank's reaction, and 'from his ambush David could see him jump like a large startled fawn in a great coat …'[4] This prank brings together two ideas from *David Blaize* and one from a short story, which I believe to be relevant. The horse pulling the furniture van is startled by Frank's leap, and begins to pull the van out of control, reminding us of the out-of-control cart that ran over David in *David Blaize*, causing the mortal injury which brought Frank back from Cambridge to hold his lover's hand. The golf ball reminds us of the golf course on which Frank told David that he was still having trouble resisting his physical desire for David. But the fact that it is David who throws the ball at Frank, suggests that he too has physical desires for Frank, albeit that he hides them, just as David himself hides behind the furniture van.

4. E.F. Benson, *David of King's* (London: Hodder & Stoughton, 1924), p. 6.

Reading the whole scene together, the fact that the ball startles Frank seems to suggest that Frank would be surprised to know that David held reciprocal sexual longings for him. David's hiding behind the van, in turn seems to suggest that he wants to keep his feelings hidden, but the fact that the horse bolts and David is revealed demonstrates the vulnerability of his position. He may be exposed for what he is at any moment, as he is by A.G.

The fear of exposure, and what might happen if he acted upon his desires, leads to another possible reference for this scene, E.F.B.'s 1912 story 'The Man Who Went Too Far.' Connections between the scene and story are slight, but compelling. Both concern a man called Frank who is beset by a problem, which can be read as his homosexuality. In the short story Frank Halton has given up being an artist and moved to St Faith's near the River Fawn in Hampshire, where he is trying to prepare himself physically for an encounter with the god Pan.[5] In the struggle between keeping faith with the church, and giving himself up to the god of Nature, Frank Halton dies, trampled to death by Pan, his naked body being found after the encounter with goat hoof prints on his back. Nicholas Freeman has discussed the story as a metaphor of keeping faith with Christianity or following one's sexuality and being destroyed by it.[6] Whether or not the story is intentionally referenced in the first scene of *David of King's* cannot be certain, though it acts as a counterpoint to my reading that the book is about David's fear of exposure, and gives an accurate account of what drives the action in the third volume of the *David Blaize* trilogy: fear that any form of sexual activity, even solo sexual activity may destroy him. Therefore, while *David Blaize and the Blue Door* might be read as offering solo masturbation as the answer to maturing sexuality in his need for asexuality to counter homosexuality, *David of King's* will be read as centring on David finding a different way of coming to terms with his mature sexuality alongside his refusal to forego the close emotional relationship with Frank. If he gives into the former he will be destroyed, but if he loses the latter he will no longer be himself. Asexuality without any form of physical pleasure is therefore the only answer he can find, and it

5. There are two parishes in Hampshire called St Faith's, one in Havant and one in Winchester. There is no River Fawn in England.

6. Nicholas Freeman, 'Paganism and Spiritual Confusion in E.F. Benson', *Literature and Theology* 19.1 (March 2005): pp. 22–33.

will take careful negotiation between him and Frank throughout the rest of their lives.

From the moment David goes up to King's College, he and Frank are inseparable:

> They had passed down the side of the back lawn at King's and gone into the building by the river where David kept rooms. Frank had not the smallest intention of coming so far, but it was always so much easier to remain with David than to go away. Indeed, it was a sheer waste of time not to be with David when you could be, for the old love, born in the days of school, had never waned, and at nineteen (just) and twenty-two, they were still knitted into each other with that taught bond of boyish affection which early manhood had done nothing to slacken. It had grown, indeed, in closeness and comprehension, when, last October, David had come up to Cambridge where Frank, having already completed his third year and taken his degree, was staying for another year to go through a second tripos in Archaeology with the view eventually of getting a fellowship. For this year they were to be together at King's, and that was sufficient for the present.[7]

While this passage might be recognized as the formal language of friendship of the early twentieth century, what has gone before between them places emphasis on 'that taught bond of boyish affection which early manhood had done nothing to slacken', and introduces the idea that the book will have to address the way their friendship will continue to survive the changes they are going through as they mature. And the most obvious change in them is discovered in the physical aspects of their relationship, a feature that shows in both David's sporting and their personal life.

Touching under God

The idea that the physical may not be as innocent as it first seems is introduced with reference to sport, and then explored in terms of touching someone of the same sex in David's and Frank's sexual development. While Frank has hitherto been the great sportsman and David his fanatical supporter, now it is David who is sought for the university rugby team and Frank who has become the bookish observer. But this is not because David has become a true sportsman: his physical actions have quite a different meaning from that for

7. Benson, *David of King's*, p. 10.

which they might be understood. David is playing rugby, watched by the 'Tooties,'[8] Tarler and Towling, the scouts for the university rugby team, and overlooked by Frank, who can see what is really happening.

> David did not possess the grim but cheerful temperament of the football player, and he had a strong objection to being collared somewhere about the knees and thrown flat on his face, which was exactly what Alston proceeded to do to him three times in the first ten minutes. The fourth time that this brutal rape appeared imminent, David gave a loud hoot of despair, and hurling the ball wildly away with no thought but to get rid of it, found that he had made a marvellously neat pass to his centre-three-quarters.[9]

What Frank can see is that David is playing well for the wrong reasons. He even scores a try to avoid being knocked down again by Alston. The rugby scouts, on the other hand, pick him for the university team, and Frank applauds their choice despite knowing they have made a mistake. To Frank, it demonstrates that the 'Tooties' cannot understand David like he can, they do not have his special connection to David. At the same time it alerts the reader to the idea that however a physical action looks, it might have another meaning to those who are involved in it. To David the tackle is a 'rape', an unwanted and undesired sexual encounter, rather than a manoeuvre in a game. Such ambivalence gives E.F.B. the chance to readdress the question of David and Frank holding hands at the end of *David Blaize*.

Just as sport has lost David's thoroughgoing participation, so too chapel has lost its charms, or at least its charms have changed. David has stopped going to chapel except to 'hear the anthem,' and it might appear that religion has become aesthetic. For example, when the boy soprano begins to sing, David 'gave a little wiggle of delight. "O-o-h Cold water down my back," he whispered.'[10] Such aestheticism in the mid 1920s would be difficult to divorce from the homosexual aesthetes who had surrounded Oscar Wilde, and of whose number E.F.B. had been. However, David's reaction to the young singer is quickly deflected by being put into another context with reference to Frank. David uses the moment of ecstasy as an opportunity to get close to his lover.

8. Two 't's', the initials of Tarler and Towling.
9. Benson, *David of King's*, p. 14.
10. Benson, *David of King's*, p. 24.

> How ripping it all was, and he wedged his shoulder against
> Frank's, for he must be in touch with him when he enjoyed himself
> particularly.[11]

Any sexual interest David has in the boy singing (who is the direct
cause of his ecstasy) is reassigned to Frank, and the deflection may be
read on at least two levels. First, if we read Frank and David as lovers,
David's overtly sensual response to another man (or at least boy) may
give rise to jealousy in Frank, so David touches him to reassure him
that he is the most important person in his life. Second, David uses
the anthem as an excuse to touch Frank in chapel, under the eyes of
God so to speak, and as such the touch is sanctioned along the lines
of the lesson David learned when he first went to school. What has
changed in the touch is that in chapel, the person sanctioning it is God.
Thus the sanction is no longer the provisional sanctioning of the Head
and the doctor, who have to trust to their chastity, but God Himself,
who knows their innermost thoughts. And so the touch, in public
and before God, can be seen as no more than a touch, and has not
developed into anything more sexual. In this way, the touch at the end
of *David Blaize* is deflected in the same fashion that David's response to
the soprano has been deflected. Nevertheless, the scene demonstrates
the growing need the two have for each other to help each other meet
the sensual assaults that the world makes on their mature sexualities.
Each knows (or at least trusts) that the other will not develop their
closeness into a physical sex act. It is as though they have decided to
join in asexual marriage with its demand for monogamy that can act
as a barrier to predation. What has not changed in their friendship is
their need for a blessing upon them touching one another. What will
change in their friendship is that Frank must go away after the end
of David's first year at Cambridge, and so David will have to learn
further ways of avoiding the onslaught of sensuality in the world
that will beset him round. At present, he has Frank to help him as
he makes mistakes with A.G., the first sexual predator who homes
in on his beauty.

Bags's Party

Arthur Gepp takes a shine to David immediately. Typical of the
pederast, his assault is not direct, and he first tries to make friends

11. Benson, *David of King's*, p. 24.

with David's friends so as to gain the trust of his target. Frank is too close to David to allow space for anyone else to get near,[12] but Bags is the perfect route for A.G. to get at David.

George Crabtree has gained a title and become a fop since coming up to Cambridge. In the late eighteenth-century mode of foppery, he dresses well, cultivates poets and sportsmen and is inveterately heterosexual. He has even begun to use prostitutes while in Paris, and regales his friends about his encounters. At this particular party, with David, he entertains Stapleton, a long-haired poet, Gowles, a golfing-blue, Vyse, a horsey young man, and 'an elderly don of Bacchic and genial disposition, who was much younger and stouter than anyone else had ever been. His name was Arthur Gepp, and he was known as A.G.'[13] Within seconds of arriving at the party, 'A.G. tucked David's hand into the crook of his own arm,'[14] and as quickly puts his arm around Vyse's waist to balance the 'Laocoon group' but more probably to take the pressure off David until after dinner when he makes his real play.

The conversation at the party is redolent with double meaning and is led by A.G. The don will talk about anything and 'golf would do as well as anything else,' which is ironic since he is playing a game with David. After telling David he would look good in a toga, he suggests a swim in the Cam. At bridge, while David and Bags sing round the piano, A.G. tells all that he 'once played bridge at Aix-les-Bains with two Queens, which with four in the pack made six.'[15] It will take A.G. several more weeks to see David naked, and the reference to six queens, the number attending Bags's party, is lost on David as he does not appear to understand the argot meaning of 'queen' as homosexual.

Drunk and contented after the meal and cards, A.G. tries his hardest to get David into bed and almost succeeds, so the seduction scene, where he sings opera and accompanies David back home, may be brief but merits close attention. The piece A.G. sings is from *The Immortal Hour* by Rutland Boughton, a choice which is anachronistic to the action of *David Blaize*. Although Boughton's music drama was

12. We later hear A.G. calling David and Frank 'David and Jonathan' and calling himself Saul among the prophets (p. 64).

13. Benson, *David of King's*, p. 29.

14. Benson, *David of King's*, p. 30.

15. Benson, *David of King's*, pp. 39–40.

first performed in 1914 at the Glastonbury festival, it did not become popular until 1922, when it ran for 612 consecutive performances in London and was attended by the Royal Family on several occasions. If we forgive the eight-year hiatus between the writing of David at school and entering university, we should realize that E.F.B. must have chosen the opera for a reason. First, the choice seems to confirm my suggestion that the short story 'The Man Who Went Too Far' is linked to this volume of the trilogy since both story and opera have the same theme: a mortal seeks sexual intercourse with a god and is destroyed. In *The Immortal Hour*, Dalua, the evil fairy, brainwashes Etain, fairy wife of Midir, so that she forgets her fairy husband and falls in love with Eochaidh, King of Eire. When Midir comes to reclaim his wife, he plays a magic harp and sings to her, she remembers him and returns home, whence Eochaidh dies of grief at his loss. While there is no homosexual theme to the opera, A.G. takes the part of Dalua, and when he leaves the party, he has 'David tucked close to him.' They cross the quad looking at the inconstant moon, and A.G. declaims:

> "Fiona Macleod!" he said. "I am convinced that if that wonderful poetess and I had ever met, I should have found that she was the one woman in the world. Or was Fiona Macleod William Sharp? How exceedingly disconcerting!"[16]

On the surface this is a comic scene, and readers (who in 1924 would be familiar with *The Immortal Hour*) seem meant to laugh at the idea of A.G. falling in love with the lyricist of Boughton's opera, only to remember that Fiona Macleod is the pseudonym of William Sharp. But the gender reversal may also be read as A.G. introducing David to the idea that men may fall in love with other men, however disconcerting that may be. Furthermore, the song A.G. chooses to sing as he and David stroll home with linked arms is 'How beautiful they are', the song Midir sings to Etain that brings her memory back, and reminds her that she is a fairy:

> How beautiful they are
> The Lordly ones
> Who dwell in the hills,
> In the hollow hills.
> They have faces like flowers
> And their breath is the wind

16. Benson, *David of King's*, p. 41.

That blows over summer meadows
Filled with dewy clover.

Their limbs are more white
Than shafts of moonshine
They are more fleet
Than the March wind
They laugh and are glad
And are terrible
When their arms shake and glitter
Every green leaf quivers.

How beautiful they are
The Lordly ones
Who dwell in the hills,
In the hollow hills.

As Dalua, we might understand what A.G. is doing, that is, trying to make David forget he is a man so they can consummate his lust. And David knows this:

The identity of the one woman in the world with William Sharp had already unsettled him, and he knew that any more music or high romance would be devastating.[17]

What is more concerning to David is that as Midir, A.G. seems to have recognized David for what he is – a fairy[18] – and has come to claim his own kind. David's response, hysterical laughter, does not seem to be so much an enjoyment of the joke as an explosion of uncontrolled relief and fear that he has been read correctly. A.G. now calms down, and after expatiating on *A Midsummer Night's Dream*, the influence of the moon and *The Second Mrs. Tanqueray*, invites David for breakfast at 8.30am. The sexual ambivalence of the Shakespeare play, the madness that the moon is supposed to induce in lovers, and the secret past of Paula Tanqueray that leads her to suicide, while her lover Captain Ardale can be forgiven, are a potent mix. It is as though A.G. is telling David to give himself up to the madness of the moment, to have sex with him, a man, and to forgive himself the act that David believes must lead to his death. Moreover, as A.G. turns into his rooms, and wishes him 'Dear old boy, good night!' he seems

17. Benson, *David of King's*, p. 41.
18. The *Oxford English Dictionary* suggests the first printed source for this use of the word to be 1895, the *American Journal of Psychology*, describing groups of inverts who pretend to womanly ways.

certain that David will follow him in, spend the night and *stay* for breakfast rather than *come* for breakfast.

After the darkness of a chapter break we discover that David has spent the night in his own rooms. He presents himself at A.G.'s at the time he was invited, only to find that A.G. has left no instructions to his bed-maker about breakfast for two, and a note on his door 'Do not wake me till half past nine'. What has happened in the interim we are not told, but we might guess if we read between the lines of A.G.'s note and of David's insouciant but ironic addition to the note: 'I didn't; and thank you for my nice breakfast. – D.B.' It is difficult to believe that A.G. would have forgotten the time of his breakfast invitation between walking into his room and going to bed, and so his note seems to confirm the idea that he expected David to follow him, that he wants them to have as much time in bed as possible and not to be discovered together in bed. It might suggest that A.G. is angry that David did not follow him and he has gone into a sulk. If it is argued that A.G. is simply drunk and wants to sleep it off, the suggestions he has made to David before bed are none the less valid. Whether or not David's note means that he did not follow A.G. because he did not want to sleep with him, or that he did not wake him, his remark about the breakfast suggests that he does not want to have anything more to do with the predatory don. But as we shall soon discover, A.G. is not so easily put off.

What is important is that David was intrigued by, and understood what was meant by A.G.'s invitation, as is suggested by his being unsettled by it. In the light of this, his next activity – smoking his meerschaum pipe before going to the morning lecture – is the more interesting. In *David Blaize and the Blue Door*, masturbation was signified by the ecstasy of flying. In *David of King's*, I would argue, masturbation is signified by the ritual of pipe smoking.

The reasons for drawing the association between pipe smoking and masturbation are many. First, his pipe is called Perpetua, virgin and martyr, in order that, it would seem, David may feel he can indulge in its pleasures without moving outside his gift of continency. Bags's meerschaum, on the other hand, is named Angelica, perhaps after the heroine of the 1724 pornographic novel *Venus in the Cloister*. Angelica is described later as having a rash, which suggests both the unwonted result of Bags's dalliances with prostitutes, and Angelica's dalliances in the cloister. David describes how his pipe must be waxed:

...when the pipe got warm, the stem of a wax match should be
carefully and lovingly rubbed on it.[19]

Wax may not be a preferred lubricant for masturbation, but many a
man masturbates with some kind of oil or soap on his penis. 'Wax'
is also a slang term for prostate fluid that leaks out of the penis tip
before ejaculation to lubricate the penis on penetration, or in this case
in the hand. 'Waxing' also suggests the growth of the penis during
erection, a process that can be enhanced by caressing. David then
tells us that:

> ... a meerschaum must only be enjoyed two or three times a day,
> and must be allowed to cool before it was smoked again.[20]

The fact is also true of masturbation, although for some men it is
possible more times, and for others less, three is probably the mean
number of times that a man might bring himself to ejaculation in
a day. If such a reading is thought to be off the mark, it must be
argued that the description of the ritual of smoking David's pipe is
so suggestive of masturbation that might even be thought to be a
primer in the art:

> He applied himself to the ritual, which was girt with ceremonial
> observances. You must never, when it began to get warm, touch
> the bowl or the stem of it with the finger, because fingers left an
> impression on that sensitive skin;[21]

Masturbation is so variable an experience, that when one has found
a way that gives the most heightened pleasure, one tends to try to
repeat the method that brought the best results, and quickly a routine,
or ritual, develops. The first lesson we learn here is not to stimulate
the glans or the end of the penis (the bowl or the stem of it) directly,
which will reduce the likelihood of an ejaculation, and which can be
unpleasant.

> ... you must never smoke fast and get it over, because that fevered
> the delicate creature; but you must never smoke so slowly that
> it went out, because then it had to be relit, which was bad for it,
> and tasted disgusting, which was bad for you.[22]

19. Benson, *David of King's*, p. 46.
20. Benson, *David of King's*, p. 47.
21. Benson, *David of King's*, p. 47.
22. Benson, *David of King's*, p. 47.

The next lesson is that stimulating oneself so fast as to bring forth a quick ejaculation reduces the pleasure of masturbation, most of which lies in the duration of the act rather than the endpoint. However, stimulating yourself too slowly can fail to keep the desire alive, and may result in the loss of erection. The third lesson is that the best orgasms are produced with the most appropriate flight of erotic imagination, and so we turn to the particular act David is engaged in:

> Perpetua was sweating heavily that morning from her waxing yesterday, and had a creaking sort of cough when she was sucked. It must have been some diptheric trouble, for a blob of bitter membrane got loose in her throat and flew up the stem into his mouth. David got rid of that by the obvious expedient of spitting between his legs into the fire, and this emission seemed to have relieved Perpetua, for she coughed no longer and only sweated.[23]

'Sweating' or 'sweated' as we shall see in the next section, is a euphemism David uses to describe physical sex. The term possibly derives from the Middle English word 'Swink' which means to work hard and to have sexual intercourse.[24] This possibility leads to the word 'wank' which the *Oxford English Dictionary* suggests is a 'low' term for masturbation, dating from about 1870, though no literary references are given before 1948.

'The waxing yesterday' seems to suggest that David's morning erection may be caused by the memory of his encounter with A.G. the previous night, and so the imaginative act he engages in to bring himself to orgasm may be him sucking A.G.'s penis to ejaculation. The fact that the 'bitter membrane' which gets into his mouth is also called an 'emission,' a word that has been associated with the ejaculate since 1646,[25] seems to confirm the reading. Furthermore, we may also consider the position David has taken up to smoke his pipe, with his chair in front of the fire and one leg on either side of the grate, the position which would keep his bottom and testicles warm, as well as stimulating his anus, can be a comfortable position for masturbation.

23. Benson, *David of King's*, p. 48.
24. See Geoffrey Chaucer, *The Canterbury Tales*, 'Miller's Tale', 'Wife of Bath's Tale', etc.
25. The *Oxford English Dictionary*, 'Night time emission' was in common use to describe spontaneous ejaculations until the 1970s.

The act he describes does not go well, but if it is thought that this may be because David was imagining a sex act with A.G., it must be remembered that in *David and the Blue Door*, his first flight is stimulated by his desire to be with the bald, old men. Much has been written about E.F.B.'s supposed adoration for beautiful young men, but for many young men, it is the older man who, with all his experience, is the more mysterious and sexually interesting, and can be an exciting proposition. However badly the masturbation has proceeded, when Tommers knocks at his door, the first thing he mentions is the stink of Perpetua, so it would seem that David was successful in bringing himself to ejaculation.

Nakedness

David's ability to substitute imagination led masturbation for actual sex with others whom he desires, allows him, at present, to feel he is maintaining his gift of continency. However, in the next scene the act becomes the only way he can deal with his growing sexual desire for Frank. What is more, the scene is a clear parallel to the bathroom scene in *David Blaize*, but one in which both he and Frank can be seen to know and understand their physical need for sexual contact with one another. In this way, *David of King's* marks the final stage of David's journey to continency, the giving up of masturbation for complete asexuality. But first, David must realize the degree to which masturbation has gained a hold over his mind, and this is achieved by realizing just how close he gets to having a physical sexual encounter with Frank, since his tension must be relieved immediately by a masturbation in which Frank nearly participates.

David has been playing rugby for the University team tryouts, and has not excelled. Frank drops in to his rooms for tea afterwards, and realizes he has to console his friend:

> "I say, do make yourself useful [David said] and make tea and toast things while I have a bath and wash off the memory of – of this Insolence!"
>
> David came back girt in a bath-towel, and wandered to and fro between his bedroom and his sitting-room as he dressed, diverting his mind with pleasant topics of the future rather than futile topics of the past.[26]

26. Benson, *David of King's*, p. 76.

Reversing their schoolboy roles, Frank becomes David's fag by making tea, but the reversal seems to highlight rather than question why it is David who is once again naked in front of his friend. His reverie will soon turn to the incident in the bathroom, but for now, he tries to justify his near nakedness with a weak joke:

> David had a shirt on after all, and he sat down in an arm-chair in front of the fire.
> "I want tea more than trousers," he said. "Besides, tea gets full of tannin if you keep it waiting, and trousers never …"[27]

The conversation in which David and Frank are engaged also lends itself to thoughts of sexuality: the Chit-Chat Society,[28] for whom A.G. is giving a paper on 'The Athletic Ideal' this week and David on *Dr Faustus* next week. A.G.'s paper will be a discussion of Hellenism, to which David's nakedness adds a present frisson. Stapleton's paper the previous week concerned Swinburne's morality, and is said to 'have been something of a flutter in this studious and celibate dovecote'.[29]

In the climate of easy sexual banter, Frank becomes nervous of his desire for David's body just as he did in the school bathroom, and in carrying out the most casual of friendly gestures, makes a blunder which gives him away.

> Frank took David's cigarette out of his hand and lit his own from it. Then by mistake he threw David's into the fire.
> "Doesn't matter," said David. "Just jaw to me!"[30]

They discuss Bags's exploits with prostitutes in Paris, but further talk of sexual relations is too apt and begins to remind David of the bathroom incident in school:

> David was silent a moment, and the dancing light in his eyes at the thought of Bags and his cocoons died out, and they became quite serious. Some memory, long buried, stirred in his mind, and he covered it up again.[31]

27. Benson, *David of King's*, p. 77.
28. The Chit-Chat Society has the air of being a debating society like The Apostles, the homoerotic society at King's which E.F.B. refused to join after A.C.B.'s disastrous homosexual liaison which might be traced to The Apostles.
29. Benson, *David of King's*, p. 76.
30. Benson, *David of King's*, p. 78.
31. Benson, *David of King's*, p. 81.

This move to close the door on the closet of nightmares is too reminiscent of his schoolboy self, so David makes an undergraduate ploy of initiating a new discussion about the nature of love and sex. It is David's first attempt to describe asexual love, that is, love without the 'sweating and mucking about,' but it goes awry, and he ends up telling Frank that he would like to kiss him.

> "There are such a lot of jollier things to do and think about," he said. "At least I think them jollier, which is all that concerns me. Interesting things, you know, funny things, and also quite serious things. Anyhow, I don't think it's got much to do with love to go sweating[32] and mucking about with a cocoon. Love's something better than that. And I shouldn't wonder if mucking about in the way of some fellows so rather spoils you for it. But, O Lord, how I do love my friends: isn't that enough for a chap till he falls in love in the regular way? If I'd *got* to kiss somebody I'd kiss one of them. You for choice, because I'm much fonder of you than the whole rest of them."
>
> Frank burst out laughing at these surprising philosophies.[33]

Whether David's suggestion that he wants to kiss a male friend is an expression of revulsion at the idea of physical sex with a woman is unclear at this stage of the novel. However, his decision that he might rather kiss Frank, as a finer substitute for sex than visiting prostitutes, is a logical if 'surprising philosophy'. Made in the context of the cocoons and Bags's pipe Angelica having a rash, David is perhaps suggesting that mutual sex between men of the same age will keep them free of sexually transmitted diseases. It also suggests that they are on the pathway towards an inevitable heterosexual future that might be spoiled by such horrors. Certainly Frank is somewhat deflated by David's suggestion that he might 'fall in love in the regular way'. David's statement will lead to a major misunderstanding that is not sorted out until the end of the book, since the question of David's attitude towards heterosexuality must first be settled by himself. For the present, the thought of kissing Frank excites David so much that he has to masturbate, or at least to smoke Perpetua. But there is a twist this time:

> "Oh, David," he [Frank] said, "there's no-one like you. You always make me feel as if I had just had a bath with plenty of soap."

32. Note the clear use of the word 'sweating' here to describe sexual intercourse.
33. Benson, *David of King's*, p. 82.

> David flushed with pleasure.
>
> "My word! You couldn't have said anything nicer than that," he observed. "But them's my sentiments. No harm in telling you, though I guess you knew it."
>
> David put down his large feet from the side of the fireplace where he had put them and held out his hands. "Pull me up," he said, and stood there a moment rather serious.
>
> "Good thing that God thought of inventing us," he said. "Which being so, I may as well dress … Gosh, I've never smoked Perpetua all day. Fill her for me frightfully carefully while I put my trousers on, and don't touch her smooth waxy bottom with your blasted fingers."[34]

By asking Frank to fill his pipe and not to touch the bowl, David has, in effect, asked him to join in with his preferred sexual activity in all its rituals. The implication of mutual masturbation pervades the air: an act that was illegal at the time E.F.B. was writing. Thus, in this case, pipe smoking may well have been a deflection of the act it implied. But there can be little doubt that both men now know that they can envisage enacted sex between them, and that they have either to express their love in a physical way, hope that they will change and become heterosexual, or find some other way to negotiate their burgeoning sexuality. A.C.B.'s 'mathematical certainty' that sexuality will be expressed is the predicament into which E.F.B. has led his characters.

A.G.'s Lust and Frank's Love

Whether or not it is possible for David to resist his desire for the consummation of his love for Frank in a physical act, albeit no more than the dream of a kiss or deflected mutual masturbation, the counterpoint to his debate about whether or not to have sex with Frank, is A.G.'s continued press for sex as physical gratification. The dilemma is highlighted in the next two sections of the novel in which we see David make a conscious religious choice not to follow the calls of his sexuality as he veers back towards continency. The mechanism for the reversion is the rivalry for David's body between Frank and A.G., which has become as obvious to the two potential suitors as it has to David himself.

---

34. Benson, *David of King's*, p. 82.

It is important to remember that while Frank represents youth, beauty and sexual gratification based on love, and A.G. age, portliness and sexual gratification based on lust, the latter is not initially presented as a comically rotund older man hopelessly chasing after a beautiful young man like a sex starved Billy Bunter. From the Head of David's first school, through to the bald, old men of *David Blaize and the Blue door*, David has always found older men sexually fascinating. Therefore, when A.G. makes a fool of himself at the Chit-Chat Society, trying to take up the pose of the discobolus, although we are meant to laugh at his antics, as does his fellow tutor Mackintosh, we must not put it beyond the bounds of possibility that David agrees to try to placate A.G. because he enjoys flirting with the older man, but if this is so, we must also find a reason why Frank asks him to do so.

A.G.'s lecture to the Chit-Chat on the Athletic Ideal concerns one of the bugbears of Victorian classical education: can you learn fully by rote or do you have to bring the words you read from classical authors into your life. The debate goes back to the end of the seventeenth century,[35] and again, here, it seems intended for comic effect as A.G.'s shadow shows in 'strong relief his enormous bulk'[36] while he tells Mackintosh, a History don, that 'Five minutes study of the Hermes at Olympia … will teach you more about the greatest civilization the world has ever seen than learning the whole of Grote's history by heart.'[37] The combination of A.G.'s obviously unathletic body with his insulting a revered Greek historian brings forth a loud report of laughter from Mackintosh, at which A.G. takes umbrage, and against whom he asks for a motion of reprehension by the society. But underlying A.G.'s thesis is the Hellenist idea that if one must bring Greek mores into one's life in order to understand Greek society, then one might also bring Greek sexuality into one's life. This returns us to the long discussion of Greek homosexuality explored in the second of these four chapters on *David Blaize*, and it is therefore hard to believe that Frank is not aware of A.G.'s interest in David when, in order to avoid an unseemly row in the Chit-Chat Society, he sends David to placate the angry A.G.

35. For instance the debate between Sir William Temple *et al* and Richard Bentley over the Epistles of Phalaris.

36. Benson, *David of King's*, p. 84.

37. Benson, *David of King's*, p. 84. George Grote, *History of Greece, 1846–1856* (London: John Murray, 1849).

Maybe Frank simply thinks, as he says, that David is so innocent that he can pour oil on troubled waters '… you're rather soothing if a man's in a bad temper. And A.G. thinks you a bright, joyous child.'[38] However, it is not out of the question to argue that since he is David's best friend, Frank knows that David is interested in older men, and that A.G. is interested in David. If this is the case, then maybe Frank is jealous of A.G., but sees it as probable that the older man will be more successful than he in getting David to fulfil his sexual needs. When he has, maybe Frank believes he and David can continue as before to be friends without indulging in sex, or maybe Frank thinks that if David gets a taste for physical sex he will bring himself to allow the consummation of their desire for each other. As we shall see, the latter will turn out to have been Frank's most likely motive, but as we shall also see, David rejects sexually both Frank and A.G. in the most uncompromising terms, and chooses instead to focus his life on the salvation from his homosexuality he believes to be offered by the blood of Christ.

Immediately Frank has put David up to pacifying A.G., the fat man sits beside 'the Athletic Blaizides.'[39] The rest of the Chit Chat Society members leave the two together, and David literally flirts with A.G. to get him to drop his motion of censure against Mackintosh. In the quad after the opera singing, David seemed to try to avoid A.G., and did not follow him to bed, now he asks A.G. 'Mayn't I come round with you one day and see [the discobolus cast in the college museum]?' As in the earlier case, David ends up laughing hysterically, which again would seem to suggest that he knows what he is doing: offering future sexual favours to A.G. in return for A.G. dropping the motion of censure against Mackintosh.

There seems therefore, to be a progression in David's association with A.G. A.G. offers himself to David after the opera singing and David refuses, or possibly does not realize exactly what has been offered, but knows that he has been recognized as homosexual. Next, Frank asks David to offer himself to A.G., and, knowing the power he has over the other man David goes ahead and flirts with A.G. and gets the result that he wants. With the knowledge of what he can do, the third step would seem to be for the two of them to have the sexual intercourse they both desire. Taking this step would turn

38. Benson, *David of King's*, p. 89.
39. Benson, *David of King's*, p. 90.

David into a queer fish, using the terminology of *David Blaize and the Blue Door*, but in that book we saw that David was as set against becoming a queer fish as he was against marriage. What follows is one of the oddest turns in the book, E.F.B. puts in a serious religious paragraph that stops frivolity in its tracks, and sets David back on the straight and narrow pathway to continency.

David is reading his paper to the Chit Chat Society the next week, on Marlowe's *Dr Faustus*. After some slight giggling at Tommers' sneezing while David is reading about the nature of Hell, David comes to his peroration on Faustus:

> "And he's lost, he's damned and he knows it," said David, "and the gain of the whole world has not profited him in comparison with that. He sees where Christ's blood streams in the firmament, and knows that a drop of it would save his soul. But between him and it there is the great gulf fixed of his deliberate choice ... Faustus dare not call on Him, a drop of whose blood from that infinite stream that suffuses from the firmament would save him, for by his own will and conscious choice he has betrayed and crucified Him, in that he has betrayed and bartered his own soul. His is the exceeding bitter cry, for the mess of pottage is finished and the birthright of his salvation forfeited."[40]

It is usual at the Chit Chat that there are questions after a paper, but there are none for David. Mackintosh asks to borrow it, apologizes to A.G., who accepts, and everyone goes home early but 'there was no doubt he had made them tense.' Alone with Frank and basking in the glory of his powerful paper, David lights Perpetua. Frank intervenes and there is a moment between them which has a haunting resemblance to the moment in the school bathroom:

> Frank ... twitched Perpetua out of his hand.
> "But that's not fair," cried David. "If Bags smokes Angelica, I'm blowed if I wont smoke Perpetua. Have some hock-cup; have a cigarette; have anything you like. But it's beyond a joke to lay hands on my stinking nymph. You'll be like Faustus ..."[41]

But for David's comment that Frank will 'be like Faustus', the moment might be put down to Frank's dislike of the smell of the pipe smoke,[42] or if we follow the metaphor of pipe smoking for masturbation, the

40. Benson, *David of King's*, pp. 96–97.
41. Benson, *David of King's*, p. 98.
42. Which is unlikely as Frank smokes a pipe himself (p. 110).

twitch of the pipe might be read as Frank telling David not to do it. However, to 'be like Faustus' is to make a 'deliberate choice' and a 'conscious choice' to do evil, in spite of the resultant damnation. To 'be like Faustus', then sits oddly with the two readings already suggested. Therefore, it would seem that Frank's 'twitching' Perpetua, the symbol of solo sex, out of David's hand might be better read as him offering himself sexually once again to David, as he had done all those years ago in the bathroom. David's squeal, in this reading would be his reaction, like the girl in William Holman Hunt's 'The Awakening Conscience' (1853), rejecting Frank's advance and warning him of the mortal danger of choosing to fulfil his homosexual desire: damnation.

Confirming a sexual reading, the next chapter begins with Bags's disconnected observation to himself that 'Maupassant was wonderful at skating over the thinnest ice and never quite falling through.'[43] The sentence, recalling the pornographic book in the first scene in the trilogy, might be read either as a comment about what E.F.B. has just written, or a comment about what David has just done.

Another disconnected comment from David seems to affirm his returning respect for Christianity. As we saw, earlier in this volume, he has begun to go to Chapel only for the anthem. Now, as he muses on different ways to run faster, he rejects the Coué method of autosuggestion since if it worked he might start running in Chapel. The reference is, once again, complex. Emile Coué was a French psychologist who discovered the placebo effect and believed that one could cure oneself by fixing ideas in one's mind by repeating words over and over again.[44] David's idea that he might use the method to help his running seems like one of his airy and ill-thought-out schemes, but he misremembers the name Coué and instead calls him 'Coue', a homophone for 'Cul' that is, anus. The combination of the method of curing oneself, chapel and a word for anus suggests that David may have been trying to find ways of getting over his sexual feelings for Frank and A.G., and rejects the Coué method in favour of Christianity. Or maybe, David realizes that repetition of words is similar to praying, so he might as well pray as pretend so to do if he wants to find the strength to maintain his gift of continency.

43. Benson, *David of King's*, p. 99.
44. The idea is used in the *Forsyte Saga* where Fleur repeats 'Every day in Every way I get better and better'.

The rest of the chapter brings together David's first moves in his Christian choice to follow the path of celibacy and chasteness, in encounters with each of his suitors. The first with Frank, lays the foundations for their asexual marriage. In the second with A.G., David sees the sexual predator as a fat, pink devil, his desire for whom must be extinguished.

Even after David's equation of Frank with Faustus, his affection for his friend remains undiminished, 'for it was natural to spend much of the day with Frank'. Nevertheless, marking the momentousness of the decision he is taking, 'some lure of the spring beckoned, making a boiling in his blood with which Demosthenes did not accord, and while he dressed, he had made up his mind to keep holiday.'[45] Holiday is, of course 'holy day', and the reference to Demosthenes, who was accused by Aeschines of ruining young men with whom he had sexual relations, would thus suggest that David was eager to spend his boiling blood in a less destructive way. His first prank reminds him of the way he must take to purity as he hits a few golf balls, one of which he slices towards Clare Chapel, whence he holds his breath hoping it will not break the 'pretty windows'. He must keep faith and redraw his relations with his potential sexual partners lest he break the law of God.

With the memory of the precariousness of his moral position fresh in his mind, he moves on to his first assignation of the day with Frank, to play Real Tennis. The game itself, which is more like squash with a net than its modern counterpart, reminds us of the game of Fives in the first volume, when Frank first had sexual feelings for David that led to the incident in the bathroom. However, in the game, which uses the term 'Love' in the scoring,[46] and which, on this day, ends in an equal score, we might look readily for the foundations of the asexual marriage that will develop between them. Even the positioning of the players in Fives and Real Tennis sends out a different message. In Fives, the players can have physical contact with each other, whereas in Real Tennis a net separates them.

Also important for my argument is that David is naturally talented at playing the game:

> Some one particular form of ball-game "sets the genius" of most athletic and quick-eyed boys, and it was evident from the

45. Benson, *David of King's*, p. 101.
46. As in the modern game.

first that the king of games was what set David's. The stooping classical stroke which most find hard to acquire, came natural [sic] to him; ...[47]

Frank introduced David to the game, and in only a year David can play equally well. On this holy day he is happy to play an equal game on the opposite side of the net from his mentor. Playing together but separately is what seems right to David: it 'sets his genius'. And on their way back after the game, it can be no surprise therefore, that David's first Headmaster's admonition about sexual maturity – that it should be no more than the singing of birds – is writ large about them in the songs of 'blackbirds ... fluting in the college gardens'.[48] David has rejected Frank's sexual advances but accepted his love, which causes Frank to muse on whether David is becoming heterosexual. But first David must continue to the second assignation of his holy day by ensuring himself he is rid of lustful thoughts about A.G.

Combining the second act with the first is the comment that '... if A.G. was a reincarnation of Heliogabalus, David was that of a tennis-marker.'[49] Heliogabalus is an apt genius to suggest motivating A.G. Elagabalus, as he is now known, ruled Rome from 218–222 AD. He removed Jupiter from the head of the pantheon and replaced him with the sun. He had five wives, and had sex with the men of his court. Gibbon wrote of him that he 'abandoned himself to the grossest pleasures and ungoverned fury.'[50]

David meets A.G. in the Turkish Bath,[51] where they see each other naked for the first time. Describing A.G., E.F.B. notes that 'Whether lying on his back or on his side, he looked the same shape.' The unlovely lump of pink sweating flesh immediately continues his assaults upon David:

> David, your shoulders are the most Praxitelean things I have ever seen.[52]

47. Benson, *David of King's*, p. 102.

48. Benson, *David of King's*, p. 103.

49. Benson, *David of King's*, p. 103. It would seem that this may be a misprint, and should read 'tennis-master'.

50. Edward Gibbon, *Decline and Fall of the Roman Empire*, Vol. 1 (London: William Strahan and Thomas Cadell in the Strand, 1776), Chapter 6.

51. Oscar Browning tried to obtain reduced rate access for the members of Footlights to the Turkish Baths in Emmanuel Street.

52. Benson, *David of King's*, p. 107.

The beauty of Praxiteles' statue of Hermes is indubitable, and A.G.'s comment a compliment. But it brings a negative thought to David's mind that A.G. 'looked even less like the Discobolus than usual.' David's silence in the presence of the naked A.G. speaks of his changed attitude to the don, who chatters on incessantly, until he leaves the steam-room with the remark:

> Why should age be attended with obesity, as well as with all its other disadvantages?

A.G. calls for his shampooer, and squeals and shrieks at the ministrations the paid servant carries out on his body. David listens as A.G. dives into the cold plunge '...accompanied, so David swore, with a hissing noise of a red-hot substance being plunged into cold water'.[53] The cooling of David's passion towards A.G. seems also to be completed in this gesture, though the fat don will re-emerge in another swimming pool in another place. The association of A.G. with water seems to suggest his 'amphibious' nature, a common eighteenth century term for bisexual, and a term that A.G. will later use of David.

Frank and David's Asexual Engagement

The rest of the volume now explores how Frank and David can set up an asexual marriage, where the two are chaste lovers and constant companions. Frank, who has noticed David's cooling sexual desire, is the first to ponder the process. Alone in his room after the game of tennis, he wonders:

> What was happiness? Was it getting what you wanted, or did it really consist in wanting?[54]

While the question may be asked about any form of happiness, it is at its most poignant when asked concerning sexual desire and fulfilment. Until a sex act has been performed it remains always possibly perfect. When it has been achieved, it may or may not have lived up to expectations. Frank, who has tried several times to have sex with David and has now been rebuffed finally with the accusation about Faustus and forgiven in the game of tennis, must decide whether a life of sexual abstinence with David can be happy.

53. Benson, *David of King's*, p. 108.
54. Benson, *David of King's*, p. 110.

He knows that he will continue to desire to have sex with David, and if he wants to remain with David he has to be happy with the thought that it will remain an impossibility, and an impossibility which might or might not have been good if they had tried it. A further unsettling thought recurs to Frank now, based on David's own declaration that he might have been passing through a phase of being homosexual, and has now become heterosexual. What upsets him most about the possibility is the thought that he might lose his access to the private side of his friend if David gets married.

> ... some day the real David would manifest himself in the ways of a man with a maid, and in a certain sense, the private David would be lost to him for ever.[55]

The thought makes him jealous:

> Frank knew that he meant more to David than any friend had ever been or would ever be. As far as David was aware of his own heart, that heart was open to him and beating for him in that sexless surrender which boys make to boys and girls to girls. But there was a chamber there of which neither he nor even David himself had the key, which was dangling round the neck of some girl unknown.[56]

Although, as we shall see, David finally decides at the end of this volume that he does not want a woman, a life of unfulfilled sexual desire and sexual jealousy is all that seems open to Frank. He is further disturbed by the fact that he must leave Cambridge soon, unless he can take a first class degree and stay on to do research for a Fellowship. For the present Frank can do no more than take into his life the neo-Pagan philosophy of Rupert Brooke and Virginia Woolf, and live each moment to the fullest extent possible without a thought for tomorrow. We see Frank learning to accept each day for what it brings in a long description of he and David bathing naked at Byron's pool. The scene recalls Brooke and Woolf swimming in the same pool sometime in the idyllic years before the Great War, when Brooke lived in the Old Vicarage in Grantchester, writing his fellowship for King's College, and Woolf visited him and unbuttoned herself from Bloomsbury manners.[57] The same sense of relaxed acceptance of beauty while the storm gathers pervades David and Frank's dip,

55. Benson, *David of King's*, p. 111.
56. Benson, *David of King's* p. 112.
57. See David Hassall, *Rupert Brooke: A Biography* (London: Faber, 1964).

but at the same time, the intensity of the imagery suggests both the intensity of the sadness at the thought of their loss of one another, and concomitantly of their love for one another. As evening draws on, David is unsettled after having lain to dry in an ants' nest:

> "... Blow it, there's some hay in my trousers. Life seems entirely to consist of dressing and undressing."
>
> David had to take them off and turn them inside out to brush off spiky grass-seeds and pieces of vegetable debris. Then he must convince himself that no ants remained in the small of his back and that the bumble-bee which had been fussing about and had unaccountably vanished was not making a nest in his socks. But presently peace and plenty of tea descended, and between speech and silence they sat on until the sun began to do its evening stunt. The light grew suffused with crimson, and the level ray shining through the tall grasses set the hayfield afire again, and the trees by the river glowed in the molten conflagration. High in the air in screeching circles the swifts went a-hunting; rooks returned from their patrol of the pastures, and a heron winged heavily by. Above the west the sun made rosy the feathery wisps of strayed cloudlets, and set them in a pale-green sea. Then he allowed a star, just one but a good one, to be lit there, and himself illuminated the gilded crescent of the moon. He spread a curtain of clear shadow as of deep and dusky water below the trees, and so slid behind a bank of remote cloud ... When they thought his stunt was over, he cleared the cloud away, and emerged redder than ever and absurdly magnified, balanced on the edge of the flat horizon.[58]

Here, the ants and bumble-bee may be read to signify David's uneasiness with his nakedness, uneasiness because he is once again naked so close to Frank. However, I would argue that they act as a counterpoint to the tension in the other scenes when David has been naked near Frank, and suggest that now nakedness is humourous rather than vulnerable. And it is for this reason that the birds[59] reappear from *David Blaize and the Blue Door*. Frank and David share the reddening ecstasy of the swifts circling in the sunset, but under the watchful eye of Parson rook. The ecstasy is not sexual; there are no bobbing flower heads and ringing bells. This is an asexual ecstasy which the two men can enjoy together, but apart as on the tennis court.

58. Benson, *David of King's*, p. 136.
59. Swifts and rooks as opposed to the dawn chorus of singing birds.

The storm of separation, which was gathering at Byron's pool, comes in David's second year when Frank, who has taken his first, has to go to Athens to get material for his fellowship dissertation. David and he spend their last days together in London at Frank's mother's house. On the very last day together, they reach the apotheosis of their asexual love in doing nothing.

> Finally came a retarded bedtime with the consciousness of a last day wonderfully well spent, for, after all, they had been together with nobody to interrupt and nothing to do, and friends cannot have better pastime than that.[60]

They do nothing because if they had chosen to be sexual they would most likely have filled the time before separation with physical intimacy. Since both have chosen to be asexual, being together 'with nobody to interrupt and nothing to do' is the fulfilment of their commitment to each other. They are now engaged to be married.

David and the Garden of Earthly Delights

Left by himself after seeing Frank off at the station, doing nothing is not an option, that pastime has now become something he does with his fiancé. But being single and alone for the first time in his life, he is not sure what to do. Though he seeks to fill his time with innocent pastimes, sexual predators lurk around every corner, both homosexual and heterosexual. His first attempt to amuse himself is with physical exercise so he goes to The Bath Club, a gentlemen's club with a sporty theme drawn from real life, at 34 Dover Street. He does some exercises by the pool, and catches sight, of a floating, pink 'orbicular' piece of flesh, which he recognizes, too late, as A.G.

> The imperial face came out of the water, and he began to talk so immediately that he must have been talking under water and only going on with what he was saying.
> "Hullo, it's Blaizides … The athletic and amphibious David – Ha! Ha! – David the son of Jesse, fair and of a ruddy countenance …"[61]

After his veiled accusation that David is at least bisexual, A.G. takes charge of David, and invites him to lunch with Prince Bumniowsky, 'One of my most intimate friends', with whom he has been reading

60. Benson, *David of King's*, p. 142.
61. Benson, *David of King's*, p. 145.

Plato. However, while A.G. might hope that David is in London, 'this modern Babylon ... Washing off the grime of Cambridge in its lascivious and sparkling flood'[62], and the prince lives up to his title, being rich, lazy and bored, David is unimpressed, leaving his flat before the prince can live up to his name.

Amid the rest of his inane prattle, A.G. makes reference to having seen a dramatization of Frank Frankfort Moore's novel of 1895 *Phyllis of Philistia*, 'an exquisite idyll out of Theocritus with all the modern improvements'.[63] The story of the novel, which as it turns out has nothing to do with the dramatization, is an account of Phyllis Ayrton, who uses her clergyman fiancé's new book questioning the morals of the biblical patriarchs as an excuse for not marrying him, though the real reason is that she does not love him. However, there is an illuminating exchange between Phyllis and her father on the first page.

> "After all," said Mr Ayrton, "what is marriage? ... Marriage means all your eggs in one basket."
>
> "Ah", sighed Phyllis once again. She wondered whether her father really thought she would be comforted in her great grief by a phrase. She did not want to know how marriage might be defined. She knew all definitions are indefinite. She knew in the case of marriage everything depends on the definer and the occasion.[64]

The passage is significant since David has just defined his marriage with Frank as an asexual link of friendship and companionship. The author of the passage reflects further on David's situation since he is most remembered for the sentence: 'He knew that to offer a man friendship when love is in his heart is like giving a loaf of bread to one who is dying of thirst.'[65] Frank, as we know, is not sure he wants the same asexual marriage as David. He wants to define their marriage as physical as well as spiritual so David's definition may

62. Benson, *David of King's*, p. 145.
63. Benson, *David of King's*, p. 146.
64. Frank Frankfort Moore, *Phyllis of Phillistia* (London: Hutchinson & Co., 1895), p. 7. In fact, when David and Bags go to see the same show, it is a review with dancers, singers and comedians who sing 'Rule Phillistia' rather than 'Rule Britannia'. This would seem to be a way of making it unexceptionable that there would be the prostitutes in the 'Red Riding Hood' theatre bar who accost David.
65. Frank Frankfort Moore, *The Jessamy Bride* (London: Hutchinson & Co., 1897), p. 106.

well be offering Frank bread. Aware of this, and in the light of the fact that Phyllis was able to break off her engagement with George Holland, David now tests whether he might be capable of finding women attractive, and that he might therefore be able to 'fall in love in the regular way'. The adventure marks the final time in the trilogy that he tries to solve the theological problem of having love and sex without sin.

David is to meet Bags to see *Phyllis of Philistia* later that evening and the opportunity arises, for the first time in his life, to be alone with a sexually available woman when a fat prostitute accosts him in the theatre bar. He knows that to remain pure he must refuse her advances, but that is not the point of his experiment. He wants to know whether he can find women attractive, in which case he can fulfil his sexual urges 'in the regular way', and remain moral so long as he is married. In pursuance of his goal, David buys the fat prostitute a glass of port and listens to her chatter, all the time looking at a second, younger and thinner prostitute over her shoulder. David's response to the situation is not black and white.

> Quite suddenly David, who, according to his admirable habit, was seeing and enjoying the comedy of this preposterous lady, felt frankly sick. This great full-blown siren, with her glasses of port, and her powdered face, her flowery hat, her fat arms, her heaving bosom, and her hopefulness that they were getting on nicely, was a huge joke, funnier than anything he had imagined about cocoons. Presently, if he played up at all, she would tell him that she shared a nice flat with a lady friend, and they both often brought a pal home in the evening for a bit of a chat. He bubbled with laughter as he thought of it, but even as his ribs shook, he felt nauseated ... And what nauseated him most was the knowledge that something in himself, even as he laughed, responded not to her indeed but to what she stood for. If it had not been she, but that slim girl over there with the narrow eyes and the tired mouth who had sat down beside him, he would have felt a need that clamoured dangerously. He would have seen nothing comic in it, nothing grotesque and incredible ...[66]

As we have already seen in David's sexual encounters with A.G., laughter is his accustomed way of circumventing his sexual desire. The fact that the fat prostitute is 'funnier than anything he had imagined about cocoons' therefore suggests that he suddenly realizes

66. Benson, *David of King's*, p. 151.

that a heterosexual encounter is a mere payment away. Since David has always been in a boarding school the only female playmate he has had was his sister and being without a mother he has no past experience of women at all, except for the school matron who presided over sexual propriety. David's response to the prostitutes therefore encompasses a wide range of mixed emotions. He is 'nauseated' because he is responding not to the fat prostitute but 'to what she stood for', and he is sure, or at least hopes, he would have felt a clamouring need if he had been closer to the 'slim girl ... with the narrow eyes and the tired mouth.' The question of what the fat prostitute 'stood for' is at the heart of the issue. Does she stand for available sexuality, for the very idea that a woman might attract him, for the degradation of women, for motherliness? It is probable that the answer would be 'all of these', which, with the inclusion of motherliness in the list marks her difference from the 'thin girl'. This is why the other prostitute is so important to the incident, for it might be out of the question that David would believe himself capable of having sex with a woman who could be his absent mother, but it is not out of the question that David would believe himself capable of having sex with the 'thin girl'. And this is why it is 'not she indeed' (the older prostitute) who nauseates David, but the 'thin girl.' The extract does not simply state that David felt sexually attracted to the 'thin girl', rather, it suggests that he felt nauseated by the idea that if she had sat next to him he 'would have felt a clamouring need'. The 'need' may be as easily to run away from the girl as feeling sexual desire for her. His sickness may as easily be fear of what would be expected of him in a heterosexual encounter, as the butterflies of sexual anticipation. The 'thin girl' might even represent his sister to him. The passage is one of E.F.B.'s most ambiguous, and does not resolve easily into a simple interpretation. Given David's decision not to enter the Marriage Meadow in *David Blaize and the Blue Door* the interpretation that David's nausea is due to homosexual panic when faced with heterosexual expectation is, I believe, the more likely. However, it remains that E.F.B. has imbued this section of the text with an ambivalence not only between David and the prostitutes, but an ambivalence of meaning, where it is not possible to decide which is preferable between competing interpretations. It might be argued that ambivalence is inherent in language, but I would rather argue that E.F.B.'s process of multiplying competing interpretations encapsulates the way one lies to oneself about how one really feels by interpreting and reinterpreting facts. David is not attracted to the fat prostitute, wildly he thinks that he is not attracted to any woman because of what she represents, the call of heterosexuality which he cannot answer, so he consoles himself that he would have been attracted to the thin prostitute had she sat by him. But at the same time he is so frightened of the idea that he might not be attracted to any woman that he adds the moral injunction against prostitution to salve his homosexual conscience and make him believe that when the right woman *is* at his side, then he'll respond to her chastely and appropriately. David's own interpretations of what happened and why, tend to support this view.

It is after David has returned to Cambridge for his second year that he gets a chance to voice his views about what happened in the theatre bar. The context of his version is as important as the interpretation itself, since it is the week before his father is coming to give the University sermon, and David is concerned that Bags is making a fool of himself with the daughter of a tobacconist in the town. Bags's involvement with 'the girl with pudgy hands' is also a reference to Frank Frankfort Moore's *Phyllis of Philistia*, since George Holland gained his substantial living at St. Chad's not by being a good student, or particularly a good preacher, but through his untangling the Earl of Earlscourt from the daughter of a tobacconist while they were both students at Cambridge. The living of St. Chad's being in the Earl's gift, it came George's way when he was ordained and the Earl old enough to believe that he had been saved from ridicule. David performs the like service to the Honourable George Crabtree, and during the recriminations from his friend works out an excuse for his lack of interest in the opposite sex.

> "I can't understand you, David," [Bags] said. "You're simply dripping with energy, and yet you never dream of going after a girl. It seems to me absolutely unnatural. You don't even want to" ...
>
> "It's nothing of the sort," said David. "You think that because I don't go messing about with girls I don't want to. But I do, if you care to know."
>
> "But you never talk about them, and you're always ragging me about them," said Bags, "and you always say they're stinkers."
>
> "I know I do. But what's the good of talking about a thing you don't mean to be mixed up in? And what's the good of thinking

about a thing if you don't intend to do it? It only makes you worse."

"But confound it all, you're twenty," said Bags.

"I know I am, and I've never kissed a girl yet, let alone the other thing. And as I don't mean to at present, it would be dam' silly always to be thinking and talking about it. Like saying you don't mean to drink, and putting a bottle of whisky on the table. But as we are talking about it – ... It isn't manly to cuddle a girl, or soak your mind in beastliness and probably your body as well. It's far more manly not to."[67]

David's declaration that he wants to 'mess about with girls' says nothing about his sexual desire for them. He *does* want to have sex with girls, he simply cannot bring himself to do it. His calling them 'stinkers' veils his lack of sexual attraction for them in schoolboy banter. The argument of the rest of the interchange is baseless, and aimed at a definition of manliness, where to be sexually active or not is an empty aesthetic judgment. To make his point David must bring in his only experience of women, and so it is the prostitutes to whom he turns:

"No, I didn't want the peony [the fat prostitute]," he said. "But there was a girl there, o-oh ... don't let's think about it. But there it is. The f-fact is" (he began to stammer) "that when the time comes that I see a girl I really want, and ask her to m-marry me, I mean to go to her clean. It's just a fad of mine, or call it pi and p-priggish. You may call it anything you please."[68]

David stammers when he is in great stress. The stress that causes him to stammer now is the need not to speak about the 'girl there,' which is a return to his juvenile strategy of hiding his desires in the closet of nightmares. But once again we do not know whether or not he desired the 'girl there'. His inarticulate 'But there it is,' which introduces his next two stammers, neither confirms his heterosexual lust nor his fear that he lacks it; it just confirms that he is tense. The two words he stammers on in the next sentence 'f-fact' and 'm-marry' tell us much more. The fact that David will marry depends on 'seeing a girl I really want', which gives him an excuse for never marrying as he may never see her. And what is more interesting is that David does not say that his marrying depends on meeting the girl he really

67. Benson, *David of King's*, p. 174.
68. Benson, *David of King's*, p. 176.

loves, just on his seeing her. While he does no more than see her she remains perfect in his imagination. Meeting a woman, becoming friends with her and either falling in love with her or not, do not fit with David's expectations. For him there will be no mistakes and no need for experimentation with the perfect woman. His point to his friend Bags is that one does not need to try out falling in love with a girl from a tobacconist's shop. His version of romance is medieval in the proper sense, he will ride up to the lady's castle on his charger and she will let open the doors of her love and they will live happily ever after. David may hold this belief since he does not have any experience of longterm relationships. His mother is never mentioned throughout the trilogy, so is presumably dead. It is therefore not surprising that he has so unworldly expectations of heterosexual love that he can call it a 'fad, and pi[ous?] and p-priggish'. What we have seen of his negotiations of homosexual relationships suggests it must be a disguise, if it is not self-deception.

However, if David's reasoning is still largely without substance, suddenly his stammering over the letter 'p' hooks his fluttering thoughts onto the peg of religion, and all becomes substantial again as 'pi' and 'p-priggish' leads him by assonance to 'preach':

> "… Good Lord, I never knew I could preach so fine. Shall I take orders? Or do you think they'll let me preach the 'Varsity sermon next Sunday instead of my father? Leave the licentious wench alone, and come round after Hall and play bridge! Do!"
>
> David paused a moment, looking frightfully gay and attractive.
>
> "Oh do," he said.
>
> "Right you are!"
>
> "Ripping," said David … "[And] we'll rook Tommers after Hall."[69]

Preaching is, of course, persuading to morality, and needs no more substance to its argument than that the proposed change of behaviour will be good. It also fits with David's experience, in that his father is an Archdeacon. What is more important is that the discourse of the sermon diverts attention from the tenseness he feels in giving his arguments about his choice of asexuality until the perfect marriage, and puts the emphasis onto Bags's need to change his behaviour and 'leave the licentious wench alone', as though it were all her fault that

---

69. Benson, *David of King's*, p. 178.

Bags is so infatuated. So successful is the redirection of emphasis, that E.F.B. can use the weasel word 'gay' to describe David: a word that can mean 'noble, beautiful, excellent, fine',[70] 'light-hearted, carefree',[71] 'wanton, lewd, lascivious',[72] and, from 1922, two years before the publication of *David of King's*, 'of a person: homosexual'.[73] The word is used to make David seem the more attractive while he is preaching, in order that he might be more effective a preacher. And in this case, David does turn Bags's mind away from the girl at the tobacconist's to play bridge with his friends in college. The fact that they will 'rook' Tommers brings in the memory of Parson Rook from *David Blaize and the Blue Door* to bless the transformation.

For the rest of the volume, David takes it upon himself to turn Bags away next from drinking too much, and then to help him to win an election that will set him up as a politician when he leaves university. And in so doing, David's own vocation becomes clear: as a writer of moral fiction, a secular priest of prose.

David's Ordination

David has lost his juvenile embarrassment about his father, and like most children who grow up with parents in prominent roles, accepts his father as preacher of the university sermon where he could not bear his preaching at his Private School. There is only one discordant note introduced in David's thoughts before his father's arrival:

> The only thing which seemed at all likely to jar the harmony of their meeting was the consideration, which must be talked about, of what David was to do in life after he had left the University. His father would certainly have liked him to be a clergyman, but it was too obvious that David wouldn't like it at all, that this project might be considered as abandoned.[74]

No reason is given why it might be 'too obvious that David wouldn't like it at all'. Although there might be a reference to a conversation that has gone on outside the action of the book, David's obvious

70. *Oxford English Dictionary*, 1a.
71. *Oxford English Dictionary*, 3a.
72. *Oxford English Dictionary*, 4a.
73. *Oxford English Dictionary*, 4d. Although the *Oxford English Dictionary* notes that the interpretation of the early uses of the word gay to mean homosexual may be based solely on the knowledge of the sexuality of the author.
74. Benson, *David of King's*, p. 180.

delight at preaching to Bags about his treatment of women, and his continuing to teach his friend how to moderate his drinking and how to set off his political career, marks him out as an excellent minister. He teaches the moral course by example with a sense of fun rather than pious priggishness. Only the question about his sexuality would seem to make him unsuitable for the ministry. And it is a question which comes up when David offers his pipe, Perpetua, to his father, in an unspoken challenge that must be resolved. The Archdeacon glosses rather than blesses the pipe for those who did not already comprehend the saintliness of the name:

> "Perpetua, Virgin and Martyr?" he asked "Let's have a look. Why Perpetua? .... Ah, a meerschaum, I see. No, my dear boy, I think I won't. Precious things Meerschaums."[75]

David's offer of the pipe, with its prior references to masturbation as a form of maintaining virginity, is startling. It is as though David is asking whether his father, in want of a wife, masturbates too. The Archdeacon's flat refusal to smoke the pipe is quickly followed by his denouncing the practice of smoking, and therefore of masturbation:

> "... My dear boy, surely that's a remarkably foul pipe, isn't it?"
> "Yes, horrid," said David. "Think I'll stop."
> "Don't mind me," said his father. "But you really can't enjoy it much, can you?"
> "I don't. I only want to make it black," said David putting it down ..."[76]

The claim only to want to make the pipe black is a flat denial of the pleasure we have seen David has taken in the ritual of smoking, like a boy caught smoking who makes a flat denial of the evidence of the burning cigarette in his hand. More importantly, it tells us he knows that in order to please his Lord and father he must give up masturbation along with the other forms of sexuality. Confirming this view, shortly afterwards, the Archdeacon sits on the pipe and breaks it: only heterosexual marriage or asexuality will do. As a reward, David gains his father's blessing on his decision to be a writer without even discussion:

---

75. Benson, *David of King's*, p. 184.
76. Benson, *David of King's*, p. 185.

He laid his hands on David's head for a moment, looking him in the face both earnestly and merrily. What he saw there gave him a full heart.[77]

Writing will become David's priestly vocation, celibate and solitary as it is, but from what has gone before, the Archdeacon's blessing lays two conditions upon his relationship with Frank. First, it defines once and for all their marriage as asexual, and second it requires that David's views be treated as equal to Frank's in order for him to be able to demand asexuality from his lover.

David and Frank's Marriage

For David, the first condition takes the form of the personal discipline not to masturbate. Once again we are reminded of A.C.B.'s mathematical certainty that masturbation will lead to homosexuality. By removing sex in all its forms, E.F.B. inhibits that certainty. But David has to be able to impose the same discipline upon his husband, which as the recessive or junior partner in their relationship, he has hitherto only been able to do by example. David needs to be able to impose his wishes upon Frank in their marriage contract, and this becomes his first task as a writer.

David lit a cigarette, and tried to determine exactly what it was that he wanted to tell [Frank]. He found it difficult to arrive at this, for his powers of self-analysis were delightfully elementary, and the written word demanded definiteness. But he knew that within the last year his attitude towards Frank had suffered considerable modification, and he was equally well aware that Frank's attitude towards him had not altered. For, up to now, ever since the beginning of their devoted friendship, Frank's mind had completely dominated his own, so that whatever in tastes and conduct Frank had commented had been to him, *ex officio*, admirable; whatever Frank thought lightly of had been contemptible. But now he was growing to maturity David was beginning to see that he could no longer take reach-me-down judgments, however nicely cut, and stuff himself into them … It was not again, that there had been open disputes or differences between them; it was mainly that David realized that a mental and moral independence of his own had grown up in him … His mind was no longer the mind of

77. Benson, *David of King's*, p. 189.

one who walked with his hand in another's and swallowed with open mouth whatever was given him.[78]

After his father's demand for asexual purity, David cannot accept a life in constant negotiation with Frank's unwavering sexual desire. He has 'a mental and moral independence of his own,' asexuality, which he now offers to Frank as the price to pay for their lifelong devotion to one another.

> He was not in the least less devoted to Frank than he had always been – that was sure enough and surely would persist through any change of relationship. That male manly love might manifest itself in many mediums, but it was not changed because the mediums vanished. Above all, now, at the ages of twenty-one and twenty-four, the three short years that separated them were immeasurably shorter than the three years that had stood between them at the ages of fourteen and seventeen.[79]

The indubitable fact of their age difference becoming less important seems here to be the given reason for David's change of emphasis on their relationship. But wedged in this quote is the much more significant sentence 'male manly love might manifest itself in many mediums, but it was not changed because the mediums vanished.' The assonance here in the plethora of 'ms' reminds us of masturbation, the medium that must vanish as it might lead to other mediums of male manly love. David has faced Frank's desire for sexual love and knows how important it is for him, therefore:

> He knew that nothing said with love behind it ought to hurt anyone, but somehow he was afraid of Frank being hurt.[80]

The sending of the letter announcing David's marriage terms to Frank gives dramatic impetus to the remainder of the trilogy since Frank does not reply, and David is left wondering (with us) whether either will get the marriage each knows he needs. Frank adds piquancy to David's discomfort by referring to other contents of the letter, but not to the demand of asexual marriage. More than 15 pages after writing the letter, David is still in suspense:

> If Frank had misunderstood him, the misunderstanding could be cleared up. If he had not misunderstood, then he had understood,

78. Benson, *David of King's*, p. 278.
79. Benson, *David of King's*, p. 280.
80. Benson, *David of King's*, p. 281.

which was precisely what David had wanted him to do. But one way or another, this waiting for Frank's arrival was as bad as waiting for the lists at Tripos.[81]

The posting of the 'lists at Tripos', that is, the degree results, becomes the moment around which the outcome of the trilogy is choreographed: will David lose Frank? What is the prize for living asexually? Will they manage to live together asexually? The first of these questions is answered after a physical gesture that mirrors David touching Frank in Chapel, that is, under God's witness:

> [Frank] paused a moment and laid his hand on David's arm, which lay conveniently along the window-sill. David saw at once that they were already on the subject of which he had written ... Frank's reticence had filled him with vague misgivings, but that gesture showed him that he need not have any about the discussion of it ...
>
> "David old chap," he said quite gravely, "we've had such a dam' good time – you know it as well as I do – that all these years I've never wanted it to be anything different to what it was. But it belonged to boyhood, and now it has changed; it couldn't possibly help that. But as for disliking it, now could any decent fellow dislike his friend's growing up? We've loved each other, thank God: I've been first in your life, and you in mine. Soon now, I shouldn't wonder, you'll meet a girl, and fall madly in love with her and be frightfully happy, and you must think me a pretty good stinkpot if you imagined I should mind that. Very likely I shall do exactly the same ... Besides our friendship is built into us. It's all there ..."
>
> "That's all right, then," said David quietly.[82]

In action and speech, Frank finally accepts David's demand for asexuality in their marriage along with the myth of the perfect heterosexual marriage to which each aspires as the outward excuse for their being together. It is interesting here that while Frank claims, echoing St Paul, that he is putting aside that which 'belonged to boyhood', at the same time he uses schoolboy banter to show he understands the fact that marriage to a woman will not happen for either of them. By calling himself a 'stinkpot' he mirrors the term 'stinkers' that Bags has told us David uses for women. The two men have by this conversation come to a tacit agreement that they will devote themselves to each

81. Benson, *David of King's*, p. 293.
82. Benson, *David of King's*, pp. 301–302.

other forever on David's terms of asexuality: a marriage contracted for men in heaven.

But nevertheless, the decision puts the two of them beyond the pale of society as we see them quietly together in David's rooms while a party goes on below to celebrate the end of the year:

> David and Frank sat up till some timeless hour, for it was really very little use going to bed while the band at the dance blared on: but probably they would not have parted any sooner if there had been no dance at King's at all. There was a lot to say, and food for silence in between, and what not.[83]

The prize for living asexually is that David takes a first class degree, a result which maybe he would not have achieved if he had been sexually involved with Frank, but a result that is nevertheless brought to him in his bed by a triumphant Frank. Despite all that has passed, however, it is not out of the question to argue that Frank has just quit that bed to go to find David's name on the 'lists at Tripos'. Certainly the innocent phrase 'and what not' at the end of the last quote, listing one of the activities they get up to when they are together, leaves room for sexual activity, or at least for their continued negotiation of it.

83. Benson, *David of King's*, p. 309.

Chapter 6

EDWARD CARPENTER: *TOWARDS DEMOCRACY* –
THE GREATEST POET ENGLAND NEVER HAD

For one reason or another, every country takes its spiritual lead
from a poet who represents a particular age. It may be for a century,
such as Alexander Pope in the eighteenth. Or it may be for a longer
period, such is Shakespeare's 400 year reign; or it may be shorter,
as with Wordsworth's 40 or so years. In the early twentieth century,
England looked to T.S. Eliot, the self-confessing Catholic, Classicist
and Conservative. But for England to take to its heart an American
poet required quite some act of forgetting of the origins of the voice
of its spiritual conscience. But the choice was not made for want of
eligible English poets. The role of spiritual guide in the early twentieth
century might well be argued, as this chapter will argue, to have been
Edward Carpenter, although his influence was disguised because of
his triple handicap of being Atheist, Homosexual and Socialist.

In this chapter I want to explore Carpenter's always faltering
reputation, not as some act designed to induce pain in the homosexual
reader, but in order to introduce Carpenter's work – once more – to
gay people who can but find it exhilarating and uplifting. I choose
the word 'exhilarating' because it exactly captures the feeling I had
when first reading Carpenter's verse which filled me with so much
excitement that I wanted to explode with joy for what I am and have
always been – recognizing myself in Carpenter's verse and prose as
though for the first time.

Beset by his failure to gain common understanding for his longest
poem, Carpenter looked back on *Towards Democracy* (1892-1902)
with the words:

> The sufferings of these years, the emotional distress and tension
> which I had experienced, poured themselves out in poetical
> effusions, outbursts, ejaculations – I know not what to call them.
> Sometimes lying full length in the train coming home at midnight
> from some lecture engagement, hardly able to move; sometimes
> in the morning with a sense of restoration, flying over the fields

in the sunlight; sometimes in my little lodging; sometimes on a long country walk – I wrote just what the necessity of my feelings compelled – formless scraps, cries, prophetic assurances – in no available metre, or shape, just as they came. In no shape that they could be given to the world; but they were a relief to me, and a consolation.[1]

If *Towards Democracy*, Carpenter's longest poetical work, about which he is writing here, marks a cycle of spiritual suffering and relief, Carpenter's modern critics have done little to develop his reputation, or a spiritual understanding of his poetry. What we shall see is a heritage based upon Carpenter's life's work, living off the land outside Sheffield in a 22 year marriage to a man (George Merrill), which concentrates on his socialism and all but ignores everything else. But along side socialism is the fact that Carpenter and Merrill changed the lives of those homosexuals who met them. E.M. Forster, for example, wrote *Maurice* after a visit to Ted and George, basing that novel's central cross-class relationship on what he had seen. And if we can believe that D.H. Lawrence read *Maurice* and repeated the story in *Lady Chatterley's Lover*, only changing the main relationship to heterosexual, we could argue that both novels, which irrevocably altered the twentieth-century view of sexuality, owed everything to Carpenter. So maybe we owe our liberated view of sexuality to someone that most people have never read: and someone whose purpose was always spiritual while at the same time wholly bound up with the physical.

For Carpenter, who left the Anglican Church after serving as a curate to the Christian Socialist, F.D. Maurice, Jesus came eating and drinking. Life was to be no ascetic road of self-denial where the aim was 'to kneel/Where prayer has been valid',[2] but had to take into account the body's desires as well as the spirit's needs. But this is also to distort Carpenter's message, which was to balance 'The Stupid old Body' against 'The Wandering Lunatic Mind'[3] and never to be a slave to either.

---

1. Edward Carpenter, *My Days and Dreams: Being Biographical Notes* (London: George Allen and Unwin, 1916), Chap. 5.

2. T.S. Eliot, *Little Gidding*.

3. Edward Carpenter, *Towards Democracy* (London: Swan Sonnenschein, 1905), pp. 484–85. Cited as TD.

Modern Carpenter Criticism

Sheila Rowbotham, writing in 1977, noticed there was a spiritual dimension to Carpenter, and suggested that 'for Carpenter, socialism and the inner life were not alternatives'.[4] Nevertheless, her study is more about socialism than sexuality or spirituality. The chapter on Carpenter's revolutionary views on sexuality gives a positive feminist reading of his exposition on housework, and a passing mention of his lack of sexual jealousy, but there is little or nothing on spirituality or the inner life. One important piece of information we are given, is about Carpenter's meeting with Merrill at which they exchanged a 'look of recognition', but nothing is made of this nexus of spiritual, sexual and political ideas, which is bound up in Carpenter's definition of 'Democracy'.

Likewise, Tony Brown's collection of essays on Carpenter concentrates upon the development of socialism at the expense of Carpenter's other interests and achievements. Beverley Thiele gives an historical account of *The Intermediate Sex* and *Love's Coming of Age,* and Scott McCracken, the only modern readings of *Towards Democracy* I have found in print. But the latter paper only quotes five sections from the poem, which in my 1905 edition covers 507 pages.[5] Nevertheless, for McCracken, Carpenter's references to Thoreau's *On Walden Pond* are seen as 'a utopian universality ... engage[d] in the breaking down of determinist structures ... to embrace a democratic world'.[6] And we must agree that to an extent Carpenter's project may be read as a form of secular Universalism. But, as we shall see, it was a very practical universalism that addresses each situation against which it found itself at odds. Thus we would argue that McCracken also seems to miss the point about Carpenter's physical and spiritual ethos, by arguing that:

> Shaped in the context of a discourse between men, in the late nineteenth-century atmosphere of strong homosocial bonds and

---

4. Sheila Rowbotham, *Socialism and the New Life: The Personal and Sexual Politics of Edward Carpenter and Havelock Ellis* (London: Pluto, 1977), p. 47.

5. This edition (London: Swan Sonnenschein & Co., Ltd., 1905) is the first complete version of *Towards Democracy* and sold 16,000 copies.

6. Scott McCracken, 'Writing the Body: Edward Carpenter, George Gissing and Late Nineteenth-Century realism' in Tony Brown (ed.), *Edward Carpenter and Late Victorian Radicalism* (London: Frank Cass, 1990), p. 185.

public homophobia, *Towards Democracy* writes an ideal, atemporal subjectivity.[7]

Carpenter and Merrill's life at Millthorpe was anything but ideal or atemporal. It was an association between two real men in love with each other, faced with the hardships of making a living from an unfriendly patch of earth in a society which, for some unexplained reason, left them to themselves, and allowed Carpenter to publish about homosexuals and homosexuality almost at will. History for them was very much 'Now and in England'.[8]

Harry Cocks's study of the Eagle Street College in Bolton[9] picks up on the notion of idealism in Carpenter. He examines the history of this group of middle and working class men who met to discuss Whitman's poetry in a way that deferred homosexual acts, replacing them with comradeship and homoeroticism. The paper is interesting since it explores the place of spirituality in a post-Darwinian society, and finds it in the Whitmanesque cosmic consciousness that these men were searching for as the next stage of human evolution, which Cocks reads as an explanation of why they were drawn to each other asexually. But Cocks avoids the point that Carpenter understood developments such as these as the result of the balance between desire and self-control.

> For (over and over again) there is nothing that is evil except because a man has not mastery over it: and there is no good thing that is not evil if it have mastery over a man;
> And there is no passion or power, or pleasure or pain, or created thing whatsoever, which is not ultimately for man and for his use – or which he need be afraid of, or ashamed at.[10]

In this section from *Towards Democracy*, Carpenter exhorts his readers that all passions should be indulged without fear or shame, despite moral injunctions against them, so long as they do not take a person over. Therefore, I would argue that Cocks's conclusion that 'For Carpenter, the [Eagle Street] College, in its intense non-physical homogenic love, may have represented the promise of his ideas in

7. McCracken, 'Writing the Body', p. 188.

8. Eliot, *Little Gidding*.

9. Harry Cocks, '*Calamus* in Bolton: Spirituality and Homosexuality in Late Victorian England' in *Gender and History* 13. 2 (August 2001): pp. 191–223.

10. TD, p. 362.

action,'[11] once again misses the point that Carpenter and Merrill were dropped into the 1890s as a fully formed homosexual couple in the midst of a world of self-alienated men who could not indulge in, conceptualize, or even write about the idea of an active same-sex sexual and loving relationship. After Forster visited Carpenter and Merrill, he wrote that 'he returned in a state of exultation feeling that the fog had cleared from his life.'[12] But as Cocks's paper demonstrates, the men of the Bolton College were still in a fog: unable as they were to touch each other sexually. They may have discovered the spiritual side of their love for one another, but in denying the body they could not be called a representation of Carpenter's ideas in action.

In a useful advance in Carpenter studies, Matt Cook's paper 'A New City of Friends: London and Homosexuality in the 1890s'[13] draws attention to the physical sexual imagery that pervades much of *Towards Democracy*:

> [*Towards Democracy*] represents the multiplicity of the urban crowd but here is also a rhythmic movement which unifies the elements into an eroticized totality: from an alienating entry to "breath of liquor, money grubbing eye, infidel skin", to an orgasmic surge ... ("Eyes and breasts of love, breathless, clutches of lust, limbs bodies, torrents, bursts"), a post orgasmic despair (of tears, entreraties, tremblings"), and finally, the passionate embrace of the crowd ... [14]

Here, however, the physical is associated with 'The power of comradeship to pull people together into a new life.'[15] The physical becomes a metaphor for the city space, and is, if not sublimated as in Cocks, then compartmentalized, mapped and little more than a cipher for personal identity in city life. Here, in Cook's move to encompass the physical as a map of cruising places in the city, the spiritual dimension has disappeared.

Introductions to Carpenter

In contrast with modern critics, his contemporaries read Carpenter more clearly and conscientiously, although with some unpleasant

11. TD, p. 218.

12. Dilip Kumar Barua, *Edward Carpenter: 1844–1929, An Apostle of Freedom* (Burdwan: University of Burdwan Press, 1991), p. 195.

13. *History Workshop Journal* 56.1 (2003): pp. 33–58.

14. *History Workshop Journal* 56.1 (2003): p. 46.

15. *History Workshop Journal* 56.1 (2003).

but not unexpected caveats. Ernest Crosby, the most prominent
radical social reformer in turn-of-the-century New York,[16] welcomed
Carpenter's *Towards Democracy*, even noting its poor reception,
writing:

> yes the world has every reason to give Carpenter a good reception
> ... Overcome with disgust for the civilization which hedged him
> in from the mass of his fellowmen, and falling in love with the
> classes that do the hard work of the world, Carpenter went in
> 1881 to share a labourer's cottage near Sheffield, and to work
> with him in the fields. There he lives, passing a part of the year
> with a mechanic in the neighbouring city, where he has built up a
> considerable business in the manufacture of sandals, ... Meanwhile
> he writes poetry and prose and lectures on matters social and
> economic. In short, Carpenter loves his neighbour in deed as
> well as word, and has of necessity ceased to be respectable. His
> so-called college "fellowship" was reputable, and from that post
> his writings might have reached polite society (as Ruskin's did),
> but the fellow of Yorkshire farm and factory hands! How could
> the world be expected to listen to such a man?[17]

The next 48 pages of his *Edward Carpenter: Poet and Prophet* give
many reasons why Carpenter should be heard. Quoting freely from
Towards Democracy, Crosby reads the poem as a paean to joyful life.
Thus, where Carpenter writes:

> Freedom! The deep breath! The word heard centuries and
> centuries beforehand: the soul singing low and passionate to
> itself: Joy! Joy!

Crosby glosses:

> Freedom and Joy in the life universal: that is the message of
> Carpenter; and who will say that there is a better one for the world
> of today? The poet felt the world's need and experienced it, and
> he has found the remedy springing up at the bottom of his heart,
> and now he comes to share his discovery with his fellow men.[18]

---

16. Crosby wrote Whitmanesque poetry and many pamphlets against
imperialism. He brought Mark Twain into the Anti-Imperialist League. Among
his publications are: *The Absurdities of Militarism* (Boston, MA: American Peace
Society, 1901) and *Captain Jinks, Hero* (New York: Funk & Wagnalls, 1902).

17. Ernest Crosby, *Edward Carpenter: Poet and Prophet* (Philadelphia, PA:
The Conservator, 1901), pp. 2–3.

18. Crosby, *Edward Carpenter*, p. 8.

In this, we can see at once how Crosby recognizes the combination of the physical and the spiritual in the idea of the experience that affects the soul of the author, who, in an advanced version of the Romantic bard writes down his experiences to cure readers' spiritual ills.

Unabashed too, by the idea of physical sex, Crosby glosses Carpenter's use of sexual language as a metaphor for spiritual and physical union with the world and one another, in a post-Christian world:

> Sex is the allegory of Love in the physical world. It is from this fact that it derives its immense power. The sum of Love is non-differentiation – absolute union of being; but absolute union can only be found at the centre of existence. Therefore whoever has truly found another has found not only that other and with that other himself, but has found also a third – who dwells at the centre and holds the plastic material of the universe in the palm of his hand, and is creator of sensible forms. [19]
>
> In short, "the prime object of Sex is union" physical, mental and spiritual.[20]

In Carpenter's use of sexual language, where the modern critic Cook sees only a map of particular areas of the city that go to make up urban homosexual identity, Crosby saw 'a third': the spiritual 'us' that is not reducible to either individual in the sexual union, and which as we shall see, is also known as 'Democracy'.

But writing so soon after the Wilde trials, Crosby, either to protect himself or to distance Carpenter's male: male theme in *Towards Democracy* which had been unequivocally explained in the privately published *Homogenic Love* (1894), appended a 'disclaimer:'

> I do not believe that much is to be expected of close friendships of a romantic nature between persons of the same sex.[21]

The point is not only homophobic (in the true sense of 'phobia' – 'afraid') but also fails to grasp the meaning of Carpenter's 'Democracy.' The concept is built upon the recognition of the existence of another across the social givens of class, race and sexuality, for which the model Carpenter uses is the same-sex look of recognition that can

19. Carpenter, *Love's Coming of Age* (Manchester: Labour Press, 1896), p. 20.

20. Crosby, *Edward Carpenter*, p. 44.

21. Crosby, *Edward Carpenter*, p. 46.

happen between any two men of any class or race, a look which collapses difference and enhances union.

A paragraph in a letter from Carpenter to Tom Swan,[22] printed in Swan's book *Edward Carpenter: the Man and the Message,* which followed Crosby's by one year, explains a little further the point of the spiritual, physical and mental aspects of 'Democracy':

> I find that my thought proceeds upon an Assumption – namely that all existence is an Emanation (an Expression, a Revelation) of one Being underlying … The rationale of all growth or evolution is recognition – recognition of the Soul, in self and others. Side by side with the egoistic or individualizing force which we must assume has the character of darkness and blindness and ignorance – comes the upbuilding illuminating power which leads the Many back to the One – which reveals to the Many that they are One.[23]

The idea of a 'One' at the heart of the 'Many' appears almost as though it is a theological statement about the existence of God – and one is reminded of the prayer of St. Chrysostom, that Jesus will be there when more than two are gathered together in His name. But for Carpenter, knowledge of the 'One' comes about through the 'desire' of the individual, as he writes: 'This force appears first in consciousness in the form of *desire.*'[24]

Access to some sort of spiritual knowledge through desire marks Carpenter off from mainstream religious ideas, where revelation or dogma is the source of truth. Instead, as Swan quotes Carpenter, it is up to the individual to prepare himself mentally in order to learn from the world around:

> It should be as easy to expel an obnoxious thought from your mind as to shake a stone from your shoe; and till a man can do it, it is just nonsense to talk about his ascendancy over nature and all the rest of it.[25]

The core of Carpenter's thought might therefore be mistaken as a development of Emerson's Transcendentalism, 'an ideal spiritual state that "transcends" the physical and empirical and is only realized

22. Swan wrote for the *Manchester Weekly Citizen* and may have been its publisher.

23. Tom Swan, *Edward Carpenter The Man and His Message* (Manchester: Tom Swan, 1902), p. 11.

24. Swan, *Edward Carpenter,* p. 14.

25. Swan, *Edward Carpenter,* p. 22.

through the individual's intuition, rather than through the doctrines of established religions.'[26] But the idealism of transcendentalism once again cannot be equated with the physicality and sexuality at the heart of Carpenter's spirituality which defines itself in the reciprocal relationship of the bodily individual with others, and with the world: with 'the problem of life':

> The racial, religious, political, professional, family and individual prejudices must be temporarily laid aside, if not entirely discarded, so that the man may stand naked, erect and free – so that he stands face to face with the problem of life, as it presents itself to him; and endeavour to solve it by the strength of his own manhood, not waiting in vain for someone else to solve it for him.[27]

Swan's interpretation of Carpenter comes closest to the idea of 'Democracy', but there is something uncomfortably like the idea of 'rugged individualism' at the heart of this last statement. As will become clear, from a reading of *Towards Democracy*, there is much more compassion in Carpenter's central notion of 'Democracy', a poem which, Swan suggests will 'be found to represent the heart and kernel of all his writings.'[28]

Towards Democracy

At the beginning of the third section of *Towards Democracy*, Carpenter defines 'The Word Democracy' in a short poem, which begins:

> Underneath all now comes this Word, turning the edges of the other words where they met it.
>
> Politics, art, science, commerce, religion, customs and methods of daily life, the very outer shows and semblances of ordinary objects ...
>
> Their meanings must all now be absorbed and recast in this word, or else fall off like dry husks before its disclosure.[29]

Thus 'Democracy' is announced as a controlling idea, and considering the list of things it will change, politics, art, science, religion, customs and methods of daily life, there is no surprise that many critics have concentrated on Carpenter's Socialism. And there is more:

26. See, www.wikipedia.com 'Transcendentalism'. Accessed 17 July 2006.
27. Swan, *Edward Carpenter*, p. 24.
28. Swan, *Edward Carpenter*, p. 7.
29. TD, p. 263.

> Do you not see that our individual life is and can only be secured
> at the cost of the continual sacrifice of other lives,
>   And that therefore you can only hold it on condition that you
> are ready in your turn to sacrifice it for others?[30]

This is the reciprocity of socialism, where, as Marx argues, one gains
one's individuality in relation to the work of others. But the rest of this
poem is unusually silent about how democracy will be recognized.
It will change the world:

> All the customs of society change, for all are significant; and
> the long-accepted axioms of every day life are dislocated like a
> hill-side in a landslip:[31]

But we must look elsewhere in the book for an example of democracy
in action, and we find it in the violent juxtapositions of the earlier
poem, 'In the Drawing Rooms' from Section I. The poem begins
describing the falseness that characterizes the 'Drawing Room' society
into which many upper class people like Carpenter were born:

> Ever the same miowls and drawls, the same half-averted sad
> uneasy looks, the same immensely busy people doing really
> nothing, the same one-legged weary idling, mutual boredom,
> and vampire business.[32]

The situation leaves the narrator desperate:

> Was this then the sum of life?
>   The grinning gibbering organisation of nations – a polite trap,
> and circle of endlessly complaisant faces bowing you back from
> all reality![33]

What is surprising is both the source of relief to which the narrator
turns and the form that relief takes:

> So I cried in my soul for the violence and outrage of Nature to
> deliver me from this barrenness.[34]

The metaphor seems to suggest that Nature has been upset by
'Drawing Room' society, and that only Nature can restore its own
inherent balance in order to become fertile again. And that fertility

---

30. TD, pp. 263–64.
31. TD, p. 264.
32. TD, p. 139.
33. TD, p. 140.
34. TD, p. 140.

comes in the form of a look of recognition of same-sex desire between two men. The narrator of the poem is on a train late at night:

> Well, as it happened just then – and as we stopped at a small way station – my eyes from their swoon-sleep opening encountering the grimy and oil-besmeared figure of a stoker.
>
> Close at my elbow on the foot-plate of his engine he was standing, devouring bread and cheese,
>
> And the firelight fell on him brightly as for the moment his eyes rested on mine.
>
> And that was all. But it was enough.
>
> The youthful face, yet so experienced and calm, was enough;
>
> The quiet look, the straight untroubled, unseeking eyes, resting upon me – giving me without any ado the thing I needed ...
>
> All these in his eyes who stood there, lusty with well-knit loins, devouring bread and cheese – all these and something more:
>
> Nature standing supreme and immensely indifferent in that man, yet condensed and prompt for decisive action: ...
>
> O eyes, O face, how in that moment without any ado you gave me all!
>
> How in a moment the whole vampire brood of flat paralytic faces fled away, and you gave me back the great breasts of Nature, when I was rejected of others and like to die of starvation.
>
> I do not forget.
>
> It is not a little thing ...[35]

It is the look of recognition between potential same-sex lovers that is here evoked, and is the nexus of physical, mental and spiritual responses that is at the heart of Carpenter's term 'Democracy'. The look is physical because – as those of us who have encountered it know – it can cause sexual excitement that is wholly disproportionate to the chance of actual fulfilment. The narrator's response is not simply to a representative of Nature 'supreme and immensely indifferent' but to the stoker 'lusty with well-knit loins.' The look is mental because it is relief for the narrator from the mental confines of the 'Drawing Room' society he abhors, so that 'in a moment the whole vampire brood of flat paralytic faces fled away, and you gave me back the great breasts of Nature, when I was rejected of others and like to die of starvation.' And the look is also spiritual. It is 'all.' When the word 'all' is used for the first time in the extract we understand

35. TD, pp. 140–43.

the sense of a fulfilling religious experience bringing unexpected calm. And in the final time the word is used in the extract, the word 'all' brings with it a sense of metonymy: the stoker stands for all the world of relationships between all people, and thus explains to us the method in which 'Democracy' works.

Thus, as physical, mental and spiritual, 'Democracy' cannot be counted as a metaphor for life. It is important that Carpenter uses 'the same-sex look' as a metonym for 'Democracy'. In this way, 'Democracy' is a real encounter between two people stripped of their 'racial, religious, political, professional, family and individual prejudices' facing each other in the same way that they face everyone else in the world in a dynamic, reciprocal, mutually-constructing relationship. It is as though the narrator and the stoker are saying to one another in the look 'I am me because you make me what I am.' The image is at once charged with sexuality but is also banal. It is the everyday look that we all give each other, but which can take us unawares when it is re-activated with the charge of sexual recognition.

Carpenter ends the poem with a more spiritually – minded explanation of the encounter with the stoker:

> Indeed I worship none more than I worship you and such as you.
> Who are no god sitting on a jasper throne,
> But the same toiling in disguise among the children of men and giving your own life for them.[36]

The banal consubstantiality of stoker and God is at the heart of Carpenter's 'Democracy.' Whether or not it is an object worthy of worship was taken up in Carpenter's later work, but that it falls under the aegis of the same-sex look of recognition sets it outside the bounds of the Anglican Church even to this day.

The Intermediate Sex

It was the power of the same-sex look of recognition which interested Carpenter for much of the rest of his writing, and in the last two sections of this chapter, I will argue that his writing becomes quasi religious in its fervour to spread the word of the normality of inter-mediate sexual types, the usefulness of their place in society, and the

36. TD, p. 144.

things people had to learn from them. Carpenter was writing at the time of the early sexologists, Ulrichs, Havelock-Ellis, Krafft-Ebing, Moll and Symonds, but his work develops theirs, possibly because he was writing from the experience of his own intermediate sexuality, rather than objectively about the scientific category of inversion. His opening position on the spectrum of types of men and women seems representative enough for the time it was written:

> It is beginning to be recognised that the sexes do not or should not normally form two groups hopelessly isolated in habit and feeling from each other, but that they rather represent the two poles of one group – which is the human race; so that while certainly the extreme specimens at either pole are vastly divergent, there are great numbers in the middle region who (though differing corporeally as men and women) are by emotion and temperament very near to each other.[37]

However, where Karl Ulrichs defines the 'Urning,' or what we would now call the effeminate male homosexual as a male body with a female soul, Carpenter is more subtle, and accounts for more and different sexual types:

> That there are distinctions and gradations of Soul-material in relation to Sex – that the inner psychical affections and affinities shade off and graduate, in a vast number of instances, most subtly from male to female, and not always in obvious correspondence with the outer bodily sex – is a thing evident enough to anyone who considers the subject; nor could any good purpose well be served by ignoring this fact – even if it were possible to do so.[38]

In modern parlance, Carpenter is arguing here that masculinity is not solely the gender of the male, and femininity is not solely the gender of the female. Men may be to a greater or lesser extent feminine and women masculine. What is more, gender is not related to body type. Thus, a woman with a male-looking body may be very feminine in her gender traits, and a man with a female-looking body may nevertheless have very masculine gender traits. What was probably most revolutionary about Carpenter's sexology was that he recognized all points between the poles of the spectrum as well.

37. Edward Carpenter, *The Intermediate Sex: A Study of Some Transitional Types of Men and Women* (London: George Allen and Unwin, 1908), Chapter 2. This text is available at www.edwardcarpenter.net from where the quotations are taken [Cited as IS].

In a further development of the idea of the spectrum or 'continuous group' of sex and gender, Carpenter suggests that there is also a spectrum of attitudes between the poles of Love and Friendship:

> ...as people are beginning to see that the sexes form in a certain sense a continuous group, so they are beginning to see that Love and Friendship – which have been so often set apart from each other as things distinct – are in reality closely related and shade imperceptibly into each other.[39]

The move allows Carpenter to redefine comradeship between men, that 'manly friendship' which was so highly prized by the Victorian society in which he was brought up. The move is at the heart of the problem of male same-sex sexuality at the turn of the century. Where Wilde had ironically called it 'The love that dare not speak its name' he ought to be taken literally. For example, when E.M. Forster, at 35, visited Carpenter and Merrill he was touched knowingly by a same-sex desiring man for the first time in his life. Rob Doll explains:

> In his 'Terminal Note' to *Maurice* Forster tells how the novel came to be written:
>
>> It was the direct result of a visit to Edward Carpenter at Millthorpe. Carpenter [was] a ... believer in the love of comrades, whom he sometimes called Uranians. It was this last aspect of him that attracted me in my loneliness ... I approached him ... as one approaches a saviour. It must have been on my second or third visit to the shrine that the spark was kindled as he and his comrade George Merrill combined to make a profound impression on me and to touch a creative spring. George Merrill also touched my backside –gently and just above the buttocks ... The sensation was unusual and I still remember it ... It was as much psychological as physical. It seemed to go straight through the small of my back into my ideas, without involving my thoughts.
>
>> Forster was thirty-five when he visited Edward Carpenter, and had never achieved physical sex.[40]

The fact that Forster was still a virgin and took the trouble to travel all the way to Sheffield, strongly suggests that it had not occurred to

38. IS, Chapter 1.
39. IS, Chapter 5.
40. http://www.emforster.info/pages/maurice.html. Accessed 21 July 2006.

him – for want of any information about same-sex relations – that a man having sex with a man was possible and not pathological, and caused him to live his life in a fog.

Doll points out that *The Intermediate Sex* is cagey about physical relations between same-sex couples, but Carpenter had privately published his ideas about the desirability of same-sex physical relations as early as 1894, in *Homogenic Love.*[41] This work is clear that physical sexual relations ought to be considered as part of a homogenic attachment, but that

> while the homogenic feeling undoubtedly requires *some* kind of physical expression, the question what degree if intimacy is in all cases fitting and natural may not be very easy to decide ...[42]

Nevertheless, Carpenter concludes:

> that it probably demands and requires some amount of physical intimacy ...[43]

If these two sentences were enough for a publisher to refuse to publish a book, then it is not hard to understand how difficult it was to pass around the idea that physical same-sex relations were not only possible, but also likely to reduce the chance of the pathology believed to be associated with same-sex sexual relations. That Carpenter's and Merrill's house in Millthorpe became a place of pilgrimage might suggest that they were visited for information about how one might live as a Uranian. Carpenter's other work on the subject was involved in producing a taxonomy of Uranian types and explaining their place in the democratic world. It is as though he was teaching homosexuals to recognize and understand themselves for the first time. Of course, the first person any homosexual must 'come out' to is him or herself.

41. Edward Carpenter, *Homogenic Love* (Manchester: The Labour Press Society, 1894). This book was to be published as part of a series on *Sex-Love, Women* and *Marriage,* but George Allen and Unwin refused to take the series for fear of prosecution. It remains a delightful possibility that Carpenter gave Forster a copy of *Homogenic Love,* which is where most of the ideas in *The Intermediate Sex* were first minted.

42. Carpenter, *Homogenic Love,* p. 16.

43. Carpenter, *Homogenic Love,* p. 35.

Uranian Types and Uranian Roles

It may seem at best pedantic or at worst limiting to give a list of characteristics of Uranian types of men and women. Nowadays in the battle between essentialist and constructionist methods of reading sexuality as a list of attributes is self-confirming in the former case and always incomplete in the latter. But for want of information from any readily available source at the turn of the century, one cannot but wonder how liberating it must have been for people to find themselves described in detail in Carpenter's texts. Self-recognition is an important part of the formation of identity, and is by no means self-evident. From my own experience of finding out about myself, I know I would have benefited from reading Carpenter. Instead I consulted the word 'homosexual' in the *Encyclopaedia Britannica* and discovered that my desire for other men was an unnatural, pathological, sexual urge that was uncontrollable but shared by humans and the higher apes. The result of my research did not make me feel too good.

However, even for modern intermediate sexual people, for a gay man to read of himself that he is:

> the more normal type of the Uranian man, [and in whom] we find a man who, while possessing thoroughly masculine powers of mind and body, combines with them the tenderer and more emotional soul-nature of the woman – and sometimes to a remarkable degree. Such men, as said, are often muscular and well-built, and not distinguishable in exterior structure and the carriage of body from others of their own sex; but emotionally they are extremely complex, tender, sensitive, pitiful and loving, "full of storm and stress, of ferment and fluctuation" of the heart; the logical faculty may or may not, in their case, be well-developed, but intuition is always strong; like women they read characters at a glance, and know, without knowing how, what is passing in the minds of others; for nursing and waiting on the needs of others they have often a peculiar gift; at the bottom lies the artist-nature, with the artist's sensibility and perception. Such a one is often a dreamer, of brooding, reserved habits, often a musician, or a man of culture, courted in society, which nevertheless does not understand him – though sometimes a child of the people, without any culture, but almost always with a peculiar inborn refinement.[44]

What must have been so powerful to the late Victorian reader of this description is the idea that there may be 'normal' types of abnormal

44. IS, Chapter 2.

men. Furthermore, that in the intermediate sexual state, a man may look and act just like any other man, even if he feels entirely different. It must have been just such a realization that E.M. Forster had when he visited Carpenter and Merrill. And it is with just such misfits that Carpenter had his secular ministry, as he had also to 'normal' intermediate women in whom:

> we find a type in which the body is thoroughly feminine and gracious, with the rondure and fullness of the female form, and the continence and aptness of its movements, but in which the inner nature is to a great extent masculine; a temperament active, brave, originative, somewhat decisive, not too emotional; fond of out-door life, of games and sports, of science, politics, or even business; good at organisation, and well-pleased with positions of responsibility, sometimes indeed making an excellent and generous leader. Such a woman, it is easily seen, from her special combination of qualities, is often fitted for remarkable work, in professional life, or as manageress of institutions, or even as ruler of a country. Her love goes out to younger and more feminine natures than her own; it is a powerful passion, almost of heroic type, and capable of inspiring to great deeds; and when held duly in leash may sometimes become an invaluable force in the teaching and training of girl-hood, or in the creation of a school of thought or action among women. Many a Santa Clara, or abbess-founder of religious houses, has probably been a woman of this type; and in all times such women – not being bound to men by the ordinary ties – have been able to work the more freely for the interests of their sex, a cause to which their own temperament impels them to devote themselves *con amore*.[45]

The two passages are worth quoting in full because they speak for themselves in the joyful recognition they seem meant to bring to the turn of the century homosexual reader. They are not merely descriptions of types, but hortatory addresses designed to imbue the reader with a sense of self that was unavailable in other contemporary literature. While still a mixture of scientific and historical documents, the texts reach out with that same-sex look of recognition Carpenter described between his narrator and the stoker in the poem from *Towards Democracy* we saw above. It is as though he is saying of these pieces: if you can see yourself in this text it is because I am looking at you with desire.

45. IS, Chapter 2.

But if the Uranian could finally recognize him or herself for the first time in dynamic relationship with Carpenter's texts, what was also important was to see their role in society. In a post-Darwinian society, there had to be a reason for non-reproductive love and the Uranian temperament. Carpenter gives an extensive history of them in *Intermediate Types among Primitive Folk*, and develops the idea in *The Intermediate Sex*, especially in chapter 5 where he begins generally:

> the Uranian spirit may lead to something like a general enthusiasm of Humanity, and that the Uranian people may be destined to form the advance guard of that great movement which will one day transform the common life by substituting the bond of personal affection and compassion for the monetary, legal and other external ties which now control and confine society.[46]

Here, we see the idea of Carpenter's spiritual socialism, the soul being seen as the source of the external relations between people. But at the same time, the Marxian idea of history moving forward with an 'advance guard' partakes of the Darwinian idea that there has to be some reason for the inheritance of fit characteristics, and in particular when they are unlikely to be passed on directly by the person who has them. The idea might be equated with Richard Dawkins's *The Selfish Gene*, in which apparently altruistic behaviour is seen as a way to secure the survival of the gene pool, and of specific characteristics. Carpenter continues on this theme:

> on its ethical and social sides [the homogenic attachment, which we could equate with altruistic behaviour] is pregnant with meaning and has received at various times in history abundant justification. It certainly does not seem impossible to suppose that as the ordinary love has a special function in the propagation of the race, so the other has its special function in social and heroic work, and in the generation – not of bodily children – but of those children of the mind, the philosophical conceptions and ideals which transform our lives and those of society.[47]

The two areas in which Carpenter gives examples of Uranians taking care of the 'children of the mind' are still challenging to the modern homosexual today: the Army and the Church. Of the military use of the Uranian temperament, Carpenter once again blends the scientific with the historical argument:

46. IS, Chapter 5.
47. IS, Chapter 5.

The Uranian, though generally high-strung and sensitive, is by no means always dreamy. He is sometimes extraordinarily and unexpectedly practical; and such a man may, and often does, command a positive enthusiasm among his subordinates in a business organisation. The same is true of military organisation. As a rule the Uranian temperament (in the male) is not militant. War with its horrors and savagery is somewhat alien to the type. But here again there are exceptions; and in all times there have been great generals (like Alexander, Cæsar, Charles XII. of Sweden, or Frederick II. of Prussia – not to speak of more modern examples) with a powerful strain in them of the homogenic nature, and a wonderful capacity for organisation and command, which combined with their personal interest in, or attachment to, their troops, and the answering enthusiasm so elicited, have made their armies well-nigh invincible.[48]

In this passage, it is once again the hortatory mode that predominates. Carpenter seems keen both to show the Uranian where his special talents may lie, and also justify by example Uranians taking up positions in the military – whether they do or do not ask or tell.

In ministry, Carpenter seems equally keen to demonstrate the use of the special sensitivity of Uranians, due to their intermediate sexual nature that partakes of degrees of both masculinity and femininity:

no one else can possibly respond to and understand, as [Uranians] do, all the fluctuations and interactions of the masculine and feminine in human life …That the Uranians do stand out as helpers and guides, not only in matters of Education, but in affairs of love and marriage, is tolerably patent to all who know them. It is a common experience for them to be consulted now by the man, now by the woman, whose matrimonial conditions are uncongenial or disastrous – not generally because the consultants in the least perceive the Uranian nature, but because they instinctively feel that here is a strong sympathy with and understanding of their side of the question. In this way it is often the fate of the Uranian, himself unrecognised, to bring about happier times and a better comprehension of each other among those with whom he may have to deal. Also he often becomes the confidant of young things of either sex, who are caught in the tangles of love or passion, and know not where to turn for assistance.[49]

48. IS, Chapter 5.
49. IS, Chapter 5.

What is perhaps most sad here is that Carpenter cannot see that he is describing the role (or at least one role) of the priest, maybe because he could find no place for himself in the body of the Anglican Church. Nevertheless, demonstrating his commitment to the special sensitivity of the Uranian, Carpenter explores the reasons why they make good mediators. That the next two paragraphs quoted appear side by side in the *Intermediate Sex* is interesting. The first seems to suggest that Uranians are usually emotionally faithful to each other for long periods, but the second, with its rejection of jealousy shows that there is less emphasis on physical faithfulness among Uranian communities. The observation certainly fits with modern experience.

> Now in the Urning societies a certain freedom (though not complete, of course) exists. Underneath the surface of general Society, and consequently unaffected to any great degree by its laws and customs, alliances are formed and maintained, or modified or broken, more in accord with inner need than with outer pressure. Thus it happens that in these societies there are such opportunities to note and observe human grouping under conditions of freedom, as do not occur in the ordinary world. And the results are both interesting and encouraging. As a rule I think it may be said that the alliances are remarkably permanent. Instead of the wild "general post" which so many good people seem to expect in the event of law being relaxed, one finds (except of course in a few individual cases) that common sense and fidelity and a strong tendency to permanence prevail. In the ordinary world so far has doubt gone that many today disbelieve in a life-long free marriage. Yet among the Uranians such a thing is, one may almost say, common and well known; and there are certainly few among them who do not believe in its possibility.
>
> Great have been the debates, in all times and places, concerning Jealousy; and as to how far jealousy is natural and instinctive and universal, and how far it is the product of social opinion and the property sense, and so on. In ordinary marriage what may be called social and proprietary jealousy is undoubtedly a very great factor. But this kind of jealousy hardly appears or operates in the Urning societies. Thus we have an opportunity in these latter of observing conditions where only the natural and instinctive jealousy exists. This of course is present among the Urnings – sometimes rampant and violent, sometimes quiescent and vanishing almost to nil. It seems to depend almost entirely upon the individual; and we certainly learn that jealousy, though

frequent and widespread, is not an absolutely necessary accompaniment of love. There are cases of Uranians (whether men or women) who, though permanently allied, do not object to lesser friendships on either side – and there are cases of very decided objection. And we may conclude that something the same would be true (is true) of the ordinary Marriage, the property considerations being once removed. The tendency anyhow to establish a dual relation more or less fixed, is seen to be very strong among the Intermediates, and may be concluded to be equally strong among the more normal folk.[50]

To conclude, these paragraphs, to a greater or lesser extent, present the modern homosexual attitude to sexuality. It is the attitude that is again and again used against us by the homophobic elements of society. The fact that society is more and more taking on this type of attitude towards sexual relations, marriage and fidelity, makes homophobia less and less logical – if fear of something that cannot hurt you can ever be logical. Thus, it would not seem to be out of the question that twentieth-century society learned its sexual morality from Edward Carpenter, albeit indirectly, and is becoming more intermediate in character.

50. IS, Chapter 5.

Chapter 7

ALAN HOLLINGHURST: *THE SWIMMING-POOL LIBRARY* – THE BELLE ÉPOQUE OF A PRODIGAL

As with most of the other novels that are explored in this book, little has been written on Alan Hollinghurst except for his Booker Prize winning *The Line of Beauty* (2004), but what has been written on the *Swimming-Pool Library* (1988) concentrates on the Queer and Post-Colonial theories of interpretation. Papers by David Alderson, Thomas Dukes and Brenda Cooper,[1] for example, use recognizably Foucauldian strategies, and Dukes and Cooper read Eve Sedgwick's *Epistemology of the Closet* (1990) back onto Hollinghurst's earlier text.

While the readings these critics give are useful in showing the developments of Queer Theory, Gender Theory and Post Colonial Theory through the 1990s, only Alderson makes contextual references that intersect with the methodology of the present chapter. The title of his paper, 'Desire as Nostalgia', draws a useful link between sexuality and history, but his paper misprises the novel as being at heart homophobic. Writing of history of the laws on homosexuality, Alderson suggests:

> There is no question that Hollinghurst indicts the legal proscription of male same-sex desire – this is one of the more obvious "messages" of the novel – but that does not mean that the past is in every way denigrated: rather, the sexual liberties of the present are in many ways presented as a violation of older ideals.[2]

1. Thomas Dukes, 'Mappings of Secrecy and Disclosure, *The Swimming-Pool Library, The Closet*, and *The Empire*', *Journal of Homosexuality* 31 (1996): pp. 95–107.

Brenda Cooper, 'Snapshots of Postcolonial Masculinities: Alan Hollinghurst's *The Swimming-Pool Library* and Ben Okri's *The Famished Road*', in *The Journal of Commonwealth Literature* 34 (1999): pp. 135–57.

David Alderson, 'Desire as Nostalgia: The Novels of Alan Hollinghurst' in David Alderson and Linda Anderson (eds), *Territories of Desire in Queer Culture* (Manchester: Manchester University Press, 2000), pp. 29–48.

2. Alderson, 'Desire as Nostalgia', p. 33.

This passage demonstrates a belief that it is necessary to erase the past in order to start anew, and because Hollinghurst has not let go of the past, the novel's nostalgia questions his positive view of law reform. In this chapter I will argue that such a negative view of Hollinghurst is only possible because Alderson misunderstands the function of nostalgia, and falls for what I will call the homonormative argument. My definition of 'homonormativity', which will develop over this paper, is distinct from that of Lisa Duggan, who has defined the word as 'a politics that does not contest dominant heteronormative assumptions and institutions but upholds and sustains them.' What we shall see is that homonormativity is an oppositional force to heteronormativity, and one that we shall find to be as destructive to happiness as its better-known counterpart.[3]

For Alderson, Hollinghurst's nostalgia is to be too captivated by the frisson of elicit homosexual activity in a way which cannot be happy with the sexual freedom that resulted from law reform. For Alderson, only a wholehearted belief in prodigal sexual expression for all homosexuals will do. For Alderson Will's happy go lucky sexual activity, falling in and out of love with whomsoever he fancies while still having endless casual sexual encounters, is the norm for all happy homosexuals. This is what I would like to call the homonormative argument. For Alderson, the homonormative is set against the repressive times before law reform, the heteronormative, against which Queer Theory is arrayed. As we shall see, his argument results from a failure to contextualize the novel to 1983, the summer of Will Beckwith's 'belle époque' when excessive sexual activity seemed to have no comeback.

This chapter will demonstrate that Hollinghurst's novel argues that although homosexual law reform was good, in its context it was not an unalloyed success. Those who followed the homonormative argument forgot the old ideals of the heteronormative argument. Nor am I arguing that *The Swimming-Pool Library* makes the case that heteronormative repression was an unalloyed success. Rather it will appear that elements of both are necessary for the continued happiness of homosexual men, while to a greater or lesser extent, the purveyors of both the heteronormative and homonormative are guilty of destroying a generation of homosexual men. Furthermore,

3. See: http://www.colum.edu/Academics/Humanities_History_and_Social_Sciences/Cultural_Landscapes/Volume_I_Issue_3.php

Hollinghurst makes it clear in his novel that the survivors of the mistakes made by both the heteronormative and homonormative ought not to seek revenge upon those who led them astray, but should forgive and remember.

It might seem odd to suggest that *The Swimming-Pool Library* is an intensely moral novel, particularly when we are confronted by a soundbite from Hollinghurst himself stating 'I Do Not Make Moral Judgments'.[4] But it seems to me that Hollinghurst is writing in the tradition of the sermon, which has a 'message' (as Alderson also notes) and which has something to teach us. As Thomas Hastings and Geoffrey Elborn write, 'Since the advent of AIDS, the moral responsibility in writing of safe sex became obligatory, something Hollinghurst is conscious of in *A Folding Star*.'[5] I would argue that the same is true of *The Swimming-Pool Library*, though within the confines of what was conceivable in 1988.

Hollinghurst seems to give readers a prompt in this direction, and clearly undercuts readings of his novel that are based on literary theoretical concerns. Marxist readings of the type Hollinghurst was probably most aware of while at university studying English are laughed off in the quasi sado-masochistic encounter between an Argentinean, Gabriel and Will Beckwith, who narrates the novel, towards the end of the text. After risible sex where neither Gabriel nor Will can get beyond the stereotypes of master and earnest lover derived from pornographic movies, comes the following exchange:

> "I could whip you," he [Gabriel] suggested, "for what you did to my country in the war." He seemed to think this was a final expedient which might really appeal to me; and I had no doubt he could have provided a pretty fearsome lash from one of the items of his luggage.
>
> "I think that might be to take the sex and politics metaphor a bit too seriously, old chap," I said. And I could see the whole thing deteriorating into a scene from some poker-faced left-wing European film.[6]

It would seem, therefore, that we should also remember the lesson of this failure of theoretical procedures to come close to understanding

4. *The Guardian*, 21 October 2004. Interview title with Stephen Moss.

5. http://biography.jrank.org/pages/4432/Hollinghurst-Alan.html#ixzz0lN6yS0zX

6. Alan Hollinghurst, *The Swimming-Pool Library* (London: Penguin, 1989), p. 275. [Cited as SPL].

the *Swimming-Pool Library* when we read about the Corinthian sports Club, described thus:

> The ground floor has a severe manner, the Portland stone punctuated by green-painted metal-framed windows; but at the centre it gathers to a curvaceous, broken pedimented doorway surmounted by two finely developed figures – one pensively Negroid, the other inspiredly Caucasian – who hold between them a banner with the device "Men of all Nations".[7]

The statues seem to welcome the Post-Colonial theory of reading employed by Alderson, Dukes and Cooper. However, an inscription inside this same building which Will calls an 'underworld full of life, purpose and sexuality,'[8] which reads 'with brother clubs in all the major cities of the world,'[9] rips the disguise off the old Tottenham Court Road YMCA, and a more contextual reading emerges. The Young Men's Christian Association, founded in London in 1844 by George Williams, was by 1983, the date of the action of the novel, a worldwide federation with the goal of putting Christian principles into practice, achieved by developing 'a healthy spirit, mind, and body.' In an irony of what quickly became a conservative arm of both Nonconformist and Episcopalian Christianity, the YMCA also became a major locus of male homosexual activity. The fact is documented in a song 'YMCA', a 'disco-music' hit from 1979 for a group called The Village People. In the gay culture to which the song appealed, the song is easily understood as celebrating the YMCA's reputation as a popular place for finding sexually available men, and Will Beckwith, the protagonist of the *Swimming-Pool Library* is certainly active in finding sexual partners at the club throughout the novel.

In the same way the gymnasium suggests we can read the novel as an exploration of the curious relationship between the church and homosexuality in the twentieth century, Will's surname and his grandfather Lord Dennis Beckwith's political background suggest a further two contextual ways into the novel. It is no great leap from the name Beckwith to Beckford. The name Beckford was shared by two eighteenth-century Williams, father and son, along with grandfather Peter Beckford, founder of the family fortune based on Jamaican sugar, and thus on the slave trade. Despite their links with that vile trade,

7. SPL, p. 9.
8. SPL, p. 9.
9. SPL, p. 10.

Peter and William the father were pillars of society, the latter twice
being Lord Mayor of London, but William the son was a notorious
sexual adventurer and writer of sexually explicit prose[10] who spent a
good deal of his life exiled from England in Portugal. With William
Beckford junior's life and exile in mind, the relationship between
Lord Beckwith, a former Director of Public Prosecutions, and Will, a
sexual outlaw who is writing explicitly about his sexual adventures,
is brought to a crisis in the novel by the revelations of Lord Charles
Nantwich's diaries which tell of his imprisonment during the anti-
homosexual pogroms by the British police and government in the
1950s, which is another era of the novel.

Hollinghurst's novel layers twentieth-century homosexual history,
with one level being Will telling of his open and rampant sexual
adventuring, while at the same time spending the summer of 1983
reading Nantwich's private diaries. These in turn tell of Nantwich's
covert sexual adventures at school and university in the 1920s, which
continued throughout an undistinguished career in the foreign service
until his arrest for cottaging by a 'pretty policeman' in the 1950s, a
misfortune that resulted in his turn to philanthropy, setting up boys
clubs and finding jobs for fellow ex-convicts. Nantwich's stated
intention is that Will writes his biography, but the novel's denouement
puts this into question when Will discovers that his grandfather, Lord
Beckwith, as DPP, instigated the purge on homosexuals, in which
Lord Charles Nantwich was imprisoned on trumped-up charges
brought by a good looking young policeman who entrapped him in
a public toilet. It consequently becomes apparent that Nantwich has
asked Will to write the biography as some sort of justified revenge
in the pro-gay climate after homosexual law reform.

An easy reading of the novel would therefore be that Lord
Beckwith is the villain of the piece and Lord Charles Nantwich the
gay hero. Nantwich's revelation provides an irony for Will's proposed
biography: which he refuses to write since he is afraid he will be disin-
herited, but which he feels he ought to write since he is gay, proud
of it and wants to help his best friend James, a doctor, who has been
similarly arrested for cottaging by a 'pretty policeman.' But to give
a reading as a parallel between two historical periods would be to
diminish Hollinghurst's achievement, and to misprise the novel.

---

10. *Vathek* is Beckford's most reprinted tale.

Hollinghurst has written an historical fiction, but he nevertheless reminds us several times that we ought to be mindful of the facts of our past. For example, James, soothing Will after the revelation about his grandfather remarks:

> "Isn't there a blind spot ... for the period just before one was born? One knows about the Second World War, one knows about Suez, I suppose, but what people were actually getting up to in those years ... There's an empty, motiveless space until one appears on the scene. What do you know about your family anyway? There's such secretive organisms, I can't be doing with them."[11]

Following this clue, and filling in the characters in the history of homosexual law reform in Britain in the 1950s we can begin to discern the novel has a much wider irony. First of all, the character of Lord Charles Nantwich may be seen loosely to be based on Edward Douglas-Scott-Montagu, third Baron Beaulieu. We read in Nantwich's prison diary:

> My case, on account I suppose of my title. Had been the subject of more talk than most – though nothing like as much as that of Lord Montagu, which shows all the signs of iniquity and hypocrisy evident in the handling of my arrest and persecution.[12]

Public disquiet at Montagu's arrest and imprisonment in 1953 was pivotal in the setting up of the Wolfenden Committee, which was the start of homosexual law reform in Britain. Since the noble Lord is still alive, and did not write his own autobiography until 2001,[13] little was known about his case before that date. Hollinghurst's novel of 1989 might therefore be seen to be giving a fictional account of a real blind spot in British homosexual history. Furthermore, with James's arrest it might be read to suggest that further reform of the law was necessary in the 1980s.

At the end of Nantwich's prison diary Hollinghurst again mixes fact and fiction, and in the paragraph that names Lord Beckwith and accuses him, writes:

> I see in *The Times* today that Sir Denis Beckwith, following calls in the House for the reform of the sexual offence law, is to leave the DPP's office and take a peerage. Oddly typical of the British way of getting rid of troublemakers by moving them up – implying

11. SPL, p. 279.
12. SPL, p. 253.
13. *Wheels within Wheels* (London: Weidenfeld and Nicholson, 2001).

as it does too some reward for the appalling things he has done
… And he is a man I could hate, the one they call the inspiration
of this 'purge' as he calls it, this *crusade to eradicate male vice*.
Though one always treated him with contempt, he will now be
a powerful voice in the Lords, with others like Winterton and
Ammon – though beside their ninnyish rant he will be the more
powerful in his cultured, bureaucratic smoothness.[14]

Working from the real-life people, and fitting them with the protag-
onists of the novel, we find some startling historical anomalies
that speak against the idea that Lord Beckwith is simply a villain.
Winterton, that is, Edward Turnour, Earl Winterton and Baron
Turnour of Shillinglee, was a suave and cool operator out of the House
but a seasoned Minister in the House of Commons until his English
Barony sent him up to the Lords in 1952,[15] where he was venomous
and direct. In a Hansard report of a debate in the House of Lords
we can hear his voice modulating in an insulting manner that must
raise our gay hackles:

I have many contemporaries in age in your Lordships' House
and I think they will agree with me that, when we were young,
this thing was never mentioned in decent mixed society. In male
society, its votaries were contemptuously described by a good
old English cognomen which I cannot use in your Lordships'
House. To-day, at any rate, to my disgust, you hear young ladies,
themselves of irreproachable morality, say, half pityingly, half
facetiously, "Of course, he is a pansy: he cannot help it." Hostesses
have been known to say: "If we ask Bill we must ask Joe. You
see, he is peculiar and they are inseparable, like two lovers." All
this to me seems to show a serious moral declension, as does this
fact. Many of the great actors of the past, in the early days of this
century, were friends of mine. I knew Sir Herbert Beerbohm Tree,
Sir John Hare, Sir Cyril Maude and others. We were members
of the same club. It is inconceivable that they would have been
guilty of the disgusting offence of male importuning, or that the
theatrical public in those days would have treated the offence with
the leniency accorded to a well-known actor of the present day.
In my opinion, there has been a moral declension.[16]

14. SPL, p. 260.

15. His Earldom of Winterton was Irish so he did not renounce it when he
was voted into The Commons at the age of 22.

16. *HL Deb*, vol. 187 (May 1954): pp. 737–67. See the Hansard website:
http://hansard.millbanksystems.com/lords/1954/may/19/homosexual-
crime#S5LV0187P0_19540519_HOL_87

The references to actors suggest Winterton used mimicry and gives the yea to his 'rant' being 'ninnyish', but if this speech sounds rather weak today, it must be noted that it was met by an exclamation of 'Oh!' by Lord Onslow when it was delivered. Winterton's 'move for Papers,' that is his call for a debate in the Lords, was precipitate. At the time of the debate, 1954, the Home Secretary had just set up the Wolfenden Committee, the committee which saw the beginning of homosexual law reform, so in effect, by 'moving for Papers' the noble Lord Winterton was putting the cart before the horse and trying to quash the chance of law reform before it had been properly explored. Few Lords spoke in favour of reform in that debate, which mentions the public uneasiness at the imprisonment of Lord Montagu, one of their number, simply because the Committee had not yet reported. What Winterton was trying to do was to gainsay the Committee and hijack its report.

In this project, Winterton was avidly supported by Ammon, Charles George Ammon, Lord Ammon of Camberwell, who was the first Labour peer, created in 1945. He was a Wesleyan Minister known to have urged Prime Minister Clement Attlee to reform the morals of the younger Labour Members of Parliament. He spoke in the same debate to support the idea that the Lords should debate homosexual law reform before the committee reported.

> My Lords, first I should like to congratulate the noble Earl who introduced this Motion on the manner in which he dealt with a subject which can be, and is, extremely unpleasant. I disagree with the noble Lord who has just spoken; I feel it is appropriate that this question should be discussed before the Committee enter upon their inquiry, so that it can be seen in all its aspects. There is one point which I think has been rather overlooked, and that is that the great increase in this beastly crime has occurred in post-war years, following a time when there was a great emotional stir-up and a disregard of the moral and legal law, coupled with the mixing of numbers of our own people with others to whom this is not an offence. Nothing, I believe, shows more the moral decline that has occurred than the particular case to which reference has been made and about which I entirely disagree with the noble Lord who has just spoken. The way that case has been accepted, as it were, by the public is one of the most serious things that we have to face at the present time.[17]

17. *HL Deb*, vol. 187 (May 1954): pp. 737-67.

The Lord who had 'just spoken' was Lord Ritchie of Dundee, whose response, typical of those who spoke against Ammon and Winterton, was simply to welcome the Wolfenden Committee, and to point out that the idea of homosexual law reform had come from the church:

> It now seems clear that considerable sections of Church opinion favour some reexamination of the law; I am assured that many members of the Judicature are of like opinion; and I believe that the majority of the general public and, if the noble Earl will forgive me, especially of the younger generation, will welcome the decision of Her Majesty's Government to set up a Committee of Inquiry. For reasons which have already been indicated, I would make no attempt to answer in detail anything which the noble Earl has said, and I am sure that at a more appropriate time there will be many noble Lords, far more able than I am, who will do so. In the meantime, I should like to congratulate Her Majesty's Government upon the decision they have reached.[18]

Ritchie was a Scottish Presbyterian, and a reformer of the Stock Exchange, which seems to suggest that in the debate it is not possible to link a particular political or idealistic background with ideas for or against homosexual law reform.

In trying to find a real-life model for the character of Lord Beckwith, we find something looser than Nantwich's historical parallel. The Director of Public Prosecutions at the time of Charles Nantwich's prosecution was Sir Theobald Mathew (appointed in 1944 and died in post in 1962), who was well-known for his advocacy of the difference between public and private morals. Although his office had to take forward the prosecution of Penguin books for the publication of *Lady Chatterley's Lover*, he has been quoted as having disapproved of his department being placed in the position 'of being a censor of novels or other literary publications.'[19] His disposition would suggest he might be in favour of homosexual law reform, although I can find no evidence that persuades either way. There are no Hansard reports of his speeches since, as a civil servant, he did not sit in the House of Commons. Nor was he ennobled to get rid of him by 'moving him up.'

However, Sir David Maxwell Fyfe, who was appointed Home Secretary in October 1951, promised 'a new drive against male vice'

---

18. *HL Deb*, vol. 187 (May 1954): pp. 737–67.
19. See, *Oxford Dictionary of National Biography*.

that would 'rid England of this plague.'[20] Furthermore, in the role of Home Secretary, he was, indirectly, responsible for imprisoning Lord Montagu in 1954. Maxwell-Fyfe was ennobled in 1955, taking the title of Lord Kilmuir and the post of Lord Chancellor in the House of Lords, but nor was this a move to get rid of a troublemaker by moving him up. Rather, he continued as a minister in the conservative government, taking the title and post when he realized that he would not succeed Churchill as Prime Minister. Maxwell-Fyfe, though not the most reforming of Home Secretaries, as a direct result of the public disquiet at the imprisonment of Lord Montagu, set up the Wolfenden Committee in 1954, the committee that Winterton and Ammon were so active to destroy. Complicating matters, as Lord Kilmuir in 1955, he argued vehemently in the House of Lords against reform of the laws on homosexuality, while at the same time he probably knew that Sir John Wolfenden, whom he appointed chair of the committee he had set up, had a gay son, Jeremy.

In order to focus the conflicting ironies and the complex positions of his characters, Hollinghurst has thrown one further model into the mix. Halfway through the novel Will, his gay 'sister' James and Lord Beckwith sit in the directors' box at the Royal Opera House to see a performance of *Billy Budd* by Benjamin Britten. The opera explores the problem of making judicial decisions under pressure, and asks whether it is possible to be forgiven for making the wrong decision. The opera itself is based on a story by Herman Melville, *Billy Budd, Sailor: (An Inside Narrative)* [1924]. Billy is a pressed sailor, who though good at his job as foretopman, is pursued by his superior, John Claggart, the Master at Arms onboard their ship *Indomitable*, who eventually accuses him of mutiny.[21] The only reason given by Melville for Claggart's action is malice, and Claggart is carefully defined as 'naturally depraved'. As one of the scorpions in God's creation he therefore poses the question of the presence of evil in the world. Captain Vere interrogates Billy in the presence of Claggart, as he believes Billy to be innocent, and watches their expressions carefully for telltale signs. However, Billy has a stammer and rather than being able to answer Claggart with words, answers his accusation with a blow, which kills the Master at Arms. At a drumhead court Billy is

20. See, *Oxford Dictionary of National Biography*.
21. More correctly the ship is the *Bellipotent*, though the name is not corrected as Melville intended in the opera libretto.

found guilty and hanged. All aboard the *Indomitable* believe that Vere has been peremptory in holding the court, but his excuse is that it is soon after the Nore Mutiny,[22] and if one sailor is not punished for mutiny the others might rise up. The story is set in 1797 when the British fleet was at war with the French Directory, so Vere's worries are not altogether unaccountable in terms of their Republican context. Vere dies in a skirmish soon after the hanging with Billy's name on his lips.

In making an opera of Melville's story, Britten, Eric Crozier and E.M. Forster altered the emphasis so that it could also be read as an eternal triangle of sexual jealousy between Claggart, Vere and Billy. More importantly they altered the plot, adding Vere as an old man in a prologue and epilogue musing on his misdeed and hoping for forgiveness.

In Melville's version Vere is no doubt guilty of precipitate action and also of directing the three drumhead judges too strongly in favour of the death penalty, probably because he believed they would be too ready to acquit if he did not. Vere is both witness and counsel for the prosecution. He is the most intelligent man on his ship and confounds the three chosen to preside at the court. Nevertheless, when Billy shouts 'God Bless Captain Vere'[23] as he has the rope around his neck, and dies without muscular spasms, we are reminded of the two hours he and Vere spent in the cell while the captain told him the court's verdict. We are not told what was said but the shout and quiet death suggest that Billy has forgiven Vere.

In the opera, Britten makes a clearer musical gesture, giving the orchestra 34 equal chords in the key of F after Vere has told Billy of his fate. The chords are much discussed,[24] but the arguments are perhaps best summed up by Philip Brett:

22. The Spithead [15 April to 16 May 1797] and Nore Mutinies [began 12 May 1797] are the political background of Billy's hanging. The Spithead Mutiny was successful as the mutineers were asking for and got better pay and conditions. The Nore Mutiny failed as the mutineers had political ambitions in the French Revolutionary mould.

23. In the opera, Billy sings 'Starry Vere, God bless you!'

24. See, for example, Arnold Whittall, '"Twisted relations": Method and meaning in Britten's Billy Budd', *Cambridge Opera Journal* 2.2 (July 1990): pp. 145–71; Mervyn Cooke and Philip Reed, *Cambridge Opera Handbooks, Billy Budd* (Cambridge: Cambridge University Press, 1993); Clifford Hindley, 'Britten's Billy Budd: The "Interview Chords" Again', *The Musical Quarterly* 78.1 (Spring 1994): pp. 99–126; Barbara Johnson, 'Melville's Fist: The Execution of Billy

Possibly the strangest and most daring moment in the score is the interlude after the trial and Vere's aria ... It evidently expresses the intent of the chapter in which Melville tells nothing definite about what takes place when Vere communicates the verdict to Billy, but gives some hints and speculations which Britten and Forster worked up into the theme of salvation. What we hear is 34 clear, triadic chords, each of them harmonising a note of the F major triad, and each scored differently ... These chords lie at the heart of the musical treatment of the metaphysical overtones of Billy Budd.

They seem to suggest that in Platonic terms, the love of Ideal Beauty can lead to wisdom, knowledge and forgiveness; and that in Christian terms, goodness and love have the power to forgive. This moment of unalloyed optimism is perhaps the crux of the opera.[25]

The opera was first performed as part of the Festival of Britain in 1951, and then reworked by Britten, Forster and Crozier from four into two acts in 1960 for the Royal Opera House, the staging which Will, James and Lord Beckwith see. With its all male cast and re-envisioned homosexual plot, the opera must be understood as part of the struggle to bring the recommendations of the Wolfenden Report (1957) into law (1967). As such, I will argue that the scene at *Billy Budd* in Hollinghurst's novel is the crux of the *Swimming-Pool Library*. This is also the only scene in the novel for which we are given two perspectives. The first is from Will's narrative, the second is from James's diary, and he writes:

There *was* something rather consoling about the opera – struck by the mystery that comes from its not being about love but about goodness...[26]

In context with the history of Maxwell Fyfe and law reform, we might read Hollinghurst's use of the opera to suggest that Will ought to forgive his grandfather for imprisoning Charles Nantwich in the same way Billy Budd forgives Captain Vere. In the opera scene of the novel,

Budd' in *The Critical Difference: Essays in the Contemporary Rhetoric of Reading* (Baltimore, MD and London: Johns Hopkins University Press, 1985), pp. 79–109; Thomas J. Scorza, *In the Time Before Steamships: Billy Budd, the Limits of Politics, and Modernity* (Dekalb, IL: Northern Illinois University Press, 1979), pp. 183–89.

25. Philip Brett, 'Salvation at Sea: Billy Budd', in Christopher Palmer (ed.), *The Britten Companion* (London: Faber, 1984), pp. 142-55.

26. SPL, p. 218.

we shall see Lord Beckwith demonstrates his love for his grandson and acceptance of his friendship with James. Furthermore, as a politician in a democracy he may perhaps be excused his homophobia in the House of Lords since he was acting in respect of the demand for heteronormativity he believed the majority of people wanted in promoting the persecution of homosexuals. And as a sop to the other aspect of public outrage at the imprisonment of Lord Montagu, he did set up the Wolfenden Committee. What more, it might be argued, could he do? But the *Swimming-Pool Library* is not a personal tragedy about an ambivalent judgment made by a politician keen to stay in power despite the cost to his family.

Set in 1983, Will describes the scene, as 'the last summer of its kind there was ever to be … [a] belle époque.'[27] It was the last summer before Acquired Immune Deficiency Syndrome (AIDS). In that sense, the novel is a celebration of the brief period between the end of homophobic laws that brought with it the flowering of a gay lifestyle of prodigal sexuality and the onset of the disease that killed so many gay men my age and sent many other gay men running for the cover and eventual misery of heterosexual marriage. But who can read Will Beckwith's sexual prodigality now without wincing at the thought of the epidemic sexual license unwittingly caused?

Therefore, I will argue that to read the *Swimming-Pool Library* as a joyful memory of an ideal time is once again to diminish it. The novel's layering of the histories of Will Beckwith and Charles Nantwich demonstrates the function of nostalgia as an organizing principle of memory. As Will says when seeing Peter Pears in the audience of the performance of *Billy Budd*: 'It [is] an irresistible elegiac need for the tenderness of an England long past.'[28] Everything always seems to have been better in time past. In a telling speech just before Nantwich hands over the prison diary that informs Will about what his grandfather has done and so brings on the denouement, Lord Nantwich remembers his uncle Ned's homosexual history with rose-coloured spectacles:

> "Oh, it was unbelievably sexy – much more so than nowadays. I'm not against Gay Lib and all that, of course, William, but it has taken a lot of the fun out of it, a lot of the *frisson*. I think that the 1880s must have been an ideal time, with brothels full of off-duty

27. SPL, p. 3.
28. SPL, p. 122.

soldiers, and luscious young dukes chasing barrow-boys. Even the Twenties and Thirties, which were quite wild in their way, it was still underground, we operated on a constantly shifting code, and it was so extraordinarily moving and exciting when that spurt of recognition came, like the flare of a match!"[29]

But we do not live in the past. The human condition is to be beset by the hardships of the eternal present, however evil they are. What we are enjoined to remember is that these hardships will themselves eventually be tinted pink with the unfailing progress of history. And if there is a lesson to be learned from the *Swimming-Pool Library*, it is that when faced with an unaccountable evil such as AIDS, Billy Budd's love and goodness and forgiveness are better weapons than Claggart's revenge. But if this is so, we must account for the fact that revenge in the novel was Lord Charles Nantwich's goal.

If we are to look for a Vere, Claggart and Billy in the characters of the *Swimming-Pool Library*, in the same way we looked for real-life models, Vere seems readily to equate to Lord Beckwith for his wrong judgment. It ought therefore to be Nantwich who is our Billy, the man whom he condemned. But it is Will who plays the role of Billy, and is called to forgive his Vere, his grandfather at the end of the novel. This leaves the role of the motiveless bringer of evil, Claggart, to Lord Charles Nantwich, the gay hero.

If Lord Beckwith is an equivocal villain, Lord Nantwich is an equivocal hero. I shall argue that the other crucial part in the novel is that leading up to Will reading the prison diary, a diary which is so akin to *De Profundis*, Wilde's prison diary, even as far as both being written after finishing the prison sentences they concern. But the reference to Wilde is a blind since Charles Nantwich is no St. Oscar. As we shall see Nantwich has a dark side. He is a manipulator of vulnerable people, a pornographer and a blackmailer: as such he is a purveyor of pornographic films that enforce unquestioning adherence to the homonormative argument, and he is, in part, responsible for the lifestyle that allowed AIDS to spread so rapidly. He is also capable of acts of great kindness and generosity, and of great love. Nevertheless, for Will, he is another Vere who has made a wrong judgment, and he too is to be forgiven.

Finally, we shall return to the question about the role of the church in homosexual law reform, but leave the answer hanging in the air.

29. SPL, p. 247.

For there seems no reason why the church, which was so influential in initiating law reform, should continue to drag its feet in reforming itself. I shall argue, the metaphor of the YMCA is the key here. Only when the church accepts the situation that already exists, that there is an active and fine homosexual clergy, and takes neither the hard line against them of Lord Beckwith, nor believes that Lord Charles Nantwich will open the floodgates of sexual profligacy to mire its reputation if it accepts the sexuality of its clergy, can it be whole again. Only then might writers of a theological turn, such as Hollinghurst, be at peace with associating themselves again with the Church of England.

Can there be a lesser of two evils? Part 1: Lord Beckwith as Captain Vere

As we have seen, the question of Lord Beckwith's view on homosexual law reform in the 1950s is made complicated by his real-life role model, who both spoke against reform and set up the Wolfenden Committee. There can be little doubt of Lord Kilmuir's disinclination towards legalizing homosexuality in a speech in the Lords (1957):

> The argument has been put forward very forcibly in different forms from different quarters that for the State to remove the sanctions of the criminal law from homosexual behaviour, even between consenting adults in private, and even with the limitation mentioned by the most reverend Primate for the full offence, would be tantamount to suggesting that there is nothing socially harmful in such behaviour and would inevitably have as its consequence that young people would be encouraged to indulge in it, and that society would be corrupted. I believe that this is not an argument which can be lightly dismissed. For every genuine invert there are many perverted by money or desire for a fresh sensation, or by imitation. I admit that there must be a subjective element in that, but that is my conviction, after much study of the subject and after the consideration of crime as a whole which my years at the Home Office gave to me.[30]

Kilmuir's view of homosexuality causing the moral declension of society places him – as Hollinghurst places Lord Beckwith – in Earl Winterton's camp. But at the opera we encounter a very different man, a fond grandfather who obviously loves his gay grandson, whom he

---

30. *HL Deb*, vol. 206 (December 1957): pp. 753–832.

addresses as 'darling' several times: someone who might appoint as chair of the Wolfenden Committee a man who had a gay son. What is more, Lord Beckwith seems to view Will's association with James with a degree of approbation that allows them to discuss homosexuality, albeit confined within the safety of the opera plot. Nevertheless, it becomes obvious during the scene that Lord Beckwith's view of homosexuality has undergone a change from that which Will expects of him, and it would seem, because of the way Beckwith regards James and Will as a couple.

Will introduces himself as half of a couple when he meets James in the foyer:

> I was in a mood of atrocious egotism, brought on by what had turned out to be absolute adoration from Phil, but I seemed to sense, as I looked across the hall and up the long mirrored stairway, a further perspective, in which James and I were together as we had been in the past.[31]

The word 'perspective' carries a lot of weight in this passage and throughout the scene. In one perspective, Will is happy because he has just come from having sex with his current infatuation, Phil. In another he is happy because he is with James, who is a more appropriate companion at the opera. Will has given Phil no chance to show an interest in high culture, but more importantly, because this is not the first time the couple have been to the opera with Lord Beckwith, though James is not his sexual partner, he looks like either a lifelong friend, or a husband. Will also feels that James is a better fit with his grandfather:

> He had a pleasantly snobbish respect for our family; my grandfather was very fond of James, whom he saw as a humane and practical person, with charming manners and a keen interest in the arts.[32]

But if Will seems to understand his own perspective, which flickers between lover and husband, the second part of this quote shows he is not sure of his grandfather's. He does not know whether Lord Beckwith recognizes James as his gay grandson's partner, or as his straight grandson's future best man. In the same way, Will and Lord Beckwith have just had lunch in a restaurant, the *Crepuscule des Dieux*, that Will reads as gay but which Lord Beckwith might easily

31. SPL, p. 117.
32. SPL, p. 117.

read as being populated with grandfathers taking their grandsons out for a meal.

> ... [My grandfather] can't have been unaware of the discreetly homosexual style of the place, the waiters in long tails and white aprons, the rich older men treating their bored and flirtatious dolly-boys.[33]

Will simply cannot fathom his grandfather's perspective, so as the opera *Billy Budd* unfolds, he decides to believe that Lord Beckwith chooses not to read the homosexual plot which Britten, Crozier and Forster added to Melville's story.

> We must all have recognised it, though it would have had an importance, even an eloquence, to James and me that would have been quite lost on my grandfather. He had spent all his adult life in circles where good manners, lofty savoir-faire and plain callousness conspired to avoid any recognition that homosexuality even existed.[34]

From Will's perspective, therefore, when Lord Beckwith questions James on the content of the opera, it confirms his expectation that his grandfather will not countenance homosexuality:

> [Lord Beckwith to James] "I don't know if it's a piece you especially care for."
> "It's always more moving and impressive than you expect," James said, as so often echoing my own feelings; but our solidarity brought us to the edge of difficult terrain.[35]

James's response is important. It highlights the problem of expectation and how it is often foiled. Will's perspective is that only he and James can see the homosexual plot of *Billy Budd*, and that it is hidden to his grandfather. The extension of this perspective is that of open and closeted homosexuality, which Will expresses in a metaphor of the opera house itself:

> The three of us in our hot little box were trapped with this intensely British problem: the opera was, but wasn't gay, the two young gay friends on good behaviour, the mandarin patriarch giving nothing of his feelings away.[36]

33. SPL, p. 118.
34. SPL, p. 120.
35. SPL, p. 120.
36. SPL, p. 120.

The opera house is a place to 'see and be seen', and the opera box is a place of privilege and possible exposure: those who can afford to sit there are probably those who will feed the tabloid newspapers with gossip. What Hollinghurst further conveys here is the variety of perspectives an auditorium gives onto a show from which apparently everyone sees the same thing in different ways. What to Will is open homosexuality – he is dressed in a pyjama suit, accompanied by a male friend and they are watching a gay opera – may be misrecognized by Lord Beckwith as an evening out with his grandson and friend to see a naval story of wartime injustice. However, since James is at his side, Will enlarges on his perspective as though to begin the process of coming out to his grandfather:

> I decided to brave it, and said: "It's an odd piece, though, partly the sex thing, of course. Claggart's bit about beauty and handsomeness could win a prize for general ghastly creepiness. He's sort of coming out with it and not coming out with it at the same time."[37]

James's diary gives another perspective on Will's intervention:

> As usual one was all discipline & good manners – *unlike* Miss W., who smirked & simmered & did her "Great Lover" number.[38]

This is the only time in the novel that we get a glimpse of Will's demeanor and accent. James is only giving his perspective, and from other evidence in the novel it is one of hopeless devotion to Will, but Hollinghurst seems to suggest to us that even his voice gives Will away as camp and probably gay. James's information (when it comes four chapters later) makes Lord Beckwith's response to his grandson all the more surprising.

> My grandfather hesitated diplomatically before saying: "That was Forster's line actually. Though I don't think it is generally known."[39]

That is, he knows that the opera was intended by its librettist to tell a gay story. Lord Beckwith goes on:

> "[Forster] seemed satisfied with it, but there was something distinctly contrary about him. I was quite surprised when he openly criticized some of the music. Claggart's monologue in particular he thought was wrong. He wanted it much more …

37. SPL, p. 120.
38. SPL, p. 218.
39. SPL, p. 120.

open, and sexy, as Willy puts it. I think *soggy* was the word he used to describe Britten's music for it."[40]

Lord Beckwith's use of the terms 'open' and 'sexy' here indicate that he is well aware of the idea of open and closeted homosexuality. What is important too, is that Hollinghurst suggests that the information Lord Beckwith is passing on is a secret, as though he is outing Forster, a move which puts him in league with Will and James, and both comment on it. Will narrates:

> I thought this was extremely interesting, and my grandfather looked pleased, as if he had belatedly discovered the use of something he had dutifully been carrying about for years. I felt matters had subtly changed, and an admission had been made.[41]

James concurs, remembering in his diary the talk he had with Lord Beckwith about Forster:

> For the first time ever I got the feeling that he would like to talk about these things which are so difficult for people of his age and standing.[42]

If we read the novel simply as a personal irony based on Will's ignorance of his grandfather's monstrously homophobic statements in the House of Lords, this is the moment on which the novel hinges. Will has discovered, wrongly, that he should not have believed his grandfather is homophobic, and will be devastated by just how wrong he was when he reads Lord Charles Nantwich's prison diary. However, if we delve deeper into the source for Lord Beckwith's knowledge about Forster and the re-write of *Billy Budd* we find another perspective for the irony of the novel, which opens up another reading as a tragedy with Lord Beckwith at the centre.

The source for the information about Forster's antipathy to the music is his letter to Britten dated 1950, the time of the original composition, which reads:

> I want *passion* – love constricted, poisoned, but nevertheless *flowing* down its agonizing channel: a sexual discharge gone evil. Not *soggy* depression or growling remorse.[43]

40. SPL, p. 121, [My emphasis].
41. SPL, p. 121.
42. SPL, p. 218.
43. See Mervyn Cooke and Philip Reed, *Cambridge Opera Handbooks: Billy Budd* (Cambridge: Cambridge University Press, 1993), p. 27, [My emphasis].

There has been some debate about Forster's and Britten's different views of the acceptability of violence within a homosexual relationship which goes beyond the scope of this chapter. Eric Crozier wrote about the difficulties between Forster and Britten in the programme notes for the 1988 English National Opera production, though the letter had been published in 1983.[44] Whatever their early differences, Forster was happy to rejoin his fellow opera makers in making the 1960 revision. Cooke and Reed[45] reprint the transcript of a radio interview in the form of a conversation between Britten, E.M. Forster and Eric Crozier at the time they were revising the opera. In it they make the point that in the new two act version Vere is made the central character, and they believed that Melville had dishonoured him. More importantly, all three believe that Vere is a tragic figure, and this renders the aria he sings before the 34 chords discussed above the most important piece.

The lyrics of the aria describe Vere's feelings when he brings the verdict of the court to Billy:

> I accept their verdict. Death is the penalty for those who break the laws of earth. And I who am king of this fragment of earth, of this floating monarchy, have exacted death. But I have seen the divine judgment of men. I've seen iniquity overthrown. Cooped in this narrow cabin I have beheld the mystery of goodness. And I am afraid. Before what tribunal do I stand if I destroy goodness? The angel of God has struck and the angel must hang, through me. Beauty, handsomeness, goodness. It is for me to destroy you.
>
> I, Edward Fairfax Vere, Captain of the *Indomitable*, lost with all hands on the infinite sea. I am the messenger of death. How can he pardon me? How receive me?

Vere's tragedy is that he knows he has allowed a wrong judgment to be made in the case of Billy Budd. Lord Beckwith's tragedy exists on at least two levels: as a speaker against homosexual law reform in the House of Lords who has a gay grandson; and as the convener of the Wolfenden Committee which brought about reform too late to prevent the AIDS crisis.

On the first and personal level of his tragedy, Beckwith just cannot say the right thing to his grandson. His discourse on homosexuality falls back into long familiar formulae:

44. P.N. Furbank and Mary Lago (eds), *Selected Letters of E.M. Forster* (London: Collins, 1983).

45. Cooke and Reed, *Cambridge Opera Handbooks*, p. 26.

"... I do remember the first night of *Billy Budd*. Britten himself was in the pit, of course. It made a fairly big impression, though I remember opinion was divided about it. Many people understandably didn't altogether care for the Britten-Pears thing."[46]

The attempt at balance in evaluating the opera falls into homophobia, giving Will space to maintain his perspective that Lord Beckwith will never be able fully to accept him:

But then that "understandable" dislike of Britten and Pears – there was a little phrase I might myself take on through life, wanting to forget it or to disprove it the unpleasant truth it hinted at.[47]

Like Will, all we homosexuals have heard ourselves traduced politely by members of our own families. But to give the tragedy only to Lord Beckwith is to miss the point of the date of the novel, the summer of 1983, and the date of its composition, 1988. By drawing attention to the life-long relationship between Britten and Pears, Lord Beckwith highlights the fact that the only solution offered at the beginning of the crisis of AIDS was monogamy and marriage, the very legal form that was forbidden to the homosexual men who were most at risk from the disease.

As I suggested above, it is too easy to cast Lord Beckwith as the villain of the piece. His voice is the least heard as it is the voice of heteronormativity against which Queer Theory set itself. All we homosexuals need to condemn him is Charles Nantwich's final statement in the prison diary:

I have an image of him [Lord Beckwith] before me now in the courtroom at my sentencing, to which he had come out of pure vindictiveness, and of a handsome suaveté in the gallery, his flush and thrill of pride as I went down ...[48]

If, like Will, we accept this statement at face value we miss out that Hollinghurst has told us to be careful in our approach to history, for we know that Maxwell-Fyfe's role in homosexual law reform was equivocal. Whether or not he wished for it, he did set civil partnerships on track, which I for one did not believe would ever happen when I read the novel first in 1989.

46. SPL, pp. 120–21.
47. SPL, p. 121.
48. SPL, p. 260.

Nor is this to suggest that Maxwell Fyfe was correct in trying to interfere in the personal sexual choices of gay men. However, if we simply condemn Lord Beckwith, Hollinghurst has led us by the nose into forgetting to question our knee-jerk reactions against the supposedly heteronormative enforcers of sexual regulation and to accept without scruple the goodness of the homonormative argument represented by Lord Charles Nantwich.

Can there be a Lesser of Two Evils? Part 2: Lord Nantwich as John Claggart

Throughout the novel Nantwich presents himself as a victim: first of repressive laws against homosexuality that curbed him from freely following his sexuality, and second as a victim of the court of law that put him into prison for a year and destroyed his public respectability.

The first aspect of Nantwich's victimhood no doubt informed his patterns of sexual activity. Because his desires did not match social expectations, fulfilling them made it difficult for him to form a long-term sexual relationship with a man, although he does form a life-long asexual relationship with Taha, his servant. At school he learned intergenerational relationships that were necessarily cut short as the older boys left school (and were killed in the Great War). At university he learned inter-class sex, where he as a member of the aristocracy would only countenance a sexual relationship with a lower class man, though all his friends were homosexuals. Moving into public service, and fearing being arrested, he started visiting clubs for orgiastic sex[49] or cottaging for anonymous sexual encounters in public toilets. Poignantly on one occasion cottaging he meets an older Chauncey Brough with whom he had been in love while at university, and with whom he might have founded a marriage or a life-long partnership if it had been legal, that is possible within the heteronormative society which created laws, but, as we shall see, that type of relationship also falls outside the homonorm, the rules that govern homosexual society. If there is a message in this phase of the novel, it would seem to be that if homosexuals had been accepted

49. In fact the novel suggests, though the diary is not explicit on the matter, that Nantwich organized orgies in the basement room in his house that housed the roman pavement and the murals by Otto Henderson.

and allowed to form life-long relationships like those of Britten and Pears, then the only two forms of sexual relationships open to them, because of the repressive laws against them, would not have predominated and homosexuals might have learned the historical lesson from marriage that re-emerged at the beginning of the AIDS scare, when the novel was written, that lifelong monogamy was the only protection from sexually transmitted diseases.

In this way, I would argue, Hollinghurst throws out a challenge to readings such as Alderson's that accept Will's pattern of sexual activity as homonormal. Will's apparently natural sexual appetite has a particular history, even as far as Will's choice of sexual partners usually being black or lower class, which we see in Nantwich's history. More importantly, the promiscuous form of sexual behaviour he indulges in promotes the rapid transmission of sexually transmitted diseases. And promiscuity is the result of laws forbidding homosexual activity and precluding homosexual marriage. However, once those laws were repealed, it would seem Hollinghurst is asking why such homonormal behaviour should continue to dominate, when there are no longer any socially constructing forces to continue to promote it. And it is in this context that Will reads Nantwich's diary.

The attractiveness of Lord Charles Nantwich to this modern gay male reader is that his story is my history. But in being so, his life is also tinted rose pink with nostalgia, his and mine. Will catches this in the *Billy Budd* scene, when he notices Peter Pears in the audience:

> ... seeing him [Peter Pears] in the flesh I felt the whole occasion subtly transform, and the opera whose ambiguity we had carped at take on a kind of heroic or historic character under the witness of one of its creators. ... I reacted to him as if he were an operatic character – just as I entered with spurious, or purely aesthetic emotion into Charles Nantwich's war-time adolescence, and the loss of his shell-damaged idol in a Hertfordshire mental hospital.[50]

Faced with nostalgia, it is important to re-focus events as they really happened rather than as they appear in the diary, which was, as are all diaries, written with a reader in mind. In doing so, we shall find that Nantwich is another ambivalent character, but as is Will's experience in the quote above, it is difficult to discover where the fiction ends and the truth begins.

50. SPL, p. 122.

The context in which Will and we the readers read the diary, I would argue, is a careful set up so as to both reveal and mask Nantwich's character, and only thorough analysis will show that it is as equivocal as Lord Beckwith's. Before dropping the bombshell of the Prison Diary, Charles lulls Will into a false sense of security, with memories of a time of safety in his life when he is in university:

> As we sat on either side of the empty hearth, I was reminded of my Oxford tutorials, ... There was a similar maleness and candour to it, the scholarly inversion of the rules of the drawing room that allowed one to talk of sodomy and priapism as though one were really talking about something else. There was a similar toleration of silence.[51]

Charles has set up the equivalent of a casual sexual encounter with Will, a time when apparently gay men can finally be gay men with one another and be their true selves without pretence. But the life that Charles has shown Will already, he believes 'was like a life set to music.'[52] When pushed, even Nantwich ventures:

> There is a book in my life, but it's almost entirely to do with the imagination, and all that.[53]

In fact, Nantwich is so taken with the fluidity of prose that, like Britten, Crozier and Forster re-writing *Billy Budd*, he re-envisions his life as he writes about it. For example, he tells the story of his arrest in many different locations, and in several different ways.

> Perhaps the strangest dream I had was one which recalled the evening of my arrest ... What puzzled me was the variations on the actual events. Always the sequence began with my leaving a group of friends and walking off briskly and excitedly, as I had done, towards the cottage. Which cottage it was, however, altered from night to night, much as it did, of course in my actual routine. Sometimes I would make my way to the merry little Yorkshire Stingo, sometimes for the more dangerous shadowy darkness of Hill Place. Sometimes I would find myself going out to Hammersmith, intent on one of those picaresque 'Lyric' evenings: ...[54]

But if his life is all about the power of imagination to alter facts, what about the truth of Lord Beckwith being in court when he was

51. SPL, p. 238.
52. SPL, p. 240.
53. SPL, p. 240.
54. SPL, p. 250.

sentenced? If we revisit the quote at the end of the last section in this light, we must ask ourselves whether it is memory or a form of nostalgia:

> I have an image of him [Lord Beckwith] before me now in the courtroom at my sentencing, to which he had come out of pure vindictiveness, and of a handsome suaveté in the gallery, his flush and thrill of pride as I went down …[55]

This is the first time we see something of John Claggart in Nantwich. The use of the adjective 'handsome' recalls Claggart's accusation of Billy, 'Handsome is as handsome does,' which, in the story is the encounter after which his relentless pursuit begins, which will end in the death of both of them. In the moment of *'passion* – love constricted, poisoned, but nevertheless *flowing* down its agonizing channel,'[56] can Nantwich not resist Lord Beckwith's beauty? Maybe Nantwich perhaps wished that he had been at school with Dennis Beckwith, and that Beckwith had been then, like his grandson was now? If so he could get his own back on the man whom he imagined as his persecutor. He comes close to saying so in an earlier diary about his school life:

> Oh there will never again be a time of such freedom. It was the epitome of pleasure. When I sink back into the mood of these days, & then think of what happened afterwards, I am amazed. Those who were not killed are running the country & the empire, examples of righteousness, & each of them knowing they have done these unspeakable things.[57]

If such rampant homosexual activity was the standard in public schools of the 1920s, Nantwich's memory highlights and complicates the commonly held view that reform of the law on homosexuality was necessary as it was a blackmailer's charter. According to Nantwich's logic, those, like Denis Beckwith, who upheld the laws against homosexuality and were running the country, seem ripe for blackmailing for their collective homosexual past in school. But this is Nantwich's imaginative memory so we have to be careful. Was he being accurate about the sexual activity in all public schools? And was there another purpose for his implying the blackmailers' charter?

---

55. SPL, p. 260.
56. To re-quote Forster.
57. SPL, p. 113.

Once again we might turn to history to discover why homosexuals were thought to be easy targets of blackmail. In the recent past before the law reform debates from which I have quoted, the Cambridge Five case (1951), had brought the link into people's minds. Philby, Blunt, Burgess and Maclean were all homosexual or bisexual, and all had been blackmailed.[58] The facts of that case suggested that being homosexual opened people in sensitive political positions, or in positions vital to the safety of the nation, to blackmail.

Will discusses the matter with Lord Nantwich in relation to his service in the Sudan, and is told that homosexuality was only recently seen as a problem when one was in a position of trust serving one's nation. Nantwich says:

> "On the gay thing [...] they were completely untroubled – even to the extent of having a slight preference for it, in my opinion. Quite unlike all this modern nonsense about how we're security risks and what-have-you. They had the wit to see that we were prone to immense idealism and dedication ..."[59]

In the Lords' debate of 1954 to which I referred earlier, Earl Winterton disbelieves that the current laws on homosexuality amounted to a blackmailers' charter, however, Earl Jowitt, William Allen Jowitt, 1st Earl Jowitt, who had been Attorney General for Ramsay MacDonald (1929) and Lord Chancellor for Clement Attlee (1945) had evidence that it was, and had been at the time Nantwich was in the Foreign Service. This is also the same time that E.M. Forster was blackmailed when he was in the Indian service. Jowitt confirms that laws against homosexuality were indeed a blackmailers' charter:

> My Lords, this is an unpleasant subject. The noble Earl who has moved the Motion, was, of course, perfectly entitled to move it, notwithstanding the fact that a Committee is to be appointed. On the other hand, I think it is manifest that the fact that a Committee is to be appointed makes it necessary that we should be exceedingly careful in what we say. I merely want to indicate, briefly, some considerations which have come to my mind after rather long legal experience. It is twenty-five years ago that I became Attorney-General. I had had a large practice in the commercial court and knew little about crime and criminals. When I became Attorney-General, I became oppressed by the discovery that

58. See, Hereth Blacker, 'Philby Burgess and Maclean' in *Alcohol and Alcoholism* 4 (1969), pp. 128–31.

59. SPL, p. 241.

there was a much larger quantity of blackmail than I had ever realised. I have no figures – I do not suppose one can get figures in a case of this sort – but I can certainly charge my recollection to this extent. It is the fact – I do not know why it is the fact, but it is the fact – that at least 95 per cent of the cases of blackmail which came to my knowledge arose out of homosexuality, either between adult males or between adult males and boys. Why on earth it should be – and the noble Earl asked the question – that it attracts so much more blackmail, or did in those days, than did other vices, I do not know; but that certainly was the fact, and I think we have to bear it in mind.[60]

Faced with Jowitt's empirical evidence, we see that Nantwich's memory is affected either by nostalgia, dementia or that he is hiding something. Nantwich uses the possibility of his dementia as a 'blanking', and I would argue that his 'blanking' here is to lull Will into the belief that Nantwich could not himself be a blackmailer as he would more likely have been the subject of blackmail.

He [Nantwich] laughed hollowly; and then lapsed into a vacant half smile. I was trying to decide whether or not he was looking at me, whether this lull was an enigmatic part of our intercourse or merely one of Charles's unsignalled abstentions, a mental trading water, "blanking" he called it. I thought not for the first time, how odd it was to know so much about someone I didn't know. A person could only reveal himself as Charles had done to me in love or from a deliberate distance[61]

Charles Nantwich has, of course, not revealed nearly as much of himself as Will believes. And Will is, in fact, becoming one of those trapped by Nantwich's web of intrigue and influence. People, whom Will believes simply to be loyal to an old and charming man:

"I hope you see me as a true friend, Charles," I said with half-pretended hurt. "And I know people – white people – who are immensely loyal to you. Old Bill Hawkins or whatever he's called; and all these servants who fight over you."
"I do command loyalty," Charles assented.[62]

Charles certainly does command loyalty, but it is not in any sense a loyalty freely given. In a brief story about one of his black servants, Makepeace, Charles all but gives himself away.

60. *HL Deb*, vol. 187 (19 May 1954), pp. 737–67.
61. SPL, p. 240.
62. SPL, p. 243.

... Otto found him [Makepeace] a job in the Trocadero, where, as
it happened he knew the head barman who was very Scottish and
respectable *apparently*, but underneath, according to Otto, wore
ladies knickers. Scottie was terribly jealous, needless to say, when
I hit it off with his black Adonis. Later on, he even threatened to
expose me, but he changed his tune when I promised to tell all
about the knickers.[63]

The homosexual society in London of which Charles is speaking is
one where knowledge is power, and knowledge of sexuality is used
for blackmail, and even the homosexuals blackmail each other. Later
in the same conversation, Will is confronted by the fact that he too
was nearly blackmailed by Charles, but dismisses it because it seems
so unlikely. They are discussing the pornographic film that Charles,
seeming innocent, has taken Will to watch being made at Ronald
Staines's house. Will left early that afternoon without joining in the
action in front of the camera, but even as they talk, Will chooses not
to believe how close he came to being yet another target for Charles's
blackmail:

"I must say I was rather amazed by the whole affair – you know,
seeing half the staff of a famous London Club about to copulate
in front of the camera."
    "I think you'll find that a good many of them do it – though
not always on film, I agree. They're a close little team there at
Wicks's, and they like to do what I want. But then I got them all
their jobs," he [Nantwich] added. It was one of those moments
when I had the feeling, chilling and flustering at the same time,
that Charles was a dangerous man, a fixer and favouritiser. In
the world beyond school, though, perhaps one could have what
favourites one wanted.[64]

In this scene Hollinghurst seems to give the answer to his question
why homonormal behaviour did not disappear after law reform.
Homosexual society was not a group of isolated individuals who
could control their own destinies, rather it had become a web of inter-
connected power struggles, which like its heteronormal counterpart
had gained a life of its own. Just as the heteronormal demanded
heterosexual marriage, monetary success and fecundity as the signs
of happiness, so the homonormal demanded open relationships,

63. SPL, p. 244.
64. SPL, p. 245.

promiscuity and an argot by which homosexuals might recognize each other.[65] Neither the heteronormal nor homonormal could guarantee the happiness each promised, but both groups policed their own kind to ensure conformity, and each group attacked the other as an enemy as a way to maintain conformity.

Thus, Lord Denis Beckwith has made a spectacle of Lord Charles Nantwich, by putting him in gaol for what the heteronormal calls a crime, as it is a crime against its idea of normal. Likewise, Lord Charles Nantwich plots revenge on Lord Denis Beckwith, using a grandson as the sacrificial victim: the product of heteronormal fecundity. As such, his attack on Will bears the same hallmarks as John Claggart's apparently unprovoked attack on Billy Budd, apparently unprovoked because it follows a logic that is opposite to what might be expected by the heteronormal. In the opera, Claggart explains himself thus:

> Oh beauty, O handsomeness, goodness! Would that I never encountered you. Would that I lived in my own world always, in that depravity to which I was born. There I found peace of a sort, there I established an order, such as reigns in Hell. But alas, alas! The light shines in the darkness, and the darkness comprehends it and suffers. O beauty, O handsomeness, goodness! Would that I had never seen you!
>
> Having seen you, what choice remains to me? None, none! I am doomed to annihilate you, I am vowed to your destruction. I will wipe you off the face of the earth, off this tiny floating fragment of earth, off this ship where fortune has led you. First I will trouble your happiness. I will mutilate and silence the body where you dwell. It shall hang from the yard arm, it shall fall into the depths of the sea, and shall be as if nothing had been. No, you cannot escape! With hate and envy I am stronger than love.
>
> So may it be! O beauty, O handsomeness, goodness! You are surely in my power tonight. Nothing can defend you. Nothing! So may it be! For what hope remains if love can escape?
>
> If love still lives and grows, where I cannot enter, what hope is there in my own dark world for me? No! I cannot believe it! That was torment too keen.
>
> I, John Claggart, Master-at-arms upon the *Indomitable*, have you in my power, and I will destroy you.[66]

65. For the argot in SPL, see, p. 66, 'It was typical of the transsexual talk of the place ...'

66. Eric Crozier and E.M. Forster, *Billy Budd: Opera in Two Acts* (London: Hawkes, 1961) p. 46.

There is no doubt that the heteronormal order is dominant in the society of the novel, and probably still is in today's society. Thus, the heteronormal may call itself heaven while the homonormal calls itself hell. What each order cannot countenance is that it is an artificial construction that constricts and constrains the people who fall victim to its own version of 'normal'. Thus, where the novel might seem to be offering Will the stark choice between accepting his closeted status in the heteronormal world of his grandfather, or being 'free' in the homonomal world, Hollinghurst seems to be asking us to question both.

At the end of the novel we discover that Nantwich had not innocently taken Will to Staines's to watch the making of the pornographic film. After doing his time in Wormwood Scrubs, Nantwich makes his fortune as a pornographer, and is financing films for the increasing number of legal sex-cinemas, such as the one at which Will first has sex with Phil, and which sets off the possibility that Will has found his own life-long partner. At the Brutus Cinema, Will notices 'a spry little chap of sixty-five or so' who is one of the few punters who go to the cinema to watch the films rather than to engage in sex themselves. It is probably the only moment that Will notices how homonormal sex has been packaged and sold (we are told that the cinema costs five pounds to enter) and once again we see the power of nostalgia to enter into even the moments when we should be most present to ourselves. He wonders how the older man feels about the films:

> Could he look back to a time when he behaved like these glowing, thoughtless teenagers ... Or was this the image of a new society we had made where every desire could find its gratification?[67]

It is dangerous to think that this form of entertainment is new. Nantwich's homonormative empire demands that only more sexual gratification with more sexual partners can lead to happiness, not marriage and monogamy. And this brings into focus Will's infatuation with Phil, at the Brutus, Will has sex with Phil, whom he sees as the perfect sexual partner. Likewise after Will leaves the filming at Staines's house, without joining in, he goes home and has chaste sex with Phil. Phil's effect on Will is a direct challenge to the homonormal order from which Nantwich gains his power and makes

67. SPL, p. 51.

his money by selling the image of perpetual sexual gratification. Will's marriage to Phil would be difficult. Phil is not well educated, and would not fit as well as James into his family. It would take some effort on all sides (Will's, Phil's and their families) for it to work. But if it did work, as we might expect from a romance novel, the resultant marriage would be neither heteronormal (because it was between two men) nor homonormal (because it would be monogamous). What makes the marriage even more difficult is that Will discovers Phil having sex with Bill Hawkins/Shillibeer, and is jealous.[68] The moment is extremely important. The fact that Will can be jealous when Phil is only doing the same thing he is, seems counter-intuitive. But it seems as though Hollinghurst is suggesting to us that if Will can learn jealousy, maybe he can maintain a monogamous relationship with Phil. What is more, Will has noticed Bill waiting around the hotel where Phil works several times, and Bill has told him that he loves Phil. Given that Nantwich is a notorious 'fixer' and Bill owes him his job at the Boys' Club in Limehouse, it is not out of the question to argue that Nantwich has put Bill up to seducing Phil in a way that Will should discover them together,[69] in order that he might foil their marriage so the homonormative imperative is maintained. In that sense, the ragged end of the novel might challenge its readers with the question: should Will and Phil get together again? And the answer might come: Yes, they should get married and live happily ever after, like the 'couple of queens' Will saw while still at school, walking arm in arm that caused him

> ... a frisson of shock [which turned]into pleasure – not at them individually (they seemed hopelessly old and refined) but at the openness of the gesture. I wanted men to *walk out* together. I wanted a man to walk out *with*.[70]

Hollinghurst's message of monogamy and marriage is clear, and typical of the date at which it was written, when there was no treatment or cure for AIDS, and therefore only marriage and monogamy could be a solution to the crisis.

---

68. SPL, p. 276.

69. The scene is reminiscent of a Brighton divorce, where photographs were staged of the husband in flagrante delicto with a prostitute in a Brighton hotel to verify adultery on which the case might be made.

70. SPL, p. 194.

But now Nantwich seems a thorough-going monster, which he is not. I shall be brief here as it is not germane to my argument, but we see Nantwich's humanity in his relationship with Taha, the Sudanese boy whom he befriends, and loves, but as a father. The irony here is that the love of Nantwich's life is entirely given to a heterosexual man who cannot return his desire. It is ironic, since Nantwich's humanity is to accept his heterosexual adopted son, Taha, in the wholehearted way which Beckwith finds it difficult to accept his homosexual grandson, Will. Nantwich even allows Taha's wife to come to live with them in his house, whereas Beckwith would, we suppose find it difficult to accept even James, let alone Phil as Will's spouse. It is then a further irony that it is Nantwich whom we see grieve at the death of his child, Taha, killed in a racist attack, while Will survives a similar homophobic attack with only a broken nose and tooth to show for it.

The Church and Homosexuality

To bring us back to the YMCA and its being one of the places that AIDS spread so rapidly among gay men, it must be noted that though the association might have taken the retrograde position that AIDS was God's punishment for the immoral activity which took place unwittingly in its confines, the 'Y' has rather become one of the world leaders in the promotion of sexual health and the prevention of HIV/AIDS.

What is important to remember, however, is that when Hollinghurst was writing his novel there was no treatment or cure for the disease, and the only form of sexual health and prevention that could be promoted was marriage and monogamy, neither of which were viable in the regimes of Lord Beckwith or Lord Nantwich.

Melville left his most influential novel, *Billy Budd*, unfinished at his death in 1891, but he did so wittingly. He noted that:

> The symmetry of form attainable in pure fiction can not so readily be achieved in a narration essentially having less to do with fable than with fact. Truth uncompromisingly told will always have its ragged edges; hence the conclusion of such a narration is apt to be less finished than an architectural finial.[71]

71. http://etext.virginia.edu/etcbin/toccer-new2?id=MelBill.sgm&images= images/modeng&data=/texts/english/modeng/parsed&tag=public&part= 29&division=div1 (Accessed 6 April 2010).

Likewise, Hollinghurst has chosen to leave his (in my estimation) most influential novel with 'ragged edges.' We shall never know whether Will is infected with HIV, nor whether his love affair with Phil shall continue or lead to marriage, nor do we know whether Will shall write his book, nor whether James shall be successful in his court case against Colin, the 'pretty policeman'. Nor do we know whether Will shall forgive his grandfather, though he knows as we do, that if law reform had been quicker and more accepting, the AIDS epidemic might have been less severe and taken fewer of our friends in the flower of their youth. Nor do we know whether he will discover that Lord Nantwich was trying to blackmail him and may have been instrumental in trying to turn him away from Phil.

We must therefore read the *Swimming-Pool Library* as an irony poised between two evils: the evil of a repressive law and the evil of AIDS. And we have introduced two noble sources of evil in Will's prodigal belle époque: Lord Denis Beckwith and Lord Charles Nantwich.

Hollinghurst, receiving the Booker Prize in 2004 for his novel *The Line of Beauty*, headlined the article about his novel in *The Guardian*[72] 'I make no moral judgments'. As we have seen, he makes a serious moral judgment which was understandable in the context of 1988, that gay men ought to marry and be monogamous, which can either be seen as retrograde, or forward looking towards the civil partnerships now available to gay men. The guilt of the crisis of AIDS is squarely laid upon the heteronormative and homonormative legislators, but as in the opera *Billy Budd*, the story ends with a clear call for absolution:

> ... For I could have saved him. He knew it, even his shipmates knew it, though the earthly laws silenced them. O what have I done? But he has saved me, and blessed me, and the love that passes all understanding has come to me. I was lost on the infinite sea, but I've sighted a sail in the storm, the far-shining sail, and I am content. I've seen where she's bound for. There's a land where she'll anchor for ever.
>
> I am an old man now, and my mind can go back in peace.
>
> To that faraway summer of seventeen hundred and ninety seven, long ago now, years ago, centuries ago, when I Edward Fairfax Vere, commanded the *Indomitable*.[73]

72. See n. 3.

73. Eric Crozier and E.M. Forster, *Billy Budd: Opera in Two Acts* (London: Boosey and Hawkes, 1961), p. 63.

Will is the inheritor of two mistaken traditions, the heteronormative and homonormative, living his life on the cusp of AIDS, as Nantwich was living his life on the cusp of the Great War, and Beckwith on the cusp of the Second World War, each a time when so many men died. Will might curse his inheritance, or, if he is true to Billy Budd, he must forgive Lord Beckwith for what he has done to him: both in making him feel guilty about being a homosexual, and also in not changing the laws on homosexuality quickly enough to allow for the only conceivable way to stop the spread of the disease in 1988. Will must too, forgive Lord Nantwich for trying to blackmail him into writing the book by getting him to make a pornographic film and also for trying to cheat him out of the monogamous ending which was the best way he might survive in 1983. Only by forgiving the worldly forces that try to mould us according to their image can we be free of them and free to be what we want to be: as St Paul said to the Galatians, 'It is for freedom that Christ has set us free.'

Chapter 8

JEANETTE WINTERSON: *LIGHTHOUSEKEEPING* AND *THE POWERBOOK* – THE THEOLOGY OF THE BODY

It is not difficult to argue that Jeanette Winterson's early writing continues to express her early life experience in Christianity. In *Art Objects*, her non-fiction work about aesthetics, she tells us that *Sexing the Cherry* is a reading of T.S. Eliot's *Four Quartets*. Eliot's complex religious poems resound throughout Winterson's oeuvre in quotation and cadence. But on the other hand, one might reply to such a position that Winterson was consciously or unconsciously quoting favourite poetry in the same way she might be using the language of her own religious upbringing.

Caroline Gonda suggested to me that Jeanette Winterson's writing has always been marked by her childhood as a preacher. I believe she was suggesting that if I thought that I found an interest in the spiritual in it, it was not necessarily intentional, but a rhetorical strategy that was 'hard wired' into Winterson's psyche, and as such could not help but appear in her writing.

I lived with a Unitarian Minister for seventeen years, and Saturday nights were always times of dread, with 'Sermon-itis' as my normal weekend stricture, and I am the inheritor of a thousand arguments about what to preach. As a 'hard-wired' Anglican myself, I could not understand my partner's need to find something new to say each week. The cycle of texts from the Bible set for the Anglican calendar, I argued, cannot ever produce a cycle of identical sermons. Even if a sermon is read again and again, word for word, there is something new in the moment of utterance and also in the interpretation. But my partner's Unitarian heritage demanded something new to be said in a new way. The only cycle he understood was of the seasons, and the Spring and Autumn sermons were therefore the easiest, with their calls to wake again after slumber, or to prepare for the clarity that coldness brings. Death and birth were remembered at what I call Easter and Christmas. At the end of Saturday evening, when the sermon was tried out, however different our expectations, in terms of sermons, we found that there was a commonality to both my partner and me: they celebrate the high points of life, its seasons and its beginnings and endings.

But if these themes are common to sermons for two people who come from such different backgrounds of Christian based religions, then are these not also likely to be the themes of a novelist like Jeanette Winterson, who shares another, different, though similarly Christian based religious heritage. But does this mean that Winterson's novels can be called theological in any sense, or they simply about the common experience of seasons, beginnings and endings?

I begin with this story (and beginnings are always troubling to Winterson too) because it would seem that while Winterson's early work still holds an interest in religion and spirituality, the novels after *Written on the Body* do not. This chapter will attempt to show that although Winterson's language changes in *The PowerBook* and *Lighthousekeeping*, and is no longer so redolent of her Elim Pentecostal heritage as are *Oranges are Not the Only Fruit* or *The Passion* or *Sexing the Cherry*, it still entertains a vivid and lively interest in theological concerns. Of course, a Christian famously lapsed because of her sexuality, Winterson's new theology could no longer be recognizably Christian, but as she writes in 'Endless Possibilities', an explanatory section published at the end of the Harper Perennial edition of *Lighthousekeeping*:

> I believe that storytelling is a way of navigating our lives, and that to read ourselves in fiction is much more liberating than to read ourselves as fact. Facts are partial. Fiction is a more complete truth. If we read ourselves as narrative, we can change the story that we are. If we read ourselves as literal and fixed, we find we can change nothing.[1]

Ideas of 'liberation' and 'navigating our lives' chime strongly with the ends of Christian theology. The emphasis on 'fiction' and 'change-ability' do not. However, the central theme of *Lighthousekeeping* – the light that guides ships safely home – Winterson remembers can lie as well as lead to safety. What seems like a lighthouse beam could as well be a wreckers' bonfire. Thus, if Winterson is writing in what I hope to be allowed to call a loosely theological way, it will not look like

---

1. Jeanette Winterson, 'Endless Possibilities', in Jeanette Winterson, *Lighthousekeeping* (London: Harper Perennial, 2005), p. 20 [The end matter in this edition is paginated separately].

Anglican theology, nor will it look like the Elim Pentecostal preaching that she gave up. The chapter will argue that Winterson is engaged in theology because she writes in a way that promotes the idea that her words will lead directly to the things she describes.

> I love words and my aim is to use them precisely, so that they become an equivalent to the feeling. So the feeling can be spoken.[2]

As such, we might see Winterson's theological telos as being in the Garden of Eden with Adam and God, carefully mapping words onto things. God's truth being lost, is to be returned at the end of prophetic time through the intercession of language as the Saviour. Winterson has been accused of being arrogant, and to believe herself the Saviour, even of language, surpasses all. But the sexual politics of Eden could not be further from the purpose of a feminist, lesbian writer. And so we are reminded of the first quote from 'Endless Possibilities', that in the Eden story things were not fixed, and were not facts: because maybe the story of the garden was just that – a story. And that it is in stories that we may find the truth.

Language Games, Religious Language or Theology

If we read Winterson contextually as a writer of the late twentieth and early twenty-first century, she ought to be classed as postmodern, no longer concerned with a reference in the world or with truth, but with the surface and style, and also the fragmentation of language. What we have just read about her concern with fiction over factual truth ticks the first of these boxes. Her use of magic realism where a glass heart may be given and kept in a box might be used to tick the second box. Any cursory glance at her novels shows that she writes in fragments, which often do not follow chronologically, and this ticks the third box in my brief characterization of postmodern fiction. But Antje Lindenmeyer notices that in *Written on the Body*, Winterson rejects the nihilism of the postmodern because of her feminism.[3] The postmodern cuts up the grand narratives that claimed to contain the truth (science, religion, politics etc.) but feminists reacted against the cutting up of women into pieces because it replicated the cutting up of women by the grand narrative societies.

2. Winterson, 'Endless Possibilities', in *Lighthousekeeping*, p. 21.
3. Antje Lindenmeyer, 'Postmodern Concepts of the Body in Jeanette Winterson's *Written on the Body*', *Feminist Review* 63.1 (1999): pp. 48–63.

Lindenmeyer argues that feminism tends to focus on a coherent female body beset by its dissection in androcentric literature, and fights vividly against images such as Flaubert's of the woman cut-up even at her last rights in *Madam Bovary*:

> The priest rose to take the crucifix; then she stretched forward her neck as one who is athirst, and glueing her lips to the body of the Man-God, she pressed upon it with all her expiring strength the fullest kiss of love that she had ever given. Then he recited the *Misereatur* and the *Indulgentiam*, dipped his right thumb in the oil, and began to give extreme unction. First upon the eyes, that had so coveted all worldly pomp; then upon the nostrils, that had been greedy of the warm breeze and amorous odours; then upon the mouth, that had uttered lies, that had curled with pride and cried out in lewdness; then upon the hands that had delighted in sensual touches; and finally upon the soles of the feet, so swift of yore, when she was running to satisfy her desires, and that would now walk no more.[4]

Faced with the representation of the whole male Christ, Emma Bovary is cut up into lips, eyes, nostrils, mouth and feet. Her desires for a man more interesting than her bovine husband are called lewd and sensual. Emma is outcast from the church, and can only be brought back under its aegis by dying. She cannot enter the church whole, except as a corpse. Such is the fate of the woman beset by heteronormal expectations of marriage, and likewise is the criticism that feminism has of postmodernism, that it carries out similar cutting up of women's texts. In *Written on the Body*, Lindenmeyer argues, Winterson offers constructive ways of theorizing the female body within a postmodern framework, because it is shaped by concepts of wholeness and fragmentation at the same time. Thus, when the unnamed protagonist and Louise meet, there is no objectification of the other by the one, in that one becomes the desired and the other desiring, but rather:

> As the love between the narrator and Louise deepens, the fleeting contact of the body parts is replaced by a feeling of total fusion … Winterson's metaphor is choice for the total fusion is molecular docking.[5]

4. http://www.bibliomania.com/0/0/136/1955/frameset.html (Accessed 15 April 2006).
5. Lindenmeyer, 'Postmodern Concepts', p. 53.

It is in the combination of metaphors of fusion in love and science, which holds the double key to Winterson in this reading. The discourse of love sees the two as whole people who experience strong attraction for one another, while the discourse of science offers a method of understanding how such feelings can come about in the physical world. As Lindenmeyer points out:

> The problem with both traditional medicine and postmodern theories, the disintegration of the body into single parts, is addressed by a concept of the body that stresses the interaction of parts within or between two bodies.[6]

Thus the body parts are seen as integral in the same way that the two bodies are seen to be integrated: the fragments make up the whole bodies and the two bodies another greater whole.

Andrea Harris, explains the process in the same novel through the metaphor of merging with the other in sexual congress as central to Winterson's use of language. Harris writes:

> Writing becomes a manifestation of passionate sexual love that enables the lover to cross the boundary between self and other and thereby fully inhabit the other's being. ... Through [writing] the flesh, typically considered the marker of the boundary between the self and other, becomes the gateway to immersion in the other's being.[7]

Here, Harris has moved forward from Lindenmeyer's position on metaphors of love and science, and instead ties the process of language itself to the body and the body in relation to others. Writing on the body, in the sense of writing *about* the body, becomes writing on the body in the sense of *inscribing* on the surface of the body. The ecstatic caress of a lover on the body of their beloved can thereby be caught in language *about* the caress.

But to no little extent, this is to equate the orgasm with meaning in language, and although this may work on the level of the story, when the reader is to be accounted for, the theory falls prey to the question of pornography. If you read something that arouses you sexually then you *are* aroused sexually, ergo, language has had its effect. But I believe this is to belittle Winterson as a writer. Surely she is no mere purveyor of high-class pornography?

6. Lindenmeyer, 'Postmodern Concepts', p. 55.
7. Andrea L. Harris, *Other Sexes: Rewriting Difference from Woolf to Winterson* (Albany, NY: SUNY Press, 2000), p. 129.

Marian Eide argues that Winterson's constant use of religious language is paramount in the metaphor of how language completes meaning and avoids falling into pornography. She writes that 'Winterson's narratives of romantic love and sexual passion seek in a different form the experience of the perfect union with another demonstrated in the ecstatic practices of charismatic Christianity.'[8] In a close reading of *The Passion*, Eide suggests that Winterson equates 'sexual passion in the language ... with the understanding of a parallel and informing spirituality and compassion.'[9] In so doing, Eide's reading makes a connection between the practice and language of Evangelical love for Christ and sexual love (and especially same-sex love). In a careful side-step from the 'merge-queens' that typify popular discourse about lesbian love (and by inference, if not by name, Lindenmeyer and Harris) Eide draws on Winterson's own declared interest in boundaries[10] and goes on to argue that *The Passion* marks a category shift in Winterson's thinking, in which 'the sublime expression of union in charismatic Christianity ... prepared Winterson to represent the shift in boundaries and experiences of exalted union in sexual passion.'[11] That is to say, the 'Passion' of the title represents both the Passion of Christ and the sexual passion of the heroine Villanelle. Likewise, St. Paul's admonishment 'It is better to marry than to burn' (1 Corinthians 7: 9) encompasses for Winterson both burning in hell as well as burning with passionate love. Hereby, the charge of pornography is avoided.

In a useful turn, the end of Eide's paper argues that Winterson's early novels draw attention to many Churches' unequal treatment of homosexuals set against Christ's demand to show compassion for the outcast. But the power of the irony is lost in Eide's reliance upon the claim that Winterson's language is a shifting in boundary from the prayer of Charismatic Christianity to the pleas of impassioned lovers. Although the language may sound the same, anyone praying knows what they are doing, and that it is radically different from making love, however impassioned either process. We all know the two are different, although the words 'which' and 'witch' may sound

---

8. Marian Eide, 'Passionate Gods and Desiring Women: Jeanette Winterson, Faith and Sexuality', *International Journal of Sexuality and Gender Studies* 6.4 (October 2001): pp. 279–91, abstract.

9. Eide, 'Passionate Gods and Desiring Women', p. 280.

10. See Jeanette Winterson, *The PowerBook* (London: Vintage, 2010).

11. Eide, 'Passionate Gods and Desiring Women', p. 284.

the same, it does not mean that we cannot tell the difference between them when we utter them.

For this reason I would argue that Eide's position on Winterson describes only the religious use of language. She has described its use in an equivocal way, but disregards the fact that language users know what they intend when they are uttering language, and hover lightly at the moment of language flickering between different meanings before landing firmly on one side or the other. Even if Winterson intended to be equivocal, as it will be argued below, this does not demonstrate an argument in favour of the religious reading over the pornographic after her ejection from the Elim Pentecostal Church. Moreover, the suggestion that Winterson is criticizing the Church in general for its casting out of homosexuals more clearly argues that Winterson is set against religion and its uses of language.

What all three of these critics have in common is their interest in how language finally means what it says – the Eden story[12] – but from a feminist perspective. Probably the best general theorization of their project is the work of Luce Irigaray, which is never mentioned directly, but alluded to over and over again.[13] Irigaray was ejected from the Lacan Institute because of her early work, which explores a female anatomical metaphor for language set up against the male metaphor of Lacan. Lacan uses the metaphor of the phallus as central to understanding meaning. The turgidity of the phallus, he argues, is the unitary meaning of a sentence, idea or book. However, words are equivocal and pull in different directions to different construc- tions – an attack on the turgid phallus. Thus, Lacan suggests the disregarding of 'useless' meanings that do not add to the unitary meaning. Language is thereby seen as coherent and teleological: but at the expense of the equivocal nature of words.

Irigaray theorizes from the metaphor of the vagina's 'lip(s)' which are not separated into two 'one(s)'. The metaphor is used in several ways. Irigaray suggests that you cannot separate off unitary meanings from words that are equivocal by nature, thus, she suggests that there cannot be a unitary meaning in a text. She also points out that words do not mean separately from the things they describe. Like the lips of the vagina they are constantly in touch with the thing(s) they describe.

---

12. How we know which words go with which things.

13. In particular, *This Sex Which Is Not One* (trans. Catherine Porter and Carolyn Burke; Ithaca NY: Cornell University Press, 1985).

Thus there is no question of choosing the best unitary meaning of a text since all meanings of the text are equally valid.

What these readings of Lacan and Irigaray introduce, is the notion that sexuality in a text may not be a veil for pornography, but rather a useful way of explaining how texts mean. Thus, when we read Winterson's stories of love, we need to be awake to the fact that they may on one level be about love, at another about religion, and at another about sexuality – or any other meaning that the equivocal words point towards. Moreover, their multi-valence suggests they are also likely to be about how texts mean.

The Language of Love

In *Lighthousekeeping* Winterson notes the radical shift in epistemology between Biblical and Darwinian times, the former understood the world in terms of stories which challenge belief, and the latter claimed to be scientific, that is, a factual statement of how things are. However, what is important is that although the old theological explanation is seen as hopelessly inadequate, she also sees scientific accounts as ultimately unsuccessful.

> In the fossil record of our existence, there is no trace of love. You cannot find it held in the earth's crust, waiting to be discovered. The long bones of our ancestors show nothing of their hearts … Darwin and his fellow scientists still had no idea how old the earth and her life forms might be, but they knew they were unimaginably older that Biblical time, which dated the earth to 4,000 years. Now time had to be understood mathematically. It could no longer be imagined as a series of lifetimes, reeled off like a genealogy from the Book of Genesis. The distances were immense… The simple image is complex. My heart is a muscle with four valves. It beats 101,000 times a day, it pumps eight pints of blood around my body. Science can bypass it, but I can't. I say I give it to you, but I never do.[14]

Read from an Irigarayan perspective, the love that Winterson describes as absent may be understood as meaning: what is life when it is reduced to facts about long bones? We live in relation to other people, and it is those relationships that give life meaning. What is time when it is reduced to a mathematical calculation? We live

14. Winterson, *Lighthousekeeping*, pp. 170–71.

expectantly, hoping for something to happen, and this gives time meaning. The Bible gave life meaning in terms of Adam and Eve and the loss of Eden, and though science has provided a new method of describing the world and its genesis, it has scorched the meaning off the bones of fact. Furthermore, both the Bible and the scientists reduce meaning to the unitary, whereas for Irigaray and Winterson, it is not. In the Bible the meaning of life was the return to God through the intercession of Christ. For the scientist, inductive empiricism posited a single story which it approached asymptotically. For Winterson, 'I say I give you my heart, but I never do' holds the idea that the giving of my heart is a metaphor (the carrier of meaning) for love, but it is undecideable whether the 'I' is lying about the metaphor of being in love, since the heart as a lump of flesh is never actually given, *and* the 'I' may simply be lying about being capable of loving.

It is the contention of the rest of this chapter that Winterson is trying to achieve what science has failed to do: to describe meaning, the essential experience of being human, for which biblical language is now inadequate, but which scientific language cannot contain either. I shall argue that Winterson achieves it with her use of the language of love. And that it is neither the language of postmodernism describing something that does not exist outside language, nor is it the recycled language of religion, but that it is her own theology of the body.

We can see the fully developed theology of the body in *Lighthousekeeping*, which Winterson describes as the beginning of a new cycle in her writing.[15] The novel is the story of Babel Dark, a nineteenth-century evangelical minister, and Silver, a twentieth-century woman in love. Dark's name suggests his inability to use language or see correctly, and his discovery of the cave of fossils is his link with Darwinism. He believes he has the key to all knowledge, but all he has is the remnants of dead life. Silver was brought up in a lighthouse, and knows that a beam of light (a metaphor for words) may lead a ship to safety or danger, may tell the truth or may lie. But more than this, she knows that sometimes, the beam of light, words, may occasionally lead to full understanding, to communication:

> We roam the labyrinths of our experience, sometimes trying to find the way out, sometimes trying to find the centre, always a bit lost unless some unexpected insight shows us the way.

15. Winterson, 'Endless Possibilities', in *Lighthousekeeping*, p. 18.

> Such insights are by their nature imaginative, heightened, revelatory. They are not the everyday accumulation of facts.[16]

The idea of being in a heightened state and receiving revelation, is language borrowed from religion. The difficulty is therefore in knowing which experiences are revelations, and which are not. In biblical religion, revelation is that which is already written in the book: and all one need do is find the correct place in the genealogy of Genesis. In Darwinian terms, the revelation is seen in terms of its coherence with the logic of natural selection, but as Winterson points out, the fossil record does not show the conscious intentions of the dead preserved in whatever medium. If we perform an archaeology of meaning we do not find bone structures that can be measured, categorized and processed mathematically, but rather we find:

> The Talmudic layering of story onto story, map onto map, [which] multiplies possibilities.[17]

When we look back at earlier stories they should become more and more simple as do anatomical structures. But what we find is more and more possibilities: in fact as many complexities as exist in any story told nowadays. In this way, Winterson suggests there cannot be a scientific study of meaning that looks for the simple former structures and records how the new is built upon the old. Rather, she offers a new metaphor of the growth and change of language:

> This is a world inventing itself. Daily new land masses form and then submerge. New continents of thought break off from the mainland.[18]

It is this that I would like to call the Theology of the Body, and we can see its development in *The PowerBook*.

The Postmodern, the Scientific and the Religious

Winterson begins *The PowerBook* by suggesting that she is going into the postmodern beyond the body: 'Take off your clothes. Take off your body. Hang them up behind the door. Tonight we can go deeper than disguise.'[19] The frame story of the book is an internet story-teller

16. Winterson, 'Endless Possibilities', in *Lighthousekeeping*, p. 22.
17. Winterson, *The PowerBook*, p. 54.
18. Winterson, *The PowerBook*, p. 63.
19. Winterson, *The PowerBook*, p. 4.

who offers 'freedom for one night' for her clients. Winterson uses the frame to explore the inevitable truth about the internet that one can be whoever one wants to be. The internet is the ultimate role-playing game, where the final disguise is the absence of the body of the player:

> This is where the story starts. Here, in the long lines of laptop DNA. Here we take your chromosomes, twenty-three pairs, and alter your height, eyes, teeth, sex. This is an invented world. You can be free for one night.[20]

However, the device allows Winterson to question the nihilism of the postmodern. Is language with its depthlessness all there really is? Or as Winterson puts the same question in terms of the reality of the body:

> What if the body is the disguise? What if skin, bone, liver, veins are the things I use to hide myself? I have put them on and I cannot take them off. Does this trap me or free me?[21]

The postmodern game of being someone else online suggests that there is nothing but language, and that the postmodern must be right. But the question is begged about the location of the 'me' which uses language. Is it in 'my' body, or is 'my body' a disguise for 'me'? If 'my body' is a disguise, then it can be changed at will, in the way the role-playing in Internet conversation allows. The final sentence in the quote above, however, begs a further question. When 'I' realize that the internet allows me to put on and take off characteristics, do 'I' become free to be that different person in a different body? Or does the realization demonstrate that 'I' am circumscribed by 'my' actual body, because 'I' cannot take it off?

Answering this basic postmodern dilemma, Winterson tells the story of the city of Antioch, the city that flourished with the bringing of water along an aqueduct that was destroyed by the Turks. The captain of the ship says at one moment that 'Only the body lives and dies' as he throws the half eaten carcass of a chicken overboard, suggesting the postmodern position that the body is less important than the flow of eternal micro-narratives. But the captain's position changes radically as his retelling of the destruction of Antioch

---

20. Winterson, *The PowerBook*, p. 4.
21. Winterson, *The PowerBook*, p. 15.

reminds him of the fragility of the body – the source and home of the language that is necessary for thinking:

> Nobody thinks without a cup of water. The dreams of the dying cannot be irrigated. The world ends, and you with it, to retreat into the mind of God.[22]

However strongly postmodernism puts forward the logic that language has no referent (even the language of 'me', 'myself' and 'I') and however strongly postmodernism argues that there is no authentic thinker at its core, it is beset by the problem of the requirements of the body for food and water. Like the reverse of Ezekiel's parable of the valley of dry bones, the body needs to support its own life to have the very thoughts that are the stuff of the postmodern theorist, and without life, the body is dry bone, parched sinew and desiccated skin. Language needs a body to think it. The inevitable fact of dying, furthermore, sets the body into a theological narrative because all life must and does end in death. The question of what happens after death is a matter of faith, and so the Grand Narrative of religion returns in the quote above, unannounced and unavoidable, but a question that has to be addressed.

The metaphor of writing on a computer also allows Winterson to address and critique the limited logic of science and its answers to the theological question posed by the inevitable facts and narrative of the body. The machinic nature of a computer, with its language of binary numbers that does not have a living body to support its production of language would seem to suggest that texts created within its medium must be as predictable as its machine code. An original story created by an artificial intelligence programme should, in some sense, be predictable with reference to the programme; an idea which suggests that writing made by human writers should likewise be predictable with reference to the human that produced the text. In this way, the human writer's knowledge of their impending death will give all narratives a sense of inevitable ending: a product of the mode of production of the text of the narrative:

> There is always the danger of automatic writing ... At a certain point the story gathers momentum. It convinces itself, and does its best to convince you that the end in sight is the only possible outcome.[23]

22. Winterson, *The PowerBook*, p. 16.
23. Winterson, *The PowerBook*, p. 53.

Reducing human logic to machine logic would suggest that all stories ought to follow a fixed pattern: they all have a beginning (birth), a middle (life) and an ending (death). But the word 'automatic' can either refer to the process of typing on the automated computer, or the process of inauthentic writing, the process of repeating the same old story over and over again, an automatism which *may be* avoided by the human writer.

> I was typing on my laptop, trying to move this story on, trying to avoid endings, trying to collide the real and the imaginary worlds, trying to be sure which is which.[24]

In this sentence, we see that Winterson highlights the fact that readers (and writers) know the difference between authentic stories and inauthentic stories. If she writes a 'real' story it will do something other than follow the predictable pattern of beginning, middle, end. It will go beyond the machine logic and the apparently inevitable human logic of birth life and death. It will address the theological question of what happens after death that must have arisen from outside human experience of human life.

In the same way, the metaphor of Internet conversations on the computer also brings certain knowledge of other human lives:

> When I sit at my computer ... I talk to people whose identity I cannot prove.[25]

While computer role-playing draws attention to the fact that it is impossible to tell whether one is dealing with a real person or an assumed persona, because one can do likewise oneself, it also draws attention to the fact that even if the computer persona *is* imaginary, then it was invented by a real person, even if it was invented by a programme: the programme was invented by a real person. Science, in its attempt to remove the human from the equation, places the human back at the centre of things as it is a human endeavour. Winterson's sentences, such as the one above, short circuit science, by both following and breaking the law of non-contradiction. It is an unsettling strategy akin to Russell's antinomy, but where Russell takes us no further than to notice the edges of logic, Winterson takes us further into theology.

24. Winterson, *The PowerBook*, p. 93.
25. Winterson, *The PowerBook*, p. 94.

Lastly, let us explore briefly how Winterson addresses the limited ideas of organized religion. This is not new in her writing, and in *The PowerBook* takes the simplistic form of The Muck House.[26] The holy family of the Muck House are limited by a self-imposed space, the Muck House itself, from which they escape only once a year to the Wilderness, which acts as their Promised Land. Their language is limited, by choice, as is their access to the buried treasure of the Promised Land. The narrator's mother tells her that the treasure exists, but she knows it only because she has seen it on a map. This is the belief structure of prophetic time, where the prophecy is the map, and its possible fulfilment gives a meagre life, while its actual fulfilment would be unthinkable. If the earth in all its beauty is seen as a 'Muck House' what can heaven be like? Organized religion is thereby presented as soiled and soiling.

The Theology of the Body

Winterson's project throughout *The PowerBook* is to find a solution to the problem of making language meaningful in a way that does not fall foul the problems of the postmodern, the scientific or the formulations of organized religion we saw in the last section. Her answer takes the form of a sketch of what I would like to call the theology of the body. The most stable of the narrators, a female writer, is first discovered in Paris having a brief sexual encounter with a woman whom she meets through a friend, and with whom she falls in love. She tells her unnamed partner that she is writing about Boundaries and Desire, which we shall come to shortly. As their conversation develops, the writer challenges her lover:

> "Suppose I put you in my book."
> "You write fiction."
> "So?"
> "So you won't lash me to the facts."
> "But I might tell the truth."[27]

Here we find the idea that the truth may not only be found in facts but also in fiction – in stories. It might therefore seem that Winterson is going to tell parables like Jesus. At its heart the parable works by similitude and comparison, and is defined as 'A (usually realistic)

26. Winterson, *The PowerBook*, p. 137.
27. Winterson, *The PowerBook*, p. 37.

story or narrative told to convey a moral or spiritual lesson or insight.'[28] The parable thus tells of one plane, the real or human, but evokes another plane, the moral or spiritual to be accessed by the 'insight' of the reader or hearer. When Jesus, who is both man and God, and the intercessor between man and God, tells parables, he and only he, can connect the real or human experience with the moral or spiritual which is part of his other, divine nature: a nature which we, who are merely human, cannot grasp. For the parable to work, the hearer of the story has to recognize their human part as though they are an actor in the story, and by 'insight' rather than by real human sight, comprehend the morally or spiritually divine aspect of the story in order to bring it into their life.

But Winterson is not Christ. Her intention however is as radical as the parable. In the exchange between the two women in love, we notice that she is interested in the intersection between the real and what was there called 'fiction' but now she calls 'the invented':

> It used to be that the real and the invented were parallel lines that never met. Then we discovered that space is curved, and in curved space parallel lines always meet.[29]

In the parable the human story and the moral or spiritual lesson are parallel lines and so human readers or hearers need Christ to draw their attention to the moral or spiritual level. And it is interesting that we commonly talk of stories having 'levels' as well as having 'higher' or 'lower' purposes. What is further interesting about the quote above is what happens when Winterson replaces the term 'fiction' which appeared in the interchange between the lovers with the word 'invented' which stands in place of the moral or spiritual level of the parable. Where 'fiction' suggests something made up that has no basis in fact, 'invented' derives from the Latin root 'invenio' meaning 'I come upon' or 'I discover'. The 'invented' is therefore not a construction of the human imagination, but something that appears unexpectedly as a hitherto unthought-of 'level' of a story. Such sudden appearances are the moments of revelation that logic cannot explain and faith is not needed to elucidate what is obvious for all to see. In this way, the truths of invented stories are like the truths of Jesus' parables, though they do not need Christ as intercessor

28. See the *Oxford English Dictionary*, meaning 2.
29. Winterson, *The PowerBook*, p. 94.

to link the levels: altered human understanding of space predicts the link, though science may not be able to predict exactly what the link will be, or when the link will occur.

This unpredictable predictable I want to call the theology of the body. It is theological because it is revelatory, but it is 'of the body' because it does not move beyond the human to glimpse the divine. To a certain extent Winterson's idea might be linked to T.S. Eliot's moment 'when the fire and the rose are one' or 'the intersection of time with the timeless' from *The Four Quartets*, but where for Eliot 'the experience in the rose garden' is meditative and alone, for Winterson, such moments occur in times of passion.

In *The PowerBook*, we see this when the narrator and her lover talk of boundaries and desire, since desire can break boundaries. And, while desire can evoke the pornographic, as we saw above, Winterson locates desire within love stories, where desire has a proper place. The idea is not new in her work, and *The Passion* discusses both the link between passionate love and the Passion of Christ, and the banality of love stories. In *The PowerBook*, however, Winterson begins with the idea that love stories have traditionally been seen as either great or ruinous, and offering only three possible endings, Revenge, Tragedy or Forgiveness.

> We go back and back to the same scenes, the same words, trying to scrape out meaning.[30]

However, as we saw in her demonstration of the limits of the logic of stories with the metaphor of the computer and the Muck House, she demonstrates that love stories can go beyond our expectations, that is, they can spontaneously make the revelatory link between the real and the invented, since love makes us go beyond ourselves:

> What we seek is love itself, revealed now and again in human form, but pushing us beyond our humanity into animal instinct or god-like success.[31]

Neither the Internet conversation on the computer, nor the story of great or ruinous love, nor scientific fact can capture the lover who is beloved, without subsuming their individuality into a previously existing idea: the beloved is always new to their lover. Nevertheless, so many banal love stories objectify the beloved, and the love story is

30. Winterson, *The PowerBook*, p. 78.
31. Winterson, *The PowerBook*, p. 78.

even the basis of patriarchy where the beloved woman is expected to subsume her individuality and react in certain ways to her husband: but this is to follow heteronormative expectations. Winterson's love stories are not between a man and a woman so there is no hierarchy to maintain, only the individuality that each unnamed partner is. And this is the gift of the homosexual writer to the heterosexual world: invent yourself in love. But nor are Winterson's same-sex lovers, as Lindenmeyer or Harris would have it, 'melded' into one, but as Irigaray would have it 'two not one(s)' connected and distinct. The lover owes her existence as a lover to the bond, which is the beloved willingly being her beloved: giving back her love in a reciprocal co-creation. Therefore the beloved is not objectified by the lover because each always 'go[es] back and back' to their story to work out whether it will be a great love story or a ruinous love story: a moment when the love story renews itself by reference to its ending, and Winterson's story gives us both possible endings. But whatever the actual ending, when the lover says 'I will love you forever' in a moment of passion she does not know whether the statement will be true or not, however the declaration breaks through the banality of these words and gives place to reinvigorated passion in her beloved. This is the breaking of the logic of non-contradiction that is animal and god-like love. And it is a theology because this animal and god-like love declares the real presence of the lover and the beloved to each other, like revealed knowledge, but gained here and now following Jesus' final commandment to us to 'love one another'.

And the theology of the body leads Winterson to further revelations about the human condition. Once again starting with the metaphor of the computer, *The PowerBook* posits the existence of many interior lives that lie behind the outward self-expression of our everyday selves.

> There are so many lives packed into one. The one life we think we know is only the window that is open on the screen. The big window full of detail, where the meaning is often lost among the facts. If we can close that window, on purpose or by chance, what we find behind is another view.[32]

Typically we think of ourselves as unitary and finite, when in fact we are multiple and infinite. And it is the moments of love that show us this aspect of ourselves. If we are in want of actual love, we can turn to the love story, and the story shows us the same thing:

32. Winterson, *The PowerBook*, p. 103.

I'm sitting at my screen reading this story. In turn the story reads me.

Did I write the story, or was it you, writing through me, the way the sun sparks fire through a piece of glass.[33]

Here Winterson draws attention to the affectivity of language. We are changed by what we read in the same way we are co-created by the lover, and so the book can act upon us to alter our frame of mind, or even the way we think. The book can show ourselves to us. And the relationship, like that of lover and beloved, is reciprocal, and not simply with cold print.

The final story in *The PowerBook*, of finding Alum in Italy, demonstrates that with imagination it is possible to find that we already have what we need under our feet: 'The world is the mirror of the mind's abundance.'[34] This is the ability to cease searching for buried treasure elsewhere, but to find it where we are. The revelation we are looking for is not necessarily deferred to another place or time, but is here with us now – would that we could see it.

33. Winterson, *The PowerBook*, p. 209.
34. Winterson, *The PowerBook*, p. 224.

CONCLUSION: BLINDNESS AND INSIGHT –
SOME REFLECTIONS

The previous chapter attempted to draw out Winterson's theology of the body that lies between the postmodern, in which everything is language, and the scientific, in which everything is reduced to fact · or discarded as irrelevant, and the traditional religious, in which the world is only to be revealed in and after the passing of time and the fulfilment of a prophecy. The theology of the body was also introduced as the gift of the homosexual writer to the heterosexual world as its revelations broke down heteronormal expectations and objectification. In this final section I want to explore the theology of the body and its implications in my daily life rather than simply in my reading of Winterson's novel.

We begin from Winterson with the idea that there is a perceiver who exists in relation with the world but who is not limited by the traditional idea of perception. In the act of visual perception as traditionally understood, the eye grasps an image of the world or of another person and objectifies it. What is seen becomes a perspective, and thus I regard it as 'an object of my vision', 'my book', 'my wife'. In Winterson's reformulation, the perceiver, at certain times, feels the revelation of a higher truth: the co-creation of the 'my' (the knowledge of the self as appercipient) and the object perceived in the moment of perception, which interaction suggests a debt owed by the 'my' to the object of perception. I am 'me' because I see that object, I therefore owe my being 'me' to the object and its individuality and thus it cannot be 'mine' in any proper sense. This revelation of humility is the moment when parallel lines cross in curved space, it is the invented, brought into being in the interface between the real perceiver making a story of the object of perception (making it 'mine').

We now move onto four statements and explanations, which make perception more complex derived from my experience as a man who has recently lost his useful sight.

- Perception of the world does not objectify it since we are co-created by what we see.

I have become increasingly aware that vision is a complex interaction between memory and the image on my retinas, and that it is not simply an act of recording 'my' perspective of a world of objects. I do not recognize the faces of friends until I hear them speak their names. At that moment a blurred general face, which could be anyone, focuses briefly as that of my friend. But memory can play tricks. I see someone who physically looks like my sister, whom I know to be someone else, but from whom I cannot remove my sister's face as I look at her. I see words on a page, or on a billboard and I know they are words, but when I try I cannot read them except letter by letter. For me space has actually become curved, and the screen of my laptop looks twisted, though I know it is flat because it closes against the keyboard in a straight line. When I walk along a street I like to hold a friend's arm, though I can see everything that is there, because everything seems unreal and I feel safer having the other reference point of touch to connect me with my surroundings. For me, visual perception has begun to lose its links with the world and, perhaps surprisingly, the revelation that I owed my former sighted self to my perceptions has become increasingly obvious. The story I tell myself about the things around me looks increasingly like fiction. The car that screeches to a halt at my side when I cross a road was not there when I began to cross. And in that moment I do not know where to run because I am not sure that the pavement is real, though I can see it in front of me. When I walk along a pavement up hill, I feel that I am somehow walking through the pavement because I can see it at eye height in front of me. For me there is no problem in understanding the idea of the co-creation of perceiver and the world because as my perceived world becomes more distorted my sense of myself becomes equally strange. If anyone asks me what my vision is now like, I say I can see everything except what I am looking at.

While I was sighted, I rarely found counterfactuals useful in helping to describe the world, so there might seem little reason for you to trust my story. But now as I give the next two statements and explanations about the way perception is multiple and infinite rather than unitary I am speaking from my own experience, which I know has recently become wildly at variance with what it once was. This is my gift to you who can, hopefully, see, as blindness is my gift from God who has given me this chance to understand differently.

- What is perceived is not fixed but is always changing.

For me this is so apparent that it is barely worth saying, but if my experience counts for anything, what I see when I look at something is not a stable projection. If I am being driven in a car and I see a street scene, even one that I know well, if there is not enough information in the glance I do not recognize where I am. Since vision is made up of a perceptual part and a memory part, it would seem that my memory has not been stimulated enough by my perception to produce recognition. When I remember back to my sighted days, I recall sometimes waking and not knowing where I was, and taking some time to build the room around me as walls, furniture and curtains, until it finally became my bedroom, or the bedroom of an hotel. Such moments of waking are the typical times when we may all comprehend the instability of vision, which I would suggest are moments that highlight the fragile connection between perception and memory. At your waking, as the moments pass before recognition comes, your memory is helplessly trying to find something that will identify the place you have awoken, and at the same time the perception you are engaged in is simply perception and not 'your' perception, because you do not know what you are perceiving.

If we take this further, I would suggest that the feeling we have that vision is unitary and stable is not a consequence simply of seeing but a conjunction between percept and memory. 'My' vision is as much constructed by 'my' expectations as it is by the seeing of things. Sometimes (as early in the morning when you wake) expectations are not met, and familiar things look strange. At other times, when 'my' emotions are engaged, an object can transform dramatically. I do not need to pull curtains at night as I do not switch on lights to see by. But I do have a large blind over one of the three windows in my studio to shield my bed from the oversight of the building beside mine while I sleep. It is a beautiful white opaque blind that raises and lowers by pulling a chain at one side. But sometimes when I try to raise it in the morning the whole thing falls down and becomes an engulfing mass of wrinkled white fabric. At these moments my anger flares up, as I know it will take several attempts to get the blind rolled up again and the chain in the right alignment. People who have seen the occurrence cannot believe the level of my anger, but it is because my perception of my space has changed; my serene space has been rudely invaded by one of its components.

I moved from a large two bedroom flat to a studio little more than a year before I went blind. It was as though I knew what was happening (on some level I probably did), and I asked a friend to design the interior so there was nothing in it. I have a bed, three pieces of dark wood furniture a glass top table, chairs and a cupboard. There is no adornment at all, and nothing rests on the surfaces of any of the furniture. There are no pictures to remind me of what I cannot see. The floor is tiled so when I drop bottles of red wine, a mop and bucket will clear up the mess in moments. Most cleverly, at the window, which is a five metre window wall, there is a long hanging fringe that gives me privacy, but also means that when I look out I do not remember that I cannot see the buildings in any kind of focus. This is my paradise, and when I come home from work I am immediately at peace. My oldest friend calls it my monk's cell. I write here most days on my laptop, and entertain as many times as I can. Blackbirds wake me in the morning and sparrows have recently begun to play on my balcony.

I have given you an exhaustive description so that you can understand how I relate to my 'heaven and earth in little space'. So when my blind falls it is not a small thing: I have been ejected from my garden of Eden and it is as though I am fighting the behemoth. My peace and paradise has been, literally, destroyed. Because I perceive it differently it has changed. 'My' space is no longer as I would have it.

Oddly then, when the bathroom in the flat above mine leaked and I came home to find my glass top table covered with water I was not angry. 'My' space had been invaded from outside, rather than from inside. There was nothing I could have done differently to stop the water. I was stoical, sorted out the mess and returned my haven to its former state as quickly as possible. But the table is no longer a safe place and I will not leave my laptop on it in case I come home again to find it spoiled. That thing has altered irrevocably.

You now have three versions of my studio. For a room with grey tiles, grey walls and a white ceiling, with next to no furniture in it, it has many other aspects to me. If it is a paradise or a haven, it is not because it is always the same, but because it is so easily changed by 'my' perception.

- Percepts may not mean in an obvious way, and other meanings may lie under the surface.

When I see writing that has been greatly distorted I cannot read it, even letter by letter. I was in Manchester visiting a market, and above a shop was a signboard with writing that was incomprehensible to me. I was certain it was a shop because the building had large glass windows at street level; it was on a street by the market next to other shops whose signboards I could recognize and, like them, it had a coloured board above the window. All the perceptions I could make out told me that there ought to be writing on the signboard, because I remember there always being writing on shop signboards, but it just looked like a design. When I was told it read 'Gordon's Sandwich Bar' I simply had to believe my companion because I still could not read what was before my eyes. The pattern in purple was garish, but to me it was just a pattern. Nevertheless, based on the information I could glean from the position of the shop, how it looked and the sandwiches for sale in the window, I believed what I had been told. In this simple example, there might seem only to be one reading of the percept, but the colouring and distortion of the letters, which made them less than obvious to me, must have meant something to Gordon, and the pattern did hold letters that were readable by my companion. Imagine me setting out to read *War and Peace* letter by letter without the aid of my laptop's text to voice facility, or looking at a vast panorama, or watching a performance of *Aida*.

The example of my vitiated sight demonstrates that what we see and understand is not based on what is there, but how our memory uses what we see: what our memory can 'make out of' the perception. And something might be so new to us, or so out of our experience that we cannot make it out at all, so we have to rely on other ways of finding out its significance. Just because we cannot make it out does not mean there is no deeper significance.

From these three statements and explanations, we now move to ourselves in relation to other people. The three revelations we work from are: that we are co-created with the world we perceive; that perception is not stable and unitary as it can change; and that just because we cannot make something out of a perception does not mean that it is not meaningful.

- Perception of people does not objectify them but allows them their own difference, and their different experience of the world.

As a blind man I am supposed to rely on the kindness of strangers when I want to cross roads. As a former cyclist I learned to weave through London traffic and was never knocked off in 20 years. Where the sluggish traffic had created me as a nimble if not entirely law-abiding rider, for the blind man, the traffic of London now rushes by at breakneck (my neck) speed. Cars appear from nowhere and I have become re-created as a sluggish walker. These two versions of me were created by the different situations I found myself in before and after my 50th birthday, but to see how the world around me has been co-created, it is the blind man who can tell more of the truth because he's seen it. The cyclist flew along streets shouting out his presence in a wild ride full of foul language aimed at cars that never seemed to have drivers in them. It was a one-way creation, or so it seemed, full of ego and 'my' ride. The cyclist never encountered other people.

After the incident when the car appeared from nowhere, the blind 'me' began to cross roads only at traffic-light crossings. Fiercely independent, I worked out routes to and from the places I visited most often. The high-walks of the city of London became my goal and my gladness, as there never are cars there and my contorted face and mouth twisted with concentration might relax. Routes had to be picked out with no side-turnings to negotiate, so I had to use pavements on main streets and march from pelican crossing to pelican crossing, to await the green man (which I could not see) and listen out for the loud bleep that registered it was safe to cross. I discovered that on the bottom surface of most crossing-alert boxes was a ribbed stub that moved when the lights turned green for walkers, so if there was no bleeper, I had my own secret device that told me when it was safe. Except that there are some crossings that only have lights, no bleep and no twisting stub: useless for the blind people for whom, I assume, the crossings were made in the first place. And at crossings such as these I have to encounter other people.

The interface between blind people and the sighted is fascinating. When I recently encountered two totally blind people who asked me for help looking for a gallery that was near my home, I knew it was pointless to tell them to take the first left and second right, so I led them to the gallery instead, told them how many steps there were to climb to get to the door and put their hands onto the handrail. One of the blind people asked as we set off for the gallery, 'You're vision impaired too, aren't you?' Blind people can recognize one another without eyes.

Sighted people do not recognize blind people even though we carry white sticks: they are like the cyclist I once was. I will not now accept their help getting across a road if I can help it, and I learned to mistrust the sighted in the oddest of places. I needed to cross Judd Street to get to the RNIB, and was waiting at the pelican crossing, finger on the stub, when a sighted person called out from across the road 'It's OK to cross, there's nothing coming!' so I set off for the other side. Immediately I heard a car coming ridiculously fast towards me. 'Quick!' the man cried. 'Quick where?' I replied, 'back or forward?' Never again, I thought. But I have done it again and it has never worked. I take the proffered arm, and halfway across the road I'm told, 'Watch out for the cyclist!' 'Which cyclist, where? I cannot hear a cyclist. Nor do I know which way to dodge.' When I tell sighted people I do not want help they get quite cross. They think that they ought to be able to help, and they sound so hurt when I say, 'I'll wait for the bleep'. It is almost comical when I feel the turn of the stub at the same time as refusing to be helped, for, when I start off crossing, the sighted would-be helper can only understand how I did it by thinking that I can really see and I am faking. This is an example of my being objectified by the sighted person. The sighted person only understands in terms of visual metaphors: 'Do you see what I mean?'; 'I saw the light!'; 'The conversation we had brought to light certain truths.' In this sense I would argue that sighted people live in the postmodern world of language, where nothing exists but language as everything is reduced to the realm of consciousness which readily fulfils the criteria of the visual.

Sighted people can typically only conceptualize blind people in the same way as they do themselves: eyes open I can see; eyes closed I am blind. But this is not simply a case of non-specialist people misunderstanding. My doctors radically cannot understand me when I say, 'I can see everything except what I'm looking at'. Until the genesis of the Spectralis scan, my consultant told me that opthalmic specialists thought people with my condition were mad. He now asks me how I see, as I am a rare case; I have no macular retinas so I cannot look at a particular thing, but since the rest of my retinas are perfect I have a general, if blurred, perception of everything out there. Because the scientist can find an anomaly in the back of my eye he no longer thinks me insane. However, since he cannot find a cause for the anomaly he is unable to talk to me about the disease, and can only say that I fall into the spectrum of problems associated with other people with the same condition. And since there is no cure, we can have no conversation because I fall outside his remit. I am not to be found within the scientific narrative of cause: disease: cure.

Faced with the imminent depression concomitant with sudden blindness, I decided to begin again to be a regular Anglican churchgoer. I chose my building carefully, as I prefer the Queen Anne auditory Churches and their sense of togetherness to gothic arches, rood screens and distant priests. I chose my parish carefully as I wanted the high service I had become used to while at school, and a service that was as different as possible from the Unitarian services, where nothing was ever done twice, that I had been going to for the past 17 years. I needed something to fall back on that I could do with my eyes closed: and I can say the services of Eucharist and Evensong without a prayer book.

The first church I went to was splendid, the sermons witty and the congregation full. But that was my downfall, literally. With so many children, going up to the altar for communion was a nightmare. The holes in my vision can swallow a child whole, and I could feel two hundred pairs of eyes on my back as I stumbled forward, daring me to tread on one of their offspring. Eventually the verger grasped the situation and my arm and frogmarched me to the altar like a prisoner. I was to communicate where he led me, and to be the perfect blind man for the children to learn patience in affliction. I am not patient, and like to decide every week whether or not I will take communion. To be led about like St Paul in later life and told what to do quickly brought on the decision to leave that church to find another with a small congregation and few, if any, children. In this first church I was pigeonholed into what was expected of me: I was objectified as 'their' blind man and even had to listen to a sermon on the ineluctable blackness that is spiritual blindness. When I told the vicar my blindness was silver he gasped. I did not fit his remit of church service as crowd control, and I don't think he was happy that I told him I found his sermon offensive. Organized religion had failed me so I had to look for a disorganized church. Now, as I blunder towards the altar in my Ray-Bans with my white stick, everyone gets out of my way. It is as though the stick is Moses' rod: I point it at the Red Sea and the waters part. In this church there is much more of a sense of co-creation, of rubbing along together, rather than good citizenship. I communicate when I want to and sometimes do not go for coffee: not because I do not want to chat with the congregation, but because I am not happy being in a crowded room where all the people merge into one. I'm not sure whether the rector or the rest of the congregation are all that happy with my oddity, and nor am I entirely happy with them. But we get on.

Having explored the difficulties of the postmodern, the scientific and the religious in terms of 'we are co-created by the world we perceive', I will now move onto the second two revelations in terms of walking with people I love. I use the term 'love' in the sense of Christ's final commandment that we love one another as He loved us because only the one example has homosexual content, and even that is not, in the end, sexual.

The idea 'that perception is not stable and unitary as it can change' takes me back to a woman who one Sunday joined the congregation at my church, where it is traditional to sit for the voluntary and applaud at the end. She was dressed in a sable coat and seemed very elegant, but talked throughout the final music, so much so that I crossed the church to listen without being annoyed. I had a blind moment when she came to talk to me at coffee afterwards, but she wouldn't be put off, and in five minutes the annoying woman had let me know that we shared a love for eighteenth-century literature and architecture, and suddenly was not annoying any more. We left to walk home together, and when I asked her if I could take her arm as we crossed the street, she stopped and looked at me and asked me if I was blind. When I assured her I was, she said, 'Oh good! Then let me tell you I am the most beautiful young woman you've ever met!' 'I'm sure you are,' I replied, 'and the most charming fibber!' I have no idea what her face really looked like, but she spoke with the voice of a woman in her late 70s. Beneath the silver sheen I could barely make out her features at all, but as far as I am concerned she was the most beautiful woman I've ever met. She was also an accomplished blind guide, telling me when to raise my foot for the kerb as we got to the other side of the road, and naming the street where she left me to continue her way home. First she changed from being annoying to charming, then she changed from being old to young and beautiful: sometimes it is useful being blind because people can change so easily and quickly.

My final point explores the idea 'that just because we cannot make something out of a perception does not mean that it is not meaningful' in terms of other people reading me. Ten years before I went blind I began to be tattooed. I told my tattooist that I wanted black tattoos, and the only other direction I gave him was that they were not to be symmetrical. The cyclist soon looked very much like a cyclist with tattoos showing on arms and legs, so they fitted with that image I was making for myself. Now my relationship with them has dramatically altered.

The cyclist became used to other cyclists telling him they liked his tattoos. Admiration is part of the ritual of being tattooed because the tattoo makes the invisible visible. Skin is skin, but skin with a design etched on it is a work of art or a cultural statement that demands comment. It is as though all cyclists are in a loosely affiliated gang. The type of tattoos I have fit readily with the cyclist, but they did not fit with my other regular persona, an English Professor. The tattoos immediately became a source for discussion with my colleagues, who would ask me what the designs meant and would tell me that they were a disguise. To the former question I would answer that the tattoos meant whatever the viewer wanted them to mean (I did not want to be objectified), to the latter suggestion I would agree as it is niggling to think that two hundred pairs of eyes are looking at you, and easier to believe that they are looking at the designs. But neither response can be a proper account. Three designs have special significance to me, so are not open signifiers, even if they appear so. And why, if the tattoos are a disguise, did I spend so much time and money having my back tattooed, which is rarely seen in public except perhaps in a swimming pool, or on a beach, or (daily but in semi-private) in the showers at the gym? To try to give a truthful answer, like Winterson, I will resort to stories in which might lie some truth.

I go to the gym nearly every day. I do my exercises then go to the wet room to shower, take a steam bath and sauna. A wet room is one of the few places in England where men are naked together to the exclusion of women and the homoerotic gaze of admiration may be sent out, understood or not understood, depending upon the men sending and receiving. My tattooist, a rampant heterosexual, asked me once how he could tell if a man was gay and I told him about the gaze. If a man looks back it is either because he wants to beat your brains out or because he wants to have sex with you, and probably if he thinks he wants the former he really wants the latter. In the gym, I had decided that I would never engage in homosexual acts, as I wanted to be able to go there for the rest of my life so did not want to lose my membership. But nevertheless, one day the manager asked to speak to me after I had finished in the wet room. That day I had sat in the steam room with several other men, and then gone into the sauna alone to shave. One man had left the steam room after I had been there for a few minutes and I guessed, rightly, that he had complained about me to the manager. Quietly, the manager told me that he was not making any accusations, but someone had told him I was staring at him inappropriately. 'Oh!' I said, 'that's interesting, did I really?' The manager continued sounding flustered. He was not making accusations, but could I modify my behaviour in the steam room. 'I'd love to,' I said, 'but unfortunately I am blind and I cannot see either in or out of the steam room, so I do not believe I was staring at anyone.' The manager was floored. 'Ah! I am so sorry. I have made a mistake …' I would not let him get away with an apology, and gave him a history of men being naked together from Roman times to the bath houses of the East End of London where men used to 'schmize' each other with huge chamois leathers full of soap. If he could not understand how men might be naked with each other, maybe he ought to find another job? But really I was angry with the man who thought I was looking at him. He had misread my staring for vision, and my tattoos for a sign that I wanted him, I suppose, to have sex there and then in front of the other men in the steam room. He felt objectified, not by me, but by his own judgment of what he thought was happening. Maybe, like the example I gave my tattooist, he wanted to have sex there and then with me, and in want of any response from me took the other course and metaphorically beat me up. I do not know what his motive was, and I probably never will. I do not know who he was because I have never seen his face.

Having told the story of the incorrect reading of my tattoos, I will finish with a story about their being correctly read in an unlikely circumstance. Every year I go to the USA to attend a conference and one year, when I still had sight, it was held in New Orleans. Landing at Louis Armstrong Airport, I was glad to have checked the weather report and was wearing a singlet and shorts. It was very hot. The long wait for immigration finally over, the officer asked me why I was in New Orleans. 'To attend the American Society for Eighteenth-Century Studies Annual Conference,' I replied. The officer looked at me quizzically, eyeing my tattoos. 'You are an English professor?' 'Yes', I replied now realizing I may have made a sartorial mistake. 'You don't look like one!' he went on, almost shifting out of that dead tone that characterizes so many immigration officers. I wondered whether I ought to get out my laptop and show him my paper, but a thought came to me. 'Have you ever seen an English professor?' 'No,' he replied quickly. 'Well this is what English professors look like because I am one.' Maybe because of my accent, maybe because he knew I was carrying $10,000 worth of tattoos, he stamped my passport and ushered me through without a further word, or a further search. Somehow, he could see through the obvious gang signification of my tattoos, possibly because of the preposterousness of what I had said. But 900 English professors had landed at Louis Armstrong Airport that day, and none of them looked anything like me. I don't think any one of them has a tattoo. The immigration officer must have heard the same answer to his question several times before he came to me, but something made him suspect the truth. I could have as well been like my tattooist, a motorcycle gang member who is automatically tagged when he goes abroad. But I am not. I am an English Lecturer, and was then, a pedal cyclist. I will never know how he read me correctly.

Now as I sit and write this on my new laptop (one that a blind man can write on, which reads back to me as I write), and which cost as much as I usually spend on tattoos each year, I am beset by another problem. My right leg is half tattooed. It was done last year before I became blind, and I do not know whether I should get it finished because I cannot see it. For ten years I have woken up and looked at my arms joyfully contemplating the new skin I have. Now I know the designs are there because I remember them. So I wonder whether there is any point in finishing the leg designs that I won't see, and which won't be shown off on my bicycle. But then I think about my back: I have never seen those tattoos except in photographs and backwards in mirrors. Tattoos are for other people to read, misread, understand and misunderstand. They are part of my individuality, which is irreducible and never finally explicable. *They* are irreducible to one meaning and never finally explicable. In that, they are a visual sign of the theology of the body, which is one body in relation to other bodies under the injunction of Christ to love one another as He loved us. Believe me, I am a blind man and I have seen it.

SELECT BIBLIOGRAPHY

a Kempis, *The Imitation of Christ* (trans. W. Benham B.D.; Leipzig: Tauchnitz, 1877).

Alderson, David, 'Desire as Nostalgia: The Novels Of Alan Hollinghurst', in David Alderson and Linda Anderson (eds), *Territories of Desire in Queer Culture* (Manchester: Manchester University Press, 2000), pp. 29–48.

— 'Momentary Pleasures: Wilde and English Verse', in Eibhear Walshe (ed.), *Sex, Nation and Dissent in Irish Writing* (New York: St. Martin's Press, 1997).

Anstruther, Ian, *Oscar Browning* (London: Murray, 1983).

Benson, Arthur C., *The Memoirs of Arthur Hamilton* (London: Keegan Paul, Trench & Co, 1886).

Benson, Edward Frederick, *David Blaize* (London: Hodder and Stoughton, 1916).

— *David Blaize and the Blue Door* (London: Hodder and Stoughton, 1918).

— *David of King's* (London: Hodder and Stoughton, 1924).

Blacker, Hereth, 'Philby Burgess and Maclean' in *Alcohol and Alcoholism* 4 (1969): pp. 128–31.

Brett, Philip, 'Salvation at Sea: Billy Budd', in Christopher Palmer (ed.), *The Britten Companion* (London: Faber, 1984), pp. 142–55.

Burton, Peter, Introduction from E.F. Benson, *David of King's* (Brighton: Millivres, 1991).

Carpenter, Edward, *Homogenic Love* (Manchester: The Labour Press Society, 1894).

— *My Days and Dreams: Being Biographical Notes* (London: George Allen and Unwin, 1916).

— *The Intermediate Sex: A Study of Some Transitional Types of Men and Women* (London: George Allen and Unwin, 1908).

— *Towards Democracy* (London: Swan Sonnenschein, 1905).

Cocks, Harry, '*Calamus* in Bolton: Spirituality and Homosexuality in Late Victorian England', in *Gender and History* 13.2 (August 2001): pp. 191–223.

Cooke, Mervyn and Philip Reed, *Cambridge Opera Handbooks, Billy Budd* (Cambridge: Cambridge University Press, 1993).

Cooper, Brenda, 'Snapshots of Postcolonial Masculinities: Alan Hollinghurst's *The Swimming-Pool Library* and Ben Okri's *The Famished Road*', in *The Journal of Commonwealth Literature* 34 (1999): pp. 135–57.

Crosby, Ernest, *The Absurdities of Militarism* (Boston, MA: American Peace Society, 1901).

— *Captain Jinks, Hero* (New York: Funk & Wagnalls, 1902).

Crozier, Eric and E.M. Forster, *Billy Budd: Opera in Two Acts* (London: Boosey and Hawkes, 1961).

Douglas-Scot-Montague, Edward, *Wheels within Wheels: An Unconventional Life* (London: Weidenfeld and Nicholson, 2001).

Dukes, Thomas, 'Mappings of Secrecy and Disclosure, *The Swimming-Pool Library*, *The Closet*, and *The Empire*', *Journal of Homosexuality* 31 (1996): pp. 95–107.

Eide, Marian, 'Passionate Gods and Desiring Women: Jeanette Winterson, Faith and Sexuality', *International Journal of Sexuality and Gender Studies* 6.4 (October 2001): pp. 279–91.

Ellman, Richard, *Oscar Wilde* (London: Hamilton, 1987).

Frankfort Moore, Frank, *Phyllis of Phillistia* (London: Hutchinson & Co., 1895).

— *The Jessamy Bride* (London: Hutchinson & Co., 1897).

Freeman, Nicholas, 'Paganism and Spiritual Confusion in E.F. Benson', *Literature and Theology* 19.1 (March 2005).

Gibbon, Edward, *Decline and Fall of the Roman Empire* (London, 1776–1788).

Grote, George, *History of Greece* 1846–1856 (London, John Murray, 1849).

Gunn, Thom, 'Courage: A Tale', in *Jack Straw's Castle* (New York: Farrar Straus Giroux, 1976).

Hanson, Ellis, *Decadence and Catholicism* (Cambridge, MA: Harvard University Press, 1997).

Harris, Andrea L., *Other Sexes: Rewriting Difference from Woolf to Winterson* (Albany, NY: SUNY Press, 2000), p. 129.

Hart-Davis, Rupert (ed.), *The Letters of Oscar Wilde* (London: Rupert Hart-Davis, 1962).

Hassall, David, *Rupert Brooke: A Biography* (London: Faber, 1964).

Hindley, Clifford, 'Britten's Billy Budd: The "Interview Chords" Again', *The Musical Quarterly* 78.1 (Spring 1994): pp. 99–126.

Hollinghurst, Alan, *The Swimming-Pool Library* (London: Penguin, 1989).

Holland, Merlin, Vyvyan Holland et al. (eds), *Collins Complete Works of Oscar Wilde* (Glasgow: Harper Collins, 1999).

Irigaray, Luce, *This Sex Which Is Not One* (trans. Catherine Porter and Carolyn Burke; Ithaca NY: Cornell University Press, 1985).

Johnson, Barbara, 'Melville's Fist: The Execution of Billy Budd' in *The Critical Difference: Essays in the Contemporary Rhetoric of Reading* (Baltimore, MD and London: Johns Hopkins University Press, 1985), pp. 79–109.

Kiernan, Robert, *Frivolity Unbound: Six Masters of the Camp Novel* (New York: Continuum, 1990).

Kumar Barua, Dilip, *Edward Carpenter: 1844–1929, An Apostle of Freedom* (Burdwan: University of Burdwan Press, 1991).

Lindenmeyer, Antje, 'Postmodern Concepts of the Body in Jeanette Winterson's *Written on the Body*', *Feminist Review* 63. 1 (1999): pp. 48–63.

Masters, Brian, *The Life of E.F. Benson* (London: Chatto & Windus, 1991).

Mather, Rachel R., *The Heirs of Jane Austen: Twentieth-Century Writers of the Comedy of Manners* (New York: Peter Lang, 1996).

McCracken, Scott, 'Writing the Body: Edward Carpenter, George Gissing and Late Nineteenth-Century Realism', in Tony Brown (ed.), *Edward Carpenter and Late Victorian Radicalism* (London: Frank Cass, 1990).

O'Malley, Patrick, 'Religion', in Frederick Roden (ed.), *Palgrave Advances in Oscar Wilde Studies* (Basingstoke: Palgrave, 2004).

Palmer, Geoffrey and Noel Lloyd, *E.F. Benson as He Was* (Luton: Lennard Publishing, 1988).

Reavell, Cynthia and Tony, *E.F. Benson: Mr Benson Remembered in Rye, and the World of Tilling* (Rye: Martello Bookshop, 1984).

Rowbotham, Sheila, *Socialism and the New Life: The Personal and Sexual Politics of Edward Carpenter and Havelock Ellis* (London: Pluto, 1977).

Scorza, Thomas J., *In the Time Before Steamships: Billy Budd, the Limits of Politics, and Modernity* (Dekalb, IL: Northern Illinois University Press, 1979), pp. 183–89.

Swan, Tom, *Edward Carpenter the Man and His Message* (Manchester: Tom Swan, 1902).

Whittall, Arnold, '"Twisted Relations": Method and Meaning in Britten's Billy Budd', Cambridge Opera Journal 2.2 (July 1990): pp. 145–71.

Winterson, Jeanette, *Lighthousekeeping* (London: Harper Perennial, 2005).

— *The PowerBook* (London: Vintage, 2010).

Zipes, Jack, *Fairy Tales and the Art of Subversion* (London: Heinemann, 1983).

SUBJECT INDEX

AUTHOR INDEX